NIETZSCHE ON GENDER

D0840871

NIETZSCHE
ON
GENDER

Beyond Man and Woman

Frances Nesbitt Oppel

University of Virginia Press

Charlottesville and London

University of Virginia Press
© 2005 by the Rector and Visitors of the University of Virginia
Printed in the United States of America on acid-free paper

First published 2005
1 3 5 7 9 8 6 4 2

Library of Congress Cataloging-in-Publication Data

Oppel, Frances Nesbitt, 1942–
    Nietzsche on gender : beyond man and woman / Frances Nesbitt Oppel.
        p.   cm.
    Includes bibliographical references and index.
    ISBN 0-8139-2319-0 (alk. paper) — ISBN 0-8139-2320-4 (pbk. : alk. paper)
        1. Nietzsche, Friedrich Wilhelm, 1844–1900. 2. Femininity (Philosophy)
3. Woman (Philosophy) 4. Sex—Philosophy. I. Title.
    B3318.F45067 2005
    305.3'092—dc22

                                                                    2004020595

That the value of the world lies in our interpretation (—that other interpretations than merely human ones are perhaps somewhere possible—); that previous interpretations have been perspective valuations by virtue of which we can survive in life, i.e., in the will to power, for the growth of power; that every elevation of man brings with it the overcoming of narrower interpretations; that every strengthening and increase of power opens up new perspectives and means believing in new horizons—this idea permeates my writings.

—Nietzsche, *The Will to Power*

CONTENTS

THIS BOOK began as a study of Nietzsche and woman, a subject of interest to feminism in the late 1980s. Nietzsche was broadly regarded (and not only by feminists) as a misogynist, or at the least as an opponent of women's liberation, yet he wrote positively about many topics on feminists' agendas. Interpretive difficulties inherent to his texts, however, made it almost impossible to decide for sure where Nietzsche stood on the subject "woman."

What does now seem clear is that Nietzsche's texts offer an interpretive challenge specifically directed to women readers. Among many other women, I took the bait, but unlike some of them, I was not convinced by the texts' misogyny. As time passed I began to understand why. By broadening my focus to include men, and considering the attitudes of the texts toward both sexes, I began to see some consistency on matters related to "woman" and "man," and to women and men, in Nietzsche's baffling and fascinating works. I can now at least frame a hypothesis about Nietzsche's attitude toward conventional gender categories, and will make the argument in the pages that follow that Nietzsche's texts eliminate "man" and "woman" altogether. They obviously do not eliminate people; they merely ask us to question the ways in which we think about gender conventions. Perhaps gender has had its day as a fundamental identifier of people? Perhaps "gender difference" (between two "opposites") could be reinterpreted as "gender differences" (between two in relation)? Perhaps?

This book seems to be joining a new subgenre in Nietzsche studies, that of the "beyond." Richard Schacht introduces his 1995 work, *Making Sense of Nietzsche,* as a book that moves beyond previous readings or interpretations: beyond nihilism, deconstruction, aestheticism, scholasticism. He comments that each new interpretation, "in an important sense," invents Nietzsche afresh (102ff.). Keith Ansell-Pearson leaps beyond the human to the posthuman in *Viroid Life: Perspectives on Nietzsche and the Transhuman Condition* (1997), where he warns of the ascendency of biotechnology, and refers us to the Overman (Übermensch) as Nietzsche's particular behest to "remain faithful to the earth" (2, 38–39ff.). *Viroid Life* alerts us to dangers of the beyond. And in an essay in an edited volume surveying Nietzsche's futures, Gary Banham argues that there are two models for the future in *Thus Spoke Zarathustra:* the Last Man, and the Übermensch (the "beyond

man"). The herd values of the Last Man prioritize happiness in the present
and so sacrifice the future. The values of the Übermensch would sacrifice
the present to the future, and would, Banham argues, focus on the "the
body as material to be formed in a continuous process of invention" (164).
As he maintains: "Conditions of hygiene, breeding, and procreation (in
every sense of the term) are the basis of any growth" (165). Thus Banham
(to oversimplify the argument) gestures "beyond" the body as it is presently
constituted; however, in his last sentence, he asks: "But supposing the
body of the future is sexed: what then?" (164–65). My book, quite inadver-
tently, addresses that question without answering it. My primary concern
is not the body of the future, or biotechnology, or science-fiction-cum-fact.
I am interested in demonstrating how Nietzsche's texts may be interpreted
as pointing toward the future of sexed bodies, beyond fixed gender identities, without spelling out the particulars. As prophecy, the writing is ambiguous and open-ended.

I approach this writing not as a philosopher, but as a literary critic,
trained in close reading of the sort, I like to think, that Nietzsche is always
encouraging when he advocates reading slowly, meditatively, ruminating
the text, "chewing the cud." Trained to read poetry, I find that Nietzsche's
texts present the kinds of problems to which the tools of poetics are particularly suited. However, as I am not a philosopher, an initial *caveat* is in order.
I appeal to the philosopher Bernard Williams, who gave a series of lectures
on ancient Greek poetry in the classics department at the University of
California at Berkeley. In the preface of the subsequently published volume, he offers the following counsel: "Philosophers who are guilty of bad
scholarship should rightly be reproached for it. It must be said at the same
time that there are some literary scholars who seem closed to the idea that
their reflections might involve some bad philosophy. They should perhaps
at least be conscious of the risk. That is not to say that they do wrong to
run the risk" (ix).

I am aware that my ruminations may, and indeed probably do involve
some bad philosophy. I am nonetheless emboldened to believe that the
risk may be worth the errors of commission or omission I may make as I
pursue my argument. Reading the texts as "literary" has enabled me to
learn something about the problems I encountered when I tried to think of
Nietzsche's works as misogynistic. Misogyny, woman-hating, depends on
woman's existence in relation to man's; it stems from a clear sense of gender dichotomy. But it is precisely this sense that Nietzsche's texts obscure,
through their use of such poetic devices as figures of speech, allusion, parody,

mimicry, and a consummate address to readers—a repertoire of rhetorical tricks that Nietzsche asserts, in his early lectures, are not supplementary but fundamental to meaning.

The interdisciplinarity of the academic programs at Griffith University in Brisbane, Australia, where I have taught a combination of gender studies, literature, history, and philosophy, provided the impetus for this project. To my colleagues, past and present, who helped me think about it, and especially to my students, I offer my sincere thanks. I also acknowledge with gratitude the study leaves that Griffith afforded me in 1991 and 1995, which gave me time to write, and the fractional appointment they offered beginning in 1998. In 1991, as I began this project, I spent a happy and productive six months at the Institute for Research on Women, then under the directorship of Carol Smith, at Douglass College of Rutgers University, New Jersey; for this too I am grateful.

The Humanities Editor at the University of Virginia Press, Cathie Brettschneider, has been supportive of this project, and I thank her for her faith in it and her efforts on its behalf. Thanks too to the editorial staff at the Press, especially to Mark Mones for his careful, thorough work on my manuscript.

I wish finally and particularly to acknowledge and to thank John Oppel, who spent evenings over the course of a year reading with me, out loud in German, *The Birth of Tragedy* and *Thus Spoke Zarathustra*.

THE FOLLOWING published texts and translations of Friedrich Nietzsche's works are cited throughout the book by short abbreviations, together with book/part/section numbers (e.g., *A* 7 or *BGE* 212), aphorism numbers (e.g., *GS* 14), or chapter titles (*D* Preface or *BT* "Attempt at a Self-Criticism")—or a combination of these elements (e.g., *GM* 3:14—which refers to part 14 of the third essay, or *Z* 1 "Of Chastity"—which denotes the named chapter in part 1, or *TI* "Maxims and Arrows" 13—which indicates part 13 of the named chapter). Citations to *Friedrich Nietzsche on Rhetoric and Language*, to *Philosophy and Truth*, and to the *Selected Letters* refer to page numbers (e.g., *RL* 23, *PT* 90, or *L* 211). For quotations from Nietzsche's untranslated notebooks, a volume number is followed by a page number (e.g., *KSA* 10:40). Full publishing details for these sources appear in the bibliography.

A	*The Anti-Christ.* Trans. R. J. Hollingdale.
BGE	*Beyond Good and Evil: Prelude to a Philosophy of the Future.* Trans. R. J. Hollingdale.
BT	*The Birth of Tragedy.* Trans. Walter Kaufmann.
CW	*The Case of Wagner.* Trans. Walter Kaufmann.
D	*Daybreak: Thoughts on the Prejudices of Morality.* Trans. R. J. Hollingdale.
EGP	*Early Greek Philosophy and Other Essays.* Trans. Maximillian A. Mugge.
EH	*Ecce Homo: How One Becomes What One Is.* Trans. Walter Kaufmann.
GM	*On the Genealogy of Morals: A Polemic.* Trans. Walter Kaufmann.
GS	*The Gay Science.* Trans. Walter Kaufmann.
HAH	*Human, All Too Human: A Book for Free Spirits.* Trans. Marion Faber and Stephen Lehmann.
KSA	*Friedrich Nietzsche: Sämtliche Werke. Kritische Studiensausgabe in 15 Einzelbänden* (Collected works. Critical studies publication in 15 volumes).
L	*Selected Letters of Friedrich Nietzsche.* Trans. Christopher Middleton.
PT	*Philosophy and Truth: Selections from Nietzsche's Notebooks of the Early 1870's.* Trans. Daniel Breazeale.
PTAG	*Philosophy in the Tragic Age of the Greeks.* Trans. Marianne Cowan.

RL   *Friedrich Nietzsche on Rhetoric and Language.* Trans. Sander L. Gilman,
        Carole Blair, David J. Parent.
TI   *Twilight of the Idols: or How to Philosophize with a Hammer.*
        Trans. R. J. Hollingdale.
TSZ   *Thus Spoke Zarathustra: A Book for None and All.* Trans.
        Walter Kaufmann.
UDH   *On the Uses and Disadvantages of History for Life.* In *Untimely Meditations.*
        Trans. R. J. Hollingdale.
WP   *The Will to Power.* Trans. Walter Kaufmann and R. J. Hollingdale.
Z   *Thus Spoke Zarathustra: A Book for Everyone and No One.* Trans.
        R. J. Hollingdale.

NIETZSCHE ON GENDER

IN THIS book I argue that Nietzsche's writings challenge interpretations of human sexuality based on a binary opposition between man and woman, and in so doing they open up a space for new perspectives on the subject. Nietzsche's works have often been considered misogynistic, for when they notice woman at all, they patronize and belittle her, assign her to the bedroom and nursery, and apparently advocate taking the whip to her when she gets out of line. I suggest that a surface reading of Nietzsche's comments on woman tells only part of the story, and propose that Nietzsche the misogynist needs to be considered alongside the Nietzsche who judges the sexual arrangements of his day negatively, whose writings urge readers to think outside and beyond the conventional and the normative, and who nominates for consideration as a "cardinal problem" the example of "man and woman" (*BGE* 231).

This other Nietzsche asks us to question our reliance on dichotomies—such as good/evil, nature/culture, mind/body—to make sense of the world. What if, he asks, rather than thinking in terms of opposition, we were to think in terms of neighborliness—of contiguity and continuity, "degrees and many subtleties of gradation" (*BGE* 24) rather than antithesis? I claim that Nietzsche directs this question toward the foundational social dichotomy, and in doing so challenges the myths and conventions that ascribe one set of fixed traits to males and another, opposing set to females.

In the chapters that follow I argue that Nietzsche's apparent misogyny is part of his overall strategy to demonstrate that our attitudes toward sex-gender are thoroughly cultural, are often destructive of our own potential as individuals and as a species, and may be changed. What looks like misogyny may be understood as part of a larger strategy whereby "woman-as-such" (the universal essence of woman with timeless character traits) is shown to be a product of male desire, a construct. Throughout the texts, "woman" as a concept referring to female persons is erased as a matter we need to take very seriously, although she may still exist as a joke, and as history. Misogynist, indeed. But this apparently misogynistic dismissal of woman is only part—exactly half—of the story. As woman is erased, so too is her dichotomous counterpart, man-as-such, for the two are entailed in our thinking. No "woman," no "man": we are left with an empty space, a potential new horizon, where our former "perspective valuations" on sex-gender used to be. This space, I argue, is not that of castration or of nihilism—unless we want it to be. Just how it is filled is, in a completely nontrivial way, up to us.

In using the hyphenated term sex-gender, I want to signal that, in my view, the terms belong together not as an opposition but as one of those continuous, contiguous relationships that Nietzsche wishes to substitute for antitheses.[1] *Sex* is a word that has been used to signify biological differences between females and males, and *gender* to signify social and cultural constructions of those differences. Separating the pair forces us to think dichotomously in terms of the raw and the cooked. Sex is the raw—natural and given, referring to our bodies and their reproductive capacities. Gender is the cooked, signifying the ways in which we think about, prepare, ornament, and distribute our natural bodies as social beings. The sex/gender opposition is common, but it is only an interpretation, a "perspective valuation."

It is a perspective on human sexuality that Nietzsche's writings helped to open up. They did so by asking whether there is anything "natural" about human sexual behavior, and thus exposed the socially and culturally contingent aspects of the dichotomous sexual division that we now call "gender," thereby questioning the cooks and the cooking. And they did so by asking whether it is possible to get "back to nature" in any case, thereby questioning the availability of raw material. In raising these issues, Nietzsche's texts made the sex/gender distinction thinkable while at the same time they collapsed it as an antithesis, revealing it as a perspective valuation and putting it on our intellectual agenda.

However, disclosing the continuity between its biological and cultural aspects was only the first step in an ambitious program of rethinking sexuality from the ground up inaugurated by Nietzsche's writings. I say "inaugurated by" because I believe we are nowhere near the end of a social revolution that is already changing the way we think about, and live, our sexed bodies. I don't in the least claim that Nietzsche instituted this "ambitious program," or even intended that it should exist. I do hold both that his writings expose the sexual habits of the middle classes in nineteenth-century Europe as conventional and thus cultural, and that they suggest another, better way to live as sexed beings.

Nietzsche's writings indicate that sexuality is a product of interpretation. They do not oppose sexual difference, unless this is defined narrowly as an innate distinction between "man" and "woman." In my estimation, Nietzsche's writings are neither essentialist nor sexist, but rather they suggest ways of thinking about human differences that encourage us to consider the needs and desires of our own bodies after the constraints of dichoto-mous thinking and social conventions have been loosened. How Nietzsche's writings hint at a future beyond "man" and "woman"—a future toward which we are moving even as the hegemony of heterosexuality is breaking down, and as we experiment with physical sex changes and transgendering—is the primary question this book seeks to address.

By demonstrating that there are codes of moral and social behavior based on the man/woman opposition, and that these codes are human constructions, or "interpretations" and value perspectives, rather than God-given dictates, Nietzsche indicates that our ideas about sex-gender can be revised. He advocates revision for ethical reasons. In asserting that religious interpretations of human purpose are losing, will lose, or have lost their power to validate and regulate people's lives in the Western world, Nietzsche's books seek to prepare humans for a future in which, having understood that there is no heavenly reward, they are able to assume respon-sibility for themselves and for their earthly home. As Heidegger writes, this process involves bringing "man," as he has in his nature been until now, "beyond himself" (67) in order to become caretaker of the earth. Nietzsche suggests that men need to overcome, especially, their resentment of their own vulnerable bodies, of time and change, and of women. One way that Nietzsche seeks to bring human beings beyond themselves is to challenge age-old conventions about sex-gender.

In place of antagonism and opposition between "man" and "woman," Nietzsche's texts substitute relation, analogy, and differences among human beings. Emphasizing the importance of perspective in evaluation, and the impossibility of writing from either a universal or an objective viewpoint, he recasts sexuality from his own vantage point, that of an intellectual middle-class European male living in the second half of the nineteenth century. Because Nietzsche's perspective is that of a male, he attends to men; to his credit, he does not prescribe for women, but he makes sugges-tions which indeed women have taken up.[2]

Nietzsche's pioneering interventions into the story of the two-category model of human sexuality can perhaps best be analyzed as occurring in stages, though in fact the shift from sexual dichotomy to plurality takes place all at once as we read any given text. I here offer a deliberately artificial breakdown of that operation into a series of steps and categorical divisions. First, Nietzsche shifts the gender emphasis in his work from masculine to feminine.[3] The feminine category is itself divided into two parts, negative and positive. The negative component is considerably smaller than the positive, but as it is articulated from various misogynistic perspectives, it commands attention. Usually taken to represent Nietzsche's views on women, it consists of stereotyped versions of the women of his own time. Here too we find two general categories: the first is the "woman" of the eternal feminine (the domestic ideal, the myth of the redeemer and moral guardian of "man" and his children), while the second is the image of emancipated women, "anarchists in the realm of the 'eternal feminine'" (*EH* "Why I Write Such Good Books" 5). Nietzsche calls the former "real" women and then shows them up as hypocritical imposters. He calls the latter "abortive women"—not real women at all—and heaps vituperation upon them. When he is finished with each type, his demolition is complete.

At the same time, the texts energetically develop a positive view of qualities of the feminine through the use of ancient myths and figurative language. As I shall show, the "feminine" that Nietzsche's works endorse is one that he formulates through his study of ancient Greek texts, and through his reading of the writings of J. J. Bachofen, the historian of ancient Roman law and author of books on archaic matriarchy, and those of the psychologist Eduard von Hartmann, author of an influential book on the unconscious. This is the feminine, I claim, that becomes the Dionysian aspect of tragedy in *The Birth of Tragedy* and Zarathustra's symbolic "eternal return," which affirms time and the natural world, and the pain of birth and death, as humanity's most important values. The effect of this revaluation, which restores to the feminine positive connotations imported from archaic times (according to Nietzsche's revisionist story), is to endow those meanings associated with "nature,"—especially its organic cycles of birth, growth, decay, and death—with positive value. The female is the privileged bearer of new life, the mother; in ancient times, she also supervised the laying out of bodies after death, and the mourning of the dead. In reaffirming the feminine, Nietzsche reaffirms the continuity of life with death.

Following Plato's "Symposium," Nietzsche's texts use the metaphor of childbirth to argue for intellectual and artistic creativity as the highest human activity. Men are the privileged creators here, but the particulars of parturition, and most especially the state of pregnancy, maintain a powerful hold on the texts, drawing meaning from the real bodies of women and their reproductive function. Receptivity and expectancy, as traits linked to pregnancy, are praised throughout as important features of an artist's (in the broadest sense) actual practice.

This privileging of the body over the reason of philosophy effectively and positively revalues the feminine's ancient metaphoric and material connections with the body and the earth. In effect, the Nietzschean polemics directed against the God of Jews and the Christians revalue positively the multiple, dynamic physical, with its feminine connotations, as against the singular transcendental, with its masculine ones. Nietzsche's use of poetic figures—metaphor, allegory, symbol, hyperbole, paradox, and irony—throughout his writings, something that the texts themselves characterize as feminine, disrupts the discourse of philosophy and opens it to its "other," in a specifically gendered sense. Symbols and images in his writings suggest the feminine psychoanalytically: the abyss, the sea, the gateway, the dance, the ring.

Following the textual affirmation of the feminine, and the elimination of "woman-as-such," Nietzsche's next move (to continue this artificial chronology) is to appropriate the feminine for the masculine, thus altering the stories about what it is to be a man. By this point, we notice that in wiping out "woman-as-such"—that is, the ideal essence of womanhood—Nietzsche has also by implication wiped out her opposite number, "man-as-such," as bearer of a complementary, idealized set of masculine character traits. In acquiring feminine traits, "man" has become a new being, beyond himself.[4] The inference for "woman" is that she too may move beyond the stereotypes to become a complete human self. Nietzsche's revisions create "whole" human beings; we might say they produce bisexual individuals, if bisexuality weren't conceptually too limiting, prescriptive, and dualistic. The suggestion that traits historically prescribed as feminine and those prescribed as masculine belong together in one individual in no way commits that individual to a half-and-halfness, to a particular sexual orientation, or even to the assumption and acceptance of those traits; rather, it opens up entirely new possibilities for self-identification.

Cultural Contexts: The Two-Sex Model in Nineteenth-Century Germany

Human conceptions and practices of sexuality are hardly timeless and changeless. In *Making Sex,* Thomas Laqueur argues that, biologically speaking, before the seventeenth century there was for all intents and purposes one sex—the male—of which the female was regarded as an imperfect variation. In ancient times, Laqueur maintains, gender, or the cultural construction of sexual difference, was far more significant than mere biology. The ancient one-sex story, which cast biological females as inferior, inside-out males, was discredited only gradually, through the general changes that constituted modernity over two centuries. In its place there arose a new story, that of the "two stable, incommensurable, opposite sexes." This "two-sex model" was presumed to be based on the scientific truth lurking below the surface, under the skin, in a newly conceptualized biological substrate. Sexual difference "in kind, not degree, seemed solidly grounded in nature," observes Laqueur (6). Where "nature" leads, culture is not far behind. On the face of it, the recognition of the existence of two incommensurable sexes should have given females as a class a new and improved status, but Laqueur argues that if anything, the change was for the worse. His general argument, supported by the examination both of specialized medical and scientific treatises and of their more readily accessible popular counterparts, is that the facts about sex are controversial, contradictory, and inseparable from their interpretation as gender. Moreover, these problematic assertions are taken as gospel and converted into everyday practice: "The political, economic, and cultural lives of men and women, their gender roles, are somehow based on these 'facts'" (6).

Nietzsche wrote his books well into the period during which the two-sex model held sway. Having examined "an endless stream of books and chapters" drawn from the late eighteenth and the nineteenth centuries, Laqueur finds a "new vision" of an "anatomical and physiological incommensurability . . . in the representation of woman in relation to man" (5–6). Anatomy was destiny, and across Europe women were schooled about the requirements of their "nature." Schopenhauer described women as "big children all their life long" ("On Woman" 106)—suited logically therefore to the company of children. Charles Darwin corroborated this notion in *The Descent of Man* (1870)—"In the formation of her skull, [the female] is said to be intermediate between the child and the man" (quoted in Dijkstra 168)—the implication being that science had proven that women's evolutionary growth "had been stunted" (Dijkstra 168). Bram Dijkstra claims that in this key work, Darwin follows Carl Vogt's *Lectures on Man* (1864), and in so doing adds a racist element to his evolutionary interpretation of sexual difference: "The skulls of man and woman are to be separated as if they belonged to two different species. . . . We may, therefore, say that the type of the female skull approaches, in many respects, that of the infant, and in a still greater degree that of the lower races" (quoted in Dijkstra 166–67). Through these influential treatises, and many more, men of science verified the incommensurability of the two sexes on a physiological level and then went effortlessly on to maintain the validity of the resulting gender role divisions and the superiority of white men.

In addition to the expansion of biological science, other cultural changes in the eighteenth and nineteenth centuries contributed to the development and elaboration of the story of a natural, ontological division between men and women. George Mosse observes that codes of sexual respectability developed as a primary value during this period in Germany, under the powerful influence of Pietism (an evangelical Protestantism to which Nietzsche's pastor father and his mother subscribed) and the rise both of the middle class and of nationalism. The masculine ideal was that of a vital, healthy, manly man, "tall and lithe" like a Greek statue. The first responsibility of this "manliness" was to marry and produce children, in order to ensure loyalty to the state: "Through the rule of the father as patriarch, the family educated its members to respect authority" (19-20). In Prussia, where Nietzsche grew up, Junker aristocracy maintained political control through the army and the church, the bureaucracy and the judiciary; Richard Evans notes that "the army's influence penetrated the whole of society" and "set the tone for society's attitudes toward women," which was characterized by intense hostility to women's emancipation (5-9). Codes of masculinity were enforced by public opinion; Evans reports that "in the circles most strongly influenced by official morality—the army, student corporations and parts of the middle class—a visit or two to a brothel was as necessary a *rite de passage* into the moral world of the adult ruling class as was the duelling scar; both were marks of honour, proofs of manhood" (17).

The feminine rules were simple: to be a good wife, mother, and moral guardian of the family. The public (masculine) and private (feminine) dichotomy was enforced not only by social pressure but by law in Prussia and Bavaria, where from the 1850s on women were barred from participating in meetings where politics were discussed (Cocalis and Goodman 20). Indeed, women were not admitted to German universities until after the turn of the twentieth century. Images of women playing like angelic children, smiling serenely amid hoards of children, soulfully gazing heavenward out of windows, reading the Bible to an assembled family, singing at the piano (birdcage artfully set to the rear of the frame), and sewing—in all the very picture of domestic bliss and moral probity—were reproduced in plays, novels, magazine stories, photographs, and portraits throughout the century. These images constitute the material of the "eternal feminine," the womanly ideal berated and parodied by Nietzsche.

Mosse notes that in the middle classes the difference between the sexes was taken as a given and an absolute; any confusion of categories "threatened chaos and loss of control. The clear and distinct roles assigned to men and women were basic" (16). "Sexual intoxication of any kind was viewed as both unmanly and inherently anti-social" (10), and any sort of perversion or deviance among males or females was a matter of deep shame and possible prosecution. A story widely circulated, especially for the benefit of the young, held that masturbation led to homosexuality, criminality, and madness (Mosse 11)—the first of these punishable by prison and loss of civil rights in Prussia (28).

This context is vital for understanding the moral climate in which Nietzsche grew to adulthood. Personally, he fell short of the ideal of the manly in almost every conceivable way. He was not tall and lithe of build, but rather of medium height and pudgy. He did make the mandatory visit to a brothel, but with either comic or tragic results, depending on whose account one accepts.[5] He was not healthy but constantly sick, possibly from a syphilitic infection picked up at the aforementioned bordello. He did not marry, and left no wife or children. By the standards of the day, he was most likely perverse, spending much of his time suspiciously alone.

In contrast to his life, Nietzsche's writings echo, from various perspectives, the moral codes and cultural expectations for men and women in his day; thus they function ironically, projecting the conventional stories for the scrutiny and evaluation of his audience. Readers have fallen into the trap of taking these cultural echoes as originals. Why, they ask, are Nietzsche's writings about women (in particular) so hackneyed—so conventional? As Kathleen Winninger concludes: "Nietzsche was a startlingly original thinker in so many ways that one is disappointed in what looks like an unthinking re-enactment in the long European tradition of misogyny" (239). The operative words in this sentence are, in my opinion, "looks like." The writings recycle conventional thinking on the roles of women and men, but they do so ironically, with intent, and usually they give themselves away as parodic reenactments, as I hope to show.

Something that makes me suspicious about taking Nietzsche straight when he echoes conventional nineteenth-century assessments of sex roles is that his writings also openly and defiantly oppose them. He advocated "sexual intoxication," which was regarded with abhorrence by the moral hegemony of the day, by asserting that the Greek god Dionysus was worthy of consideration, and by making sexual ecstasy an artistic attribute, or even a requirement. The texts also revalue passivity and suffering, assigning the former positive connotations of receptivity and arguing that the latter is indispensable for attaining a clearer knowledge of what it is to be human. All of these qualities—sexuality, passivity, suffering—fall under the general category "the body," which Nietzsche revalued in relation to the mind, and all have been conventionally aligned with femininity rather than with masculinity.

The fact that Nietzsche turned to the feminine to bolster his confrontation with the sex-gender stereotypes of his day is significant but not unprecedented. Romantic poets, dramatists, and novelists, for example, made claims for the sensitive souls of their male personae or heroes, who defied or resisted social conventions in order to be free spirits and cultivate their individuality. In the second half of the century, bohemians and decadents (the latter self-described artists with an "aestheticized and feminized" lifestyle) sustained the battle against normalcy, the middle-class heterosexual propriety supported by church and state. In *The Gender of Modernity,* Rita Felski writes, "Thus an imaginary identification with the feminine emerged as a key stratagem in the literary avant-garde's subversion of sexual and textual norms" (91). Felski notes that these textual subversions took the form of self-conscious attacks on realist representation, "turning toward a decadent aesthetic of surface, style, and parody that was explicitly coded as both 'feminine' and 'modern.'" For the decadents, as with the romantic writers, femininity "loosened itself from the body of woman" and joined the attributes of the male artist and/or his creations (Felski 91).

This description of the male artist/decadent fits Nietzsche himself. His writing style defies conventions of normal philosophical discourse, and he identifies with the avant-garde: "Need I say . . . that in questions of decadence I am experienced? I have spelled them forward and backward" (*EH* "Why I Am So Wise" 1). According to Joachim Köhler, in *Zarathustra's Secret* (2002), Nietzsche was unarguably homosexual.[6] I find Köhler's assessment convincing, and my own reading of Nietzsche's works tends to provide it with substantial textual support. However, I am more interested in Nietzsche's ideas about sexuality than in his practices of it, and as his texts go beyond the strict dichotomy of man/woman, so too do they disrupt the gay/straight distinction. Clearly his style—hyperbolic, metaphoric, symbolic, ironic—is disruptive and subversive; it both attracts and repels readers, and is difficult to reduce to a single interpretation. A similar ambiguity, a refusal to be pinned down, may hold true for Nietzsche as a sexual being.

The Philosophical *Agon*

Nietzsche's unconventional style often generates two seemingly opposed interpretative possibilities; the texts can be read both as truth and as falsehood simultaneously, creating the effect of double exposure or of contradiction.

In *Nietzsche on Truth and Philosophy,* Maudemarie Clark identifies two strategies for dealing with the self-contradiction of Nietzsche's texts. The first (which is her own approach) is "to show that the self-contradiction is only apparent"; the second is "to admit the contradiction but to argue that its presence in Nietzsche's work teaches us something about truth" (4). I prefer to think of the doubleness of Nietzsche's texts as expressions of his finely-tuned and almost pervasive irony, a literary style that is both witty and subversive. I agree with Clark about the determination of meaning in the texts; self-contradictions are only apparent and usually strategic. They serve to make us question the text and to read carefully.

To make readers think is part of Nietzsche's purpose as a writer. He made several private and public statements to the effect that good writing must engage and challenge its readers. In the notebook he kept during the summer of 1882, there is a series of writer's guidelines that he set down privately for his friend Lou Salomé, which concludes: "It isn't polite or clever to anticipate the easier objections of our reader. It is very polite and clever to leave the quintessence of our wisdom for the reader to articulate for himself" (*KSA* 10:23). And in the preface to *Human, All Too Human* (1886), we find this somewhat ambiguous summary of the effect of Nietzsche's writings on his exercised readers: "All [of my writings], I have been given to understand, contain snares and nets for unwary birds and in effect a persistent invitation to the overturning of habitual evaluations and valued habits. . . . My writings have been called a schooling in suspicion, even more in contempt, but fortunately also in courage, indeed in audacity." In this short passage Nietzsche creates an *agon,* a power struggle. He alleges that his readers have brought on the competition between himself and them (he is the hunter, they are the unwary birds). His texts generate a number of perspectives, but by necessity the two most active are those of the writer and the reader. In Nietzsche's estimation, alert readers will contest his assertions, spot his snares, and gain the strength and courage to use their wings.

Such readers are not easy to create. They have to be engaged viscerally. Nietzsche describes the philosophy he approves in terms analogous to erotic sexuality: "Philosophy in the manner of Plato should be defined as an erotic contest, as a further development of the old agonal gymnastics and their presuppositions" (*TI* "Expeditions of an Untimely Man" 23). These presuppositions are those of the competitive power struggles that formed the basis for Greek athletics, social rivalries, war, tragic dialogue, and eventually law and dialectics. Though the "eros" that fostered most of these cultural events was homoerotic, Nietzsche carries over the analogy of erotic contest to many of his descriptions of heterosexuality. He does not exclude hate from his definition of erotic love, in that both love and hate are powerful, ultimately creative emotions: "Has my definition of love been heard? . . . Love—in its means, war; at bottom, the deadly hatred of the sexes" (*EH* "Why I Write Such Good Books" 5). There is clearly nothing sentimental about the erotic love Nietzsche has in mind. The sexual agon, or contest, involves bodies—muscles, sinews, posture, emotions, brains.

I suggest that Nietzsche would like us to read as actively as if we were engaged in such an agon. His texts are a "schooling," a training in athletic reading as an erotic contest, where eroticism includes both passionate love and hatred. If the eroticism is heterosexual, then there are at least two sets of possible players. The author/narrator is a biological male, and he speaks, very often, from an aggressively masculine position. He assumes an antagonistic stance toward female readers—often by addressing himself explicitly to a male audience, or through disparagement and belittlement, letting the negative have full play as he goads his female opponents. Or he addresses male readers, and by doing so sets up an internal *agon*, where the sexual distinction is a self-division. In both cases, Nietzsche is able to elicit a physiological response in his readers, encouraging them to become active contributors to the process of valuation that his texts promote.

"I further recall," Nietzsche notes in the passage about Platonic philosophy, "that the entire higher culture and literature of classical France also grew up on the soil of sexual interest. One may seek everywhere in it for gallantry, sensuality, sexual contest, 'woman'—one will never seek in vain" (*TI* "Expeditions of an Untimely Man" 23). That Nietzsche here puts "woman" in quotation marks alerts us to a duplicity of intention. He refers to the French proverb "Cherchez la femme" ("look for the woman"—at the bottom of a mystery, for example), but uses this "woman" as a marker for sexuality, and not necessarily a female person. Higher culture "grows" up on the "soil" of sexual interest. The metaphor connects sex and the earth, basic conditions for human survival and growth, and Nietzsche associates these earthy qualities with the flowering of the two cultures he most cherished— those of ancient Greece and the French Enlightenment. Both grew and flourished by valuing the erotic contest and keeping sex in the foreground.

The analogy that Nietzsche draws in this passage, however, is to writing (and reading) philosophy "in the manner of Plato." It is a kind of "dialogic" writing—to use a term coined by the translators of the work of the Russian formalist Bakhtin. Dialogic writing in the manner of Nietzsche often works toward the discovery of truth through the collision of or contest between several points of view. Because different viewpoints clash, and Nietzsche's texts often cast this metaphorically as a struggle between the sexes, interpretation becomes a matter of participation in the erotic agon, with senses, nerves, sinews, and passions engaged.

Interpretation becomes the reader's challenge, and it is clear that the interpretive challenge is intentional. Nietzsche explicitly raises questions of interpretation, as he confronts the implications of the death of God—a "death" he has diagnosed and pronounced. In the Judeo-Christian tradition God had figured, metaphorically, as the Author and Creator of the text of the universe; humans were part of the divine text as well as its intended audience. As readers created by the divine Author, they had been compelled to interpret that text, and had done so under the imprimatur of divine authority, knowing that their answers were accountable—that is, they could be wrong, but also could be right. For Nietzsche, the dawning of a secular era meant the end of truth as a set of "givens," the divine knowledge that guaranteed life meaning, purpose, and value. In such a transition, there was no guarantee that life meant one thing rather than another, or anything at all; humans now had to be their own authors, create their own texts, and serve as their own interpreters. Nietzsche thought that this amount of self-responsibility would be an impossibility for many, and a crushing weight for all. He saw it as an awesome burden. The worst calamity facing modern Europeans, in Nietzsche's view, was the insidious spread of nihilism, the debacle of meaning and value, the "no" to life.

Nietzsche's own texts say "no" to values that he believes are worn out, serve to deaden or tyrannize people, and contribute to the spread of nihilism. They say "yes" to those values that he thinks will strengthen people and give them self-confidence. People must become strong enough in themselves, powerful enough, to be creators; in *The Will to Power* he notes "that every strengthening and increase of power opens up new perspectives" (616).

Nietzsche on Gender focuses on Nietzsche's "no" to the old laws (or conventions) governing people's sexual behavior and his "yes" to the feminine as part of his ambitious program to revalue all values. In the pages that follow, I support my interpretations through close readings of a number of Nietzsche's texts. In addition, I focus on some of the works he read during his formative years in Basel, and consider his relationship with Lou Salomé, which I believe helped him develop his revaluation of the feminine. I expect that many readers will disagree both with my assertions and with my proofs. Clearly, questions about sex-gender in Nietzsche's writings are complicated, and they have no obvious answers—which is to say that they are the best sort of questions.

One difficulty that we encounter in addressing these questions is a problem fundamental to language. For example, if we are to dispense with "man" and "woman," what then do we call the resulting humans? Do we need new names? In *The Gay Science,* Nietzsche asserts that names are at least as important as things, that "it is enough to create new names and estimations and probabilities in order to create in the long run new 'things'" (59). He has given us new estimations and new perspectives on sex-gender, but no new vocabulary as such. For the purposes of this study, we are thus stuck with the old terminology (as I write in English and use English translations of Nietzsche, with terms to match). Nomenclature that differentiates the sexes is a complicated matter both in English and in German, and may itself be symptomatic of problems in fitting language to complex realities.

In English, there are four words that are commonly used to refer to each sex-gender: male, man, men, and masculine on the one hand, and female, woman, women, and feminine on the other. Generally, and in this study, "male" and "female" are used to indicate biological sexual beings (thus unavoidably tearing apart the carefully cultivated term "sex-gender"); "man" and "woman" refer to gendered individuals; "men" and "women" denote historical (or "real") persons; and "masculine" and "feminine" mark character traits conventionally associated with each gender. Unlike English, German has one category that encompasses both sex and gender. The German *das Weib* (a neuter word) is translated as both "female" and "woman" at the translator's discretion, and *der Mann* as both "male" and "man." In addition, German has a polite (feminine) word that signifies an adult woman, *die Frau.* The nuances evoked by the use of *die Frau* rather than *das Weib* are naturally lost in translation, since both appear as "woman." German has plural forms for all of these, which are translated as "women" and "men," as well as a form of address that corresponds to the English "ladies" and "gentlemen" *(Damen und Herren).*

The adjectival forms of "man" and "woman" in German are the counterparts of the English "feminine" and "masculine" and are equally stereotyped. In German as in English, the connotations of "womanly" and "manly" exaggerate virtues attributed to each distinct gender. And in both languages, the attribution of characteristics of one gender to the other is belittling. In mockery and denigration, Nietzsche frequently uses the word "womanish" *(weibisch)* to refer to a man and "mannish" *(männisch)* to describe a woman, thereby calling attention to the stereotypes.

Finally, as in English, in German we face the problem of the generic *Mensch* or "man." Nietzsche uses *Mensch* to indicate the human. Neither Walter Kaufmann nor R. J. Hollingdale, his two most widely read English translators, render *Mensch* as "human being," save on rare occasions; both use the generic "man," and this usage alone gives the texts a more sexist bias than they otherwise need to have. The now-familiar word Übermensch has been popularly translated either as "superman" (with connotations of a male superhero wearing underpants on the outside and a red cape) or as "overman" (with little meaning other than an implied masculinity). In *Ecce Homo,* Nietzsche states it does not refer to a person—much less to a person of the masculine persuasion—but to a "type of supreme achievement" (*EH* "Why I Write Such Good Books" 1). I argue in chapter 6 that the type of supreme achievement the Übermensch symbolizes is in fact the exact opposite of the heroic male image conjured by "superman"; it symbolizes instead the overcoming of resentment of women and of ties to birth and death— the complete acceptance of oneself and one's mortality. Rather than adopt a clumsy translation, I will follow Nietzsche's example and use his original term to signify this supreme achievement.

What follows can be simply plotted. I begin with the negative, as chapter 1 takes up Nietzsche's dismissal of "woman." In chapter 2, I trace the sources of Nietzsche's positive work on the feminine, focusing on two of his intellectual forebears—Bachofen and Hartmann—in particular detail. Chapter 3 offers an interpretation of *The Birth of Tragedy,* which springs from these sources; chapter 4 shows how, through the use of metaphor and irony, the positive and the negative feminine are set at odds in passages in *The Gay Science.* Chapters 5 and 6 are devoted to *Thus Spoke Zarathustra: A Book for Everyone and No One,* a crucial text in which positive values associated with the Dionysian feminine return. The conclusion addresses criticisms of my argument and, drawing on material from biologists and the media about transgender research and practice, sets forth some of its implications.

Nietzsche's No to Woman
Knocking Down an Ideal

THE WORD "woman" is used in two ways in Nietzsche's texts: literally, to refer to a person of the female sex, and metaphorically, to illustrate abstract concepts such as life, truth, happiness, wisdom, and sensuality. When "woman" refers to a person of the female sex, the texts almost always treat the concept as an ideal whose use-by date has expired. In *On the Genealogy of Morals,* anticipating questions about his demolition projects, Nietzsche admits that he may be asked whether he is "erecting an ideal or knocking one down?" He answers with another question: "Have you ever asked yourselves sufficiently how much the erection of *every* ideal on earth has cost? How much reality has had to be misunderstood and slandered, how many lies have had to be sanctified . . . ?" (2:24). In the case of "woman," we don't need to ask whether Nietzsche is erecting an ideal or knocking one down: woman is taking the knocks, and being carted off to the dump with other old and now worthless ideals.

An ideal is a standard of perfection, excellence, or beauty; it is a value and can act as a goal. Nietzsche thinks that ideals are necessary for human life, and he works painstakingly to create them—the positive, metaphoric "woman" among them, as I shall argue in subsequent chapters. However, his work also makes clear how misleading and deceptive most ideals can be; they slander reality and "sanctify" lies. *Twilight of the Idols* claims that many of our most cherished ideals have become idols that can be sounded out for their false ring by tapping them ever so slightly with a hammer, "as with a tuning fork" (*TI* Foreword). In this way—sounding out ideals that have become idols—Nietzsche clears the ground for the creation of new ideals.

Twilight of the Idols begins with a number of "maxims," one of which reads, "Man created woman—but what out of? Out of a rib of his God, of his 'ideal'" ("Maxims and Arrows" 13). In this instance, Nietzsche uses his tuning fork on the biblical story that God created woman out of one of man's ribs. The central ideal under the hammer here is God, but through reversal and substitution Nietzsche makes us examine all the terms of the story. "Man" is substituted for God; man then creates woman from one of God's ribs. The maxim implies that God, like woman, is an ideal created by man. Neither exists apart from man; both exist as man's fiction, a product of his creative will to power.

In tying "God" and "woman" together, Nietzsche asks us to ponder the hypothetical connection. As a rib of God, is woman a part of man's God-ideal? If "woman" is part of God, even if only his rib, then God's death, pronounced by Nietzsche, has grave implications for man's other ideal, "woman." Are the two ideals so connected that the death of the one means the death of the other? What sort of a thing is woman, after all? The references to "woman" as a female person that are scattered throughout Nietzsche's texts ask us to think about these questions and others. Of what does the ideal of "woman" consist, and what is at stake in holding onto it? Whose purposes does it serve? In posing the questions, the texts simultaneously expose the ideal as a "misunderstanding" of reality and, in the interest of truth, knock it down.

The Ideal of the "Eternal Feminine"

According to R. J. Ackermann, there are "three or four" social positions constantly considered in Nietzsche's work: the artist, the scientist, the philosopher, and the saint or prophet. He adds that "one also finds a sharp distinction between the social positions of noble and herd men, and a recognition that women must be reckoned with, this last an obscure but compelling demand" (107). This assertion calls attention to the fact that Nietzsche's texts set women apart as a singular class, whose social role is to be women, whereas men come in many different classes, whose social roles are differentiated according to avocation and skills, not according to sex-gender. The description also suggests that women figure significantly in the texts, but how they figure, or why their figuring is important and compelling, remains obscure, a mystery.

In using the words "obscure but compelling" to describe references to women in Nietzsche's texts, Ackermann may be responding to allusions to the myth of the eternal feminine, which was current and powerful in Nietzsche's day. The phrase appears at the climactic, melodramatic end of Goethe's *Faust*, signifying in the context of that poem the obscure but compelling attraction of the feminine to the good, the innocent, the pure and the holy—and given these terms, the obscure but compelling attraction of the masculine to the feminine—and finally through the feminine, the redemption of the masculine. This mode of the eternal feminine reproduces the social injunction to females on the two-sex model to be wives, mothers, and moral guardians of men, and of their families. Goethe's poem ends with a mystical chorus singing in paradise: "The eternal feminine / Draws us upward" ("Das Ewigweibliche / Zieht uns hinan," Goethe 351)—upward, that is, out of body, to a region of unmixed spiritual blessedness. Goethe's female characters generally represent an ideal of "transcendent moral nobility" (Grundlehner 152)—a conscientiousness weaker or wholly lacking in the male characters, and symbolized by the mysterious transmogrification of Faust to heaven through its agency.

The well-known nineteenth-century image of the woman as moral inspiration and redeemer, the "angel"—whether in the house or in heaven (as in *Faust*) or mysteriously linked to a magical sacred power equated with redemptive love (as in Wagner's operas)—has a content as sentimental as it is unrealistic. It is this ideal that Nietzsche's writing deplores, debunks, and temporizes, linking it to cultural fashions of the times. By suggesting that man created woman out of a rib of God, Nietzsche is obliquely or obscurely, to use Ackermann's word, referring to this ideal of the eternal feminine, whereby an idealized "woman" is more spiritual and closer to God than man, and can therefore save and redeem him.

The Nietzschean polemic aimed at exposing this ideal is particularly passionate because it is tied to another equally provocative polemic directed at Christianity. The latter demolition project is, in turn, a major target of the Nietzschean critique of modernity. From the perspective of *On the Genealogy of Morals* and *The Anti-Christ* (to name two texts where the critique of modernity is central), modern European culture is suffering from the effects of a two-thousand-year-long disease, brought on by an injection of toxic Platonism which located the true and the just elsewhere, out-of-this-world, in a separate metaphysical sphere only dimly and imperfectly perceptible to humans. With Christianity ("Platonism for the people" [*BGE* Preface]), the disease became full blown: "heaven" became the object of the peoples' hopes, and "earth" or "the world" a term of derision, abuse, despair, evil.

Because the world is defined negatively in Christianity, *The Anti-Christ* argues, "values of decline, nihilistic values hold sway under the holiest names," but "one does not say 'nothingness': one says 'the Beyond'; or 'God'; or 'true life'; or Nirvana, redemption, blessedness" (7). Furthermore, Christianity, as a result of despising the world for embodying "the instinct for growth, for continuance, for accumulation of forces, for power" (*A* 6), has willed, bred and achieved weakness, contentment, "the domestic animal, the herd animal, the sick animal man" (*A* 3), who makes a virtue of "active sympathy for the ill-constituted and weak" (*A* 2) known as pity.

Pity, the feeling through which "suffering itself becomes contagious" (*A* 7), is for Nietzsche a symptom of a democratic culture or herd morality in which members are "at one in the religion of pity, in sympathy with whatever feels, lives, suffers . . . in their almost feminine incapacity to remain spectators of suffering" (*BGE* 202). The preface to *On the Genealogy of Morals* introduces as one of its central concerns "the problem of the value of pity and of the morality of pity (—I am opposed to the pernicious modern effeminacy of feeling—)" (6). Psychologically, pity weakens and depresses; philosophically, it is life-denying: "Pity is practical nihilism" (*A* 7). Connected to a pathological condition present "almost everywhere in Europe today," pity manifests itself as "a morbid sensitivity and susceptibility to pain . . . a downright cult of suffering. The unmanliness of that which is in such fanatic circles baptized 'pity' is, I think, the first thing which leaps to the eye" (*BGE* 293). Men who pity are assuming traits of the eternal feminine; by extension, women are its embodiment. "Nothing in our unhealthy modernity is more unhealthy than Christian pity" (*A* 7); Christianity, "the religion of pity" (*A* 7), is also feminine—or at any rate, not masculine— "emasculated" (*GM* 2:14).

Christianity's practitioners are not feminists, but they commit "feminism" [*Feminismus*]. Nietzsche's texts will confuse readers who interpret the "feminism" they find there as a movement supporting women's claims to political equality and personal autonomy. Nietzsche's "feminism" means "of the feminine," the eternal feminine as it appears in *Faust,* connoting "belief in God and Christian conscience: that is . . . feminism" (*GS* 357). It means idealism, in whatever form: "[We are] still men of conscience: namely, in that we do not want to return to that which we consider outlived. . . . [we are] hostile to the half-and-halfness of all romanticism and fatherland-worship; hostile, too, to the pleasure-seeking and lack of conscience of the artists . . . ; hostile, in short, to the whole of European feminism (or idealism, if you prefer that word), which is forever 'drawing us upward' and precisely thereby 'bringing us down'" (*D* Preface 4).

This passage links idealism and the eternal feminine through the allusion to the ending of *Faust.* Nietzsche reverses the valuations generally accorded the ideal: for him up is down; the ideal, the belief in an unchanging Place of Truth—heaven, nation, or artwork—is a symptom of cultural decadence. "Everything modern will serve posterity as an emetic—and that on account of its moral mawkishness and falseness, its innermost feminism that likes to call itself 'idealism' and at any rate believes it is idealism" (*GM* 3:19). This is an idealism encoded in sacred and secular texts of Christianity:

"The *Imitatio Christi* is one of the books I cannot hold in my hands without experiencing a physiological resistance: it exhales a parfum of the 'eternal feminine' for which one has to be French—or a Wagnerian. . . [*sic*]. This saint has a way of talking about love that makes even Parisiennes curious" (*TI* "Expeditions" 4). Using his favorite set of rhetorical tools, Nietzsche "sounds out" in this passage the connection between a canonical late medieval Christian text (Saint Thomas à Kempis's *The Imitation of Christ*) and the ideal of the eternal feminine.

The first obvious polemical tool exhibited here is name-calling, the *argumentum ad hominem* that reduces the message to a personal attack on its object, or focuses attention on subjective aspects of the message that distract the reader from its more impersonal, abstract, or universal significance. Here, in under forty words, the text insults the work *Imitatio Christi*, Christianity, the feminine, the French, Wagner and Wagnerians, the sainted author of the text, and Parisiennes (women of Paris). It does so furthermore on the basis of physical, sensual, and thus highly individualized and private—rather than general and public—objections. The reader learns nothing about the book in question but a great deal about the prejudices of its reader—Nietzsche. Name-calling calls attention in the most explicit way to the valuing subject and to the very personal biases, arising in this case from the body's responses to an object, that attach to valuation.

A second feature of the Nietzschean polemic is also illustrated by this passage: its use of guilt-by-association, or collective vituperation. Here, the book in question activates in Nietzsche-the-reader a "physiological resistance" as to a bad smell—or at least, as to the scent of the eternal feminine—an odor that attracts and seduces the likes of the French and Wagnerians. The passage douses all French people and all Wagnerians—and Saint Thomas à Kempis—with the same perfume, and in doing so makes several points. One is a point about the book in question: that the *Imitatio Christi* seduces the reader's mind in the same manner that French perfume seduces the senses—sexually—and that this is a form of seduction well known to readers of French texts and aficianados of Wagner's operas. Another is a point about the eternal feminine: that for all its high-minded rhetoric about "drawing us upward," its appeal is not only connected to the physical but its basis is in the physical, like all bases. Finally, if the use of "labeling" or name-calling attracts attention to the prejudices of its writer (and by extension of its readers), the use collective vituperation demonstrates how prejudices work by association—even that of accidental proximity, as a bad smell permeates a space.

A third characteristic of the Nietzschean polemic is its militant use, and its unphilosophical abuse, of the rhetorical antithesis (pair of terms of opposite or sharply contrasted meaning)—a tool Aristotle recommends "because the significance of contrasted ideas is easily felt, and also because it has the effect of a logical argument" (*Rhetoric* 3.9.20-24:185). Antithesis holds opposites apart in order to differentiate, categorize, and evaluate each member of the pair. Aristotle's *Rhetoric* makes the listener's judgment of the speaker's argument crucial, and that judgment depends on the speaker's careful deployment of antithesis: "It is by putting two opposing conclusions side by side that you prove one of them false" (3.9.23-24:185). The *Imitatio Christi* passage establishes a short set of antitheses. On the one side, *The Imitation of Christ* attracts the terms "eternal feminine" and "saint"— signifiers connoting the sacred, the pure, the truth, the eternal—Christian ideals. On the other side of the antithesis, there are the terms "parfum" and "Parisiennes"—signifiers connoting a sensual, sexual femininity. The phrase "parfum of the 'eternal feminine'" yokes the pair of antithetical terms closely in what is almost an oxymoron, a figure of speech that subverts the antithesis by combining—rather than holding apart—a pair of contradictory terms. Whereas antithesis is a rhetorical form congenial to the prose of rational argument, oxymoron is poetic, and because it encodes paradox, it is often used to gesture toward the limits of language. In the passage under consideration, the antithesis between the sacred text and the sexual feminine body is revealed to be unstable—antithesis slipping toward oxymoron—and in the process another antithesis is maintained: that between the reader/writer Nietzsche and his revulsion on the one hand and the hypocritical text on the other. In this instance, the terms are held firmly apart.

The eternal feminine as an ideal of Christian and democratic industrial cultures enthrones values of piety, mediocrity, moderation, tranquility, modesty, and obedience (all words with which Nietzsche describes "herd morality"—see *BGE* 199-202). Starting with *Beyond Good and Evil* (1886), Nietzsche's texts turn to a serious reflection on the difference between the noble and the ignoble, variously labeled master/slave morality or noble/herd morality. For the most part, they align Christianity, the feminine ("feminism," the eternal feminine), and the ignoble herd. A passage from *The Anti-Christ* both demonstrates and explains the antithesis:

> Freedom from convictions of any kind, the capacity for an unconstrained view, pertains to strength.... The "believer" does not belong to himself, he can only be a means, he has to be used, he needs someone who will use him. His

instinct accords the highest honour to a morality of selflessness. . . . Belief of any kind is itself an expression of selflessness, of self-alienation. . . [sic]. If one considers what need people have of an external regulation to constrain and steady them, how compulsion, slavery in a higher sense, is the sole and final condition under which the person of weaker will, woman especially, can prosper: then one also understands the nature of conviction, "faith." (54)

This passage sets up an opposition between strength and weakness, and then makes woman the chief exemplar of weakness; because woman is a "person of weaker will," she (rather than the "he" of the translation) is the prime example of the believer, the person who does not belong to "himself," the person of conviction and of religious faith. The passage draws an explicit analogy between religious faith and slavery, and diagnoses the extraordinary moral value placed upon selflessness as a psychological condition of self-alienation and as a symptom of the need for external regulation. Selflessness—altruism—is one of the central character traits of the eternal feminine. This "angel in the house" possesses the tyrannical power of resentment and the moral high ground, well diagnosed by Nietzsche's descriptions of slave morality.

The passage from *The Anti-Christ* briefly indicates the other side of its antithesis: the opposite of the believer is the "person of truth" as seen from the perspective of classical Rome—that is (in Nietzsche's system), the perspective of the self-affirming individual who has attained self-mastery. The dissection of "the person of weaker will, woman especially" in this passage signals the notion of autonomy lying for the most part unstated but available for thinking, as the other half of the dichotomy. "—What is noble?" Nietzsche asks in *Beyond Good and Evil;* there is "some fundamental certainty which a noble soul possesses in regard to itself, something which may not be sought or found, and perhaps may not be lost either.—The noble soul has reverence for itself—" (*BGE* 287).

Nobility is so nearly and exclusively masculine in Nietzsche's texts that when the condition is attributed to a woman we take notice. An aphorism in *Beyond Good and Evil* points to the formulation of the eternal feminine as an ideal in the Middle Ages, to its recycled version in the nineteenth century, and finally to its reception: "That which Dante and Goethe believed of woman—the former when he sang 'ella guardava suso, ed io in lei' [she looked upward, and I with/through her], the latter when he translated it 'the eternal womanly draws us upward'—I do not doubt that every nobler woman will resist this belief, for that is precisely what she believes of the eternal manly" (*BGE* 236).

The text holds the sexes apart, the sexual "antagonism" intact, maintain-ing sexual difference and the norm of heterosexuality, and indicating its awareness that readers are gendered, with gender identity cards assigned by their reading. The aphorism anticipates late twentieth-century feminist reader-response criticism by asking: If the eternal feminine draws us up-ward, how does a woman read this line? If she is "noble," she "resists" inter-pellation, or taking up the subject position offered by the text—positioning as a man—and maintains her identity as a woman reader, capable of being drawn aloft only by the ideal of the opposite sex, the "eternal manly."

What this aphorism omits, implies through its omission, and invites consideration of (among other things) is the response of the less noble woman reader to the texts of Dante and Goethe. If "every nobler woman" will resist the pull of the text, what will happen to the others—the herd animals, the "believers," whose chief characteristic is weakness of will and willingness to be led? If the woman reader of Dante and Goethe is not noble but only a herd animal, like most women in Nietzsche's view, the aphorism implies that she will not resist the pull of the text. Therefore she, like the text's masculine readers, will be drawn upward by the feminine ideal. She will believe it herself, and her vanity will be gratified; she will become self-alienated, watching herself being watched. Her attitude toward the opposite sex, and indeed to her own sex, will become complex and hypo-critical. She will become an actress of the masculine ideal of woman; she will enact the eternal feminine, the Angel in the House.

Woman as actress of man's ideal notions of her: Nietzsche's texts not only diagnose this condition but seek its genealogy and its implications. It is a masculine ideal that some women have internalized—but not every woman has fallen for it or "believes" in it. The ones who resist it in their hearts merely "play," or become actresses of, the eternal feminine. Of all the masks that Nietzsche wears in front of women, the attitude he takes toward these actresses is most ambivalent. Does he admire them? Does he detest them? Sometimes he counsels them to put on their own masks more securely—here for example, sounding very much like an advice column for teenage girls: "You want to make him interested in you? Then pretend to be embarrassed in his presence" (BGE 113). Usually, however, he notes that the "tremendous subtlety of woman's instinct" (WP 806) alerts her to the necessity of playing her part: "All women are subtle in exaggerating their weaknesses; they are inventive when it comes to weakness in order to appear as utterly fragile ornaments who are hurt even by a speck of dust. Their existence is supposed to make men feel clumsy, and guilty on that score.

Thus they defend themselves against the strong and the 'law of the jungle'" (*GS* 66). Acting a part is an instinctive defense for women, and as other Nietzschean texts imply, it is something with which the writer sympathizes. He discusses the necessity for "profound spirits" to adopt masks, for life roles to be "played": "What? A great man? I always see only the actor of his own ideal" (*BGE* 97).

An aphorism on the actor in *The Gay Science* concludes with these famous words:

> Finally, *women*. Reflect on the whole history of women: do they not *have* to be first of all and above all actresses? Listen to the physicians who have hypnotized women; finally, love them—let yourself be "hypnotized by them!" What is always the end result? That they "put on something" even when they take off everything.
>
> Woman is so artistic. (*GS* 361)

The implication of the phrase in quotation marks—women "put on something"—is that even in bed they have to act. Commenting on this passage, Gayatri Chakravorty Spivak names what Nietzsche implies: women can fake orgasm, whereas men can't (170), which is one of the real unfakable differences between the sexes.[1]

In the case of women, the text stresses the necessity of playing a part: "Do they not *have* to be actresses?" Why this necessity? In this aphorism Nietzsche leaves the question open, but in others he answers it. That woman's play-acting secures economic support for her entire life is a "secret" that Nietzsche's texts give away several times. There are telling passages on women's well-developed hypocrisy in the posthumously published notes that constitute *The Will to Power,* but if we focus on the texts Nietzsche himself sent to the printer, we find plenty of evidence to suggest that something is at stake in letting this particular cat out of the bag: "Honor and honesty.—Those girls who want to owe their whole life's maintenance to their youthful charms alone, and whose cunning is prompted by their shrewd mothers, want the same thing as courtesans—only the girls are more clever and less honest" (*HAH* 1:404). The word "owe" needs attention here; the "girls" will pay for their maintenance throughout their entire lives, and the payment will require cleverness—shrewd mothers and youthful charms in the first place, and then their own shrewdness, to "maintain" the charade: "Simulating—oneself!—Now she loves him and looks ahead with quiet confidence—like a cow. Alas, what bewitched him was precisely that she seemed utterly changeable and unfathomable. . . . Wouldn't she do well to simulate a lack of love? Is this not the counsel of—love? *Vivat como-edia*" (GS 67). Long live the comedy.

Another example illustrates Nietzsche's genealogical approach to this social distribution of roles in particularly interesting terms: "It is a sign of the shrewdness of women that almost everywhere they have known how to get themselves fed, like drones in a beehive. One should consider, however, what that fact means originally, and why men do not have themselves fed by women. It is certainly because male vanity and respect are greater than female shrewdness; for women have known how through subordination to secure for themselves the preponderant advantage, even indeed the dominion" (HAH 1:412). The paradox of women's domination over men through (hypocritical) submission to them is fully consistent with the argument, developed in *Genealogy of Morals* and elsewhere, that the weak dominate the strong and indeed that slave morality, the morality of submission, "has won" over that of strength (GM 1:9). But as this passage implies, the women's domination is a mixed privilege: drones in a beehive may live lives of indulgence but they are slaves all the same. Similarly, the masculine position is made up of parts of strength and weakness; its mastery is only apparent (for the real master is the "submissive" woman) and it is based on the superior "strength" of the male's vanity and ambition.

The reason that a woman can "subdue" and "conquer" a man through love, and so "redeem" him (we are in the realm of poetry, fiction, opera, and melodrama now) is that she embodies the values of the community, the herd, before which most men must bow down: "Man is a coward when confronted with the Eternal Feminine—and the females know it" (CW 3). At least, the females used to know it—and although some remember, some have forgotten that their "submission" to the male is a power play: "Love. The idolization of love practiced by women is fundamentally and originally an invention of their shrewdness, inasmuch as it enhances their power and makes them seem ever more desirable in the eyes of men. But through centuries-long habituation to this exaggerated evaluation of love it has come to pass that they have become entangled in their own net and forgotten how it originated. They themselves are now more deceived than men are" (HAH 1:415).

Nietzsche suggests here, and in all the passages where "woman" is unmasked as an actress of the eternal feminine, that woman has been at least an active collaborator in her own "submission" to man. We begin to discern a split in the category "woman." There are those who still enjoy playing the part of woman, Nietzsche suggests, and those who do not, for they have "become entangled in their own net." When women forget the masquerade, and the eternal feminine grows into their skin, they become truly selfless: "Women in love come to be just as they are in the image that the men by whom they are loved have of them" (*HAH* 1:400). Then they are vulnerable; then they solicit men's pity and protection; then what was positive enjoyment of power becomes negative dependence, slavery: "It indicates a complete lack of nobility of disposition when someone prefers to live in dependency, at the expense of others, merely so as not to have to work and usually with a secret animosity towards those he is dependent on.—Such a disposition is much more frequent among women than among men, also much more excusable (for historical reasons)" (*HAH* 1:356).

"For historical reasons" most women are ignoble—that is to say, over long periods of time women have been economically dependent on men; their dependence is a result of social conditioning and is not "natural." This dependence has made women especially easy prey for the ascetic priest: "When he [the ascetic priest] was dealing with sufferers or the lower classes, with work-slaves or prisoners (or with women—who are mostly both at once, work-slaves and prisoners), he required hardly more than a little ingenuity in name-changing and rebaptizing to make them see benefits and a relative happiness in things they formerly hated" (*GM* 2:18). If there is a moral here—and clearly the polemic is directed at present manners, as it reports the situation of women as work-slaves and prisoners in the present tense—it is that the alliance of institutional Christianity (via the priesthood) and the weak (via the telling example of womankind) has been particularly destructive for those whose suffering it set out particularly to assuage. If women's plight (as weak, as slaves, as dependents) has been historically determined, it is therefore "more forgivable" for women (than for men) to harbor a secret resentment toward their masters.

An aphorism in *The Gay Science* is instructive regarding the subject of "forgiveness" toward or kindness to women. This passage has received attention from readers who think it insightful on the issue of women's vulnerability, but I offer it here as an example of a text whose meaning is perspectival and ambiguous:

> *Will and willingness.* Someone took a youth to a sage and said: "Look, he is being corrupted by women." The sage shook his head and smiled. "It is men," he said, "that corrupt women; and all the failings of women should be atoned by and improved in men. For it is man who creates for himself the image of woman, and woman forms herself according to this image."

"You are too kind-hearted about women," said one of those present; "you do not know them." The sage replied: "Will is the manner of men; willingness that of women. That is the law of the sexes—truly, a hard law for women. All of humanity is innocent of its existence; but women are doubly innocent.[2] Who could have oil and kindness enough for them?"

"Damn oil! Damn kindness!" someone else shouted out of the crowd; "women need to be educated better!"—"Men need to be educated better," said the sage and beckoned to the youth to follow him.—The youth, however, did not follow him. (GS 68)

There are four clearly defined masculine perspectives dramatized in this aphorism: those of the youth, the sage, and two different bystanders. The sage, typical of the tribal elder, a Zarathustra precursor and principal actor or character in the narrative, describes women's situation from the supposed pinnacle of years and wisdom. His central point—that men create the eternal feminine as an ideal and that women strive to live up to it—places the question of women's "nature" or natural attributes (purity, idealism, moral integrity, kindness, gentleness, and so on) on the masculine agenda. Man desires the eternal feminine, creates it as a model in religion, art, philosophy, science, psychology, even in bed—wherever culture extends—and women "willingly" imitate it. This is a point that Nietzsche makes in several of his ideal-destroying texts on "woman," as we have seen.

Having put forth the notion that man creates for himself the image of woman by which woman forms herself, the sage then produces an example of exactly such masculine image-formation. By handing down a "law" of the sexes that constructs the masculine as the active and the feminine as the passive partner in the sexual dualism—"Will is the manner of men; willingness that of women"—the sage exemplifies his own doctrine. The passage drips with his patronizing condescension not only to women but to his (presumably masculine) audience of textual narratees.

If I were determined to interpret the sage's pronouncements as signifying the position of truth in the aphorism, the text's construction of three other positions would at least make me reflect on the possibility of other points of view on the Woman Question. The two other speakers presumably represent positions contemporary with the text (1882). The first questions the sage's benevolent attitude to women on the grounds of his lack of experience, implying that the sage's theory lacks empirical evidence, in the form of personal or carnal knowledge of women, to support it. If the sage really knew women, this speaker hints, he might even carry a whip when he visited them. This speaker represents the voice of the masculine realist, for whom the difference between men and women is apparent; he is not given to pondering the problem of "images" and his practical view inclines him toward misogyny—or at least toward keeping women in their place. He is a centrist, a man of his time. The other masculine speaker is equally offended by the sage's benevolence toward women—"Damn oil! Damn kindness!"—and suggests that women need better education. This speaker represents the liberal or socialist, for whom the sage's recommended kindness is elitist or aristocratic, certainly retrograde. He implies that if women had the same educational advantages as men they wouldn't need men to create an image for them.

The sage's response—"men need to be educated better"—is consistent with his argument that men make the images to which women conform. If, by being educated better, men made superior images or established a new ideal of woman, then we might get different, better women. Again, the idea that there is anything natural or essential about "woman" is called into question. But the view of the relationship between man and woman, where man is "will" and woman "willingness," assumes that woman is passive and responsive to man, as a moon is to the gravitational pull of its planet. This view also assumes that man's identity is related to, or even constituted by, the idealized image of the other (the "eternal feminine") that he receives from a hegemonic masculine cultural ideal; this ideal "serves to affirm the self as unchanging" (Diprose 16)—as long, that is, as woman continues to play the supporting (and supportive) role mandated by the "law of the sexes," which, the sage admits, is "truly, a hard law for women." Now as a "law," there is nothing eternal or essential about this feminine role; even so-called "laws of nature" are human fabrications, as Nietzsche argues elsewhere (see for example *BGE* 21). The sage has caught himself in a contradiction: If it is man who creates for himself the image of woman, and woman forms herself according to this image, as the sage maintains, then the law of the sexes, created or at any rate rehearsed by the sage, can be changed or repealed. Such a change would then of course also change the role of man, something perhaps the sage is unwilling to contemplate.

We come finally to the important fourth character in this mini-drama, the youth who is being "corrupted" by women. He doesn't have a speaking role, but his actions, as it were, speak louder than words. The youth clearly represents the future, and as its representative his action is decisive with regard to the overall effect of the drama. He listens to the sage and his interlocutors, and when solicited by the sage to "follow him" (the language suggests discipleship) he turns the offer down flat: "the youth, however, did not follow him." This twist at the end of the aphorism carries many meanings, depending on the position from which it is viewed or read. The youth's rejection of the sage's nod may mean that the youth is wedded to his corruption and therefore not redeemable; it may mean that he rejects the sage's construction of women; it may mean he has been persuaded by one of the other speaker's interventions; it may mean that he plans to make up his own mind on the subject of women.

If for the youth the Woman Question is open, it may be so, Nietzsche implies in other aphorisms, because the old ideal, the eternal feminine, is shopworn. Nietzsche's attacks are even, he hints, belated: there are cultural indicators that the old textual role models have lost their attraction for young people. The example he chooses is, for him, the *Urtext* of his own indoctrination to the eternal feminine—Goethe's *Faust*—where the part is played by an innocent maiden, Gretchen, good as gold and pure as crystal until she is seduced (and betrayed) by Faust. She eventually dies and goes to Heaven, from whence she draws Faust upward and redeems him. Nietzsche comments, in an aphorism in *Human, All Too Human* (1878): "*Faust and Gretchen dying out.*—As a very discerning scholar has remarked, the educated men of present-day Germany resemble a cross between Mephistopheles [the devil who tempts Faust] and Wagner [Faust's pedantic student], but certainly do not resemble Fausts, whom their grandfathers (in their youth at least) felt rumbling within them. For two reasons, therefore—to continue this proposition—Gretchens are no longer suited to them. And because they are no longer desired they are, it seems, dying out" (1:408).

This text makes the same point as the sage in *Gay Science* 68: men construct images (ideals) of women to match their own desires and women conform to these ideals. This Faustian example goes a step further, however, in attributing men's desires to images (ideals) present in their culture to which they themselves conform. Yet another aphorism in *Human, All Too Human* further complicates the sage's dualistic law by speculating about what post-Freudians might label the narcissistic self-referentiality of human ideals of the opposite sex: "If, in the choice of their marriage partner, men seek above all a deep nature full of feeling, while women seek a shrewd, lively-minded and brilliant nature, it is clear that at bottom the man is seeking an idealized man, the woman an idealized woman—what they are seeking, that is to say, is not a complement but a perfecting of their own best qualities" (1:411).

This aphorism suggests that the sexes desire more of the same—that is, something in the other that matches something in themselves, rather than heterosexual difference. At this point, the "rib of God" aphorism which served as our point of departure may take on additional meaning. To reiterate—man, that aphorism holds, created woman out of a rib of God, of his ideal (*TI*, "Maxims and Arrows" 13). In inventing woman or in seeking a marriage partner, man also invents "woman's" desire for himself; her love for his idealized "masculine" qualities mirrors his own love for himself. In fact he is his own God, his own ideal. Psychologically, Nietzsche suggests, the two-sex model, as an ideal of complementarity—as "man and woman"—"slanders," misunderstands, and misrepresents human realities.

In these passages, culled from Nietzsche's work written in the last decade of his productive life (1878 to 1888), the ideal of the eternal feminine is exposed either as a crucial stay and support of a degenerate Christian religion and of herd morality, or as a cleverly acted role. Nietzsche condemns "man" for creating it and so training women to play the part of the weaker sex, the part of "willingness." He implies that "man" is the one who is willing, though he can't see this and is thus self-deceived, blinded to self-knowledge by his adherence to the ideal of the eternally feminine, something eternally different from himself. Nietzsche condemns the eternal feminine for training women to act the role of the loving redeemer of man (even in bed), and to sell themselves and their economic independence for lifelong maintenance that breeds in them a powerful unspoken resentment. The ideal infantilizes men by telling them that they need to be saved or redeemed (or mothered) by the love of a good woman; in league with Christianity it instills guilt about the enjoyment of the body and especially about sex; and by maintaining the sexual dichotomy, it produces an antagonistic situation where "the eternal hostility between the sexes" is inevitable.

Emancipated Women

However, when it comes to modifying or repealing the "law of the sexes" that his own texts have revealed as a pernicious and worn-out cultural construct, Nietzsche dismisses the actions of the women's movement. Indeed, his vitriolic sarcasm, his below-the-belt polemical techniques, are given full play in those texts that oppose the movement for women's emancipation and "equal rights." This is strange. Since the movement shares many of Nietzsche's own objections to the status quo, why does he object to it? When "the emancipated woman" comes on stage, the textual climate changes. The emancipated woman seems to open in Nietzsche's texts a vein of illogicality that seems deeply suspicious. In a passage in his last book, *Ecce Homo,* Nietzsche constructs an antithesis between women who exemplify the ideals of the eternal feminine and emancipated women. "At bottom," he concludes, "the emancipated are anarchists in the world of the eternal feminine" ("Why I Write Such Good Books" 5). Given what we have surveyed of Nietzsche's own approach to the eternal feminine, the phrase "anarchists in the world of the eternal feminine" describes none other than Nietzsche himself, and aligns him with emancipated women.

When women's rights are the issue, Nietzsche's attacks on the values of the eternal feminine cease; the female bearer of those values, conscious of her role (i.e. as actress) now becomes "the complete woman" (*TI* "Maxims and Arrows" 20) or "the woman who is turned out well" (*EH* "Good Books" 5). In Nietzsche's scenario she is the "real woman" who plays the feminine role and scorns the movement for women's emancipation because she discerns that emancipation means loss of power, not gain. That is, in aphorisms where the perspectives are divided between "real women" and the emancipated, the narrator sides with, and speaks for, the eternal feminine, and against supporters of the women's movement:

> There is stupidity in this movement, an almost masculine stupidity, of which a real woman—who is always a clever woman—would have to be ashamed from the very heart. To lose her sense for the ground on which she is most sure of victory; to neglect to practice the use of her own proper weapons; to let herself go before the man, perhaps even "to the extent of producing a book," where formerly she kept herself in check and in subtle cunning humility; to seek with virtuous assurance to destroy man's belief that a fundamentally different ideal is wrapped up in woman, that there is something eternally, necessarily feminine; emphatically and loquaciously to talk man out of the idea that woman has to be maintained, cared for, protected, indulged like a delicate, strangely wild and often agreeable domestic animal. (*BGE* 239)

This passage appears in a series of the most apparently misogynist aphorisms that Nietzsche wrote (*BGE* 231–239), in which the narrator is telling "*my* truths" about "woman-as-such," aphorisms that are explicitly addressed to men: "Already female voices are raised which, by holy Aristophanes! make one tremble; there are threatening and medically explicit statements of what woman wants of man. Is it not in the worst of taste when woman sets about becoming scientific in that fashion? Enlightenment in this field has hitherto been the affair and endowment of men—we remained 'among ourselves' in this" (*BGE* 232).

The speaker of these texts is ostentatiously masculine—so much so in fact that the masculine itself is foregrounded as a perspective among others, or rather, as the masculine counterpart to the feminine. The narrator speaks for the entire class of European males, constructing a "boys' only" territory, enforcing the binary division between the sexes, and through the ostentation of its mode of address, exposing the constructed nature of that division. It is a metatextual effect like Brechtian alienation—an instance of the text pointing to itself not as a transparent medium of truth, but as a text, a product of human prejudice. This alienating move then shifts the interpretation to the readers.

In "Nietzsche's Misogyny" (1998), one such reader, Maudemarie Clark, argues that Nietzsche sets up a parallel between the emancipated woman and the philosopher as truth-seeker based on the fact that both turn against themselves and refuse to use their own proper weapons. In the case of the woman, the weapons are the ruses of the eternal feminine, as we have seen; in the case of the philosopher, they are the lies of metaphysics, which the "ascetic ideal" of *On the Genealogy of Morals* finally denies the truth-seeker. "Philosophers probably abandoned the ground on which they were most sure of victory," Clark states, "when they abandoned God and metaphysics" and sought naturalistic explanations, as Nietzsche does in *Beyond Good and Evil*. In order to lend these explanations power, Nietzsche advocates a judicious use of deception (195-196).

Clark observes, "If the interpretation I have offered is on the right track, Nietzsche must think of himself as employing precisely this strategy [deception] when he conceals from us what he is actually asserting about women and feminism [that is, women's emancipation]—while leaving it fully accessible to the careful reader" (196). In section 227 of *Beyond Good and Evil*, Nietzsche claims that his only virtue is honesty—but he worries nonetheless because honesty is such a very stolid and boring virtue. Let us therefore "send to the aid of our honesty whatever we have of devilry in us . . . our subtlest, most disguised, most spiritual will to power." Then, as though commenting on the reception of his passages on woman, he admits that this practice of disguise and devilry carries its risk: "It is probable that we shall be misunderstood and taken for what we are not: but what of that!" At least, he remarks, we won't be taken for "saints and bores!" (*BGE* 227).

In aphorisms 231-239 of *Beyond Good and Evil*, Nietzsche's truths about "woman as such"—the metaphysical ideal of the eternal feminine—exemplify his honesty because, according to Clark, "he has an interest in believing things about women that would justify those [misogynist] sentiments. What would justify such sentiments is precisely his 'truths' about 'woman as such,' if they were truths about women." As they exist only in the realm of myth and fantasy, Nietzsche's comments can be interpreted "as overcoming what he would like to believe about women, out of his own commitment to truth" ("Misogyny" 197).

What evidence is there that Nietzsche wants to "believe in" the eternal feminine? For Clark, this construct is one of the comforting lies of metaphysics that the philosopher, out of his commitment to truth, denies himself. I'm not convinced that Nietzsche ever makes us think that the eternal feminine is comforting, but in the first of the aphorisms on woman-as-such in *Beyond Good and Evil* he tries to make us think that the womanly ideal is, for him, a matter of indelible prejudice. He begins the series by stating in a matter-of-fact way that although it is possible to be transformed by learning, some things one knows cannot be changed: "At the bottom of us, 'right down deep,' there is, to be sure, something unteachable, a granite stratum of spiritual fate, of predetermined decision and answer to predetermined selected questions. In the case of every cardinal problem there speaks an unchangeable 'this is I'; about man and woman, for example, a thinker cannot relearn but only fully learn—only discover all that is 'firm and settled' within him on this subject" (*BGE* 231).

He implies that the stories about man and woman as the necessary couple, beginning with Adam and Eve, have been bred into him. They are practically genetic. The subtext suggests that it is precisely these stories that are hardest to change: they are set in granite. He then goes on to announce his intention to discuss "his" truths about "woman-as-such"—the truths he finds all around him in his culture. He writes that believing these truths is his spiritual fate, but adds that these convictions point to the problem, or the "great stupidity" which he is (*BGE* 231). With this confession, Nietzsche slips us a wink; he virtually tells us that the truths he is about to express are both problematic and stupid! Finally, he emphasizes that the truths are particular to himself; we must understand, he tells us, "to how great an extent these are only—*my* truths—" (*BGE* 231). He then speaks as a man for "us men," as we have seen, leading us to understand that the extent to which these are solely his personal truths is practically nil. What we hear in the passages about "*my* truths about woman-as-such" are, ironically, typical masculine prejudices: "[Woman] does not *want* truth: what is truth to a woman! . . . her great art is the lie, her supreme concern is appearance and beauty. Let us confess it, we men: it is precisely *this* art and *this* instinct in woman which we love and honour" (*BGE* 232).

Aphorism 238 of *Beyond Good and Evil* begins by announcing that the antithesis "man and woman" is a "fundamental problem." Nietzsche then goes on to note: "To deny here the most abysmal antagonism and the necessity of an eternally hostile tension, perhaps to dream here of equal rights, equal education, equal claims and duties: this is a *typical* sign of shallow-mindedness." The passage claims that the man of depth, on the other hand, thinks of woman in "an *oriental* way . . . as a possession, as property with lock and key, as something predestined for service and attaining her fulfillment in service." The aphorism then concludes: "How necessary, how logical, how humanly desirable even, this [oriental solution to the problem "man and woman"] was: let each ponder for himself!" R. J. Hollingdale's commentary on this aphorism draws attention to the text's major contradiction—that having asserted the necessity of an "abysmal antagonism" and "eternally hostile tension" between the sexes, the second half of the text obliterates it (*BGE* 232). There is no antagonism or tension once the woman has become a property under lock and key. If man is "will" and woman "willingness," as the sage holds in aphorism 68 of *The Gay Science*, woman's willing servitude eliminates the antagonism (which to deny is a sign of shallow-mindedness). The passage undoes its own logic through its own contradictory rhetorical stances, and it even asks us at the end to consider the argument's "logic"—a strong hint, perhaps, that we should do so!

To return to the "almost masculine stupidity" of the women's movement as it is maligned in the passage that inscribes it: the text that constructs "a real woman—who is always a clever woman," unwilling to relinquish her real power base in domesticity where she wields actual influence, indeed her "ascendancy over men" (*BGE* 239), is curious in its mode of address. As we have seen, the texts that take up women's emancipation are often ostensibly directed to masculine readers. To whom is this text addressed? And whose perspective or point of view is being conveyed here? It breaks rank with others in the series by apparently addressing women (or if it addresses men, it does so to give away woman's secret of domination through clever role-playing). And though the speaker or narrator is masculine, the perspective or point of view is that of the "real woman." Now if there is any truth in the narrator's claim that the real woman uses her own "proper weapons" to reassure the real man of her difference—to bolster masculine belief that a "fundamentally different ideal is wrapped up in woman, that there is something eternally, necessarily feminine"—then this text pulls the veil off woman's act, and reveals it as an act. Why? What purpose is served by revealing this "truth" about woman? If this passage supports the values and methods of the eternal feminine as those of the "real woman" against those of the emancipated, this is a strange way to go about it, for it makes the absurd statement that a "real woman" is a fake woman. If the real woman is not real at all, we can dismiss her. What, then, of the emancipated woman? There is an "almost masculine stupidity" in her movement. But the almost masculine stupidity of the women's movement is no longer stupid, because it was only so from the point of view of the real woman, who no longer exists. And it is no longer masculine, because if the real woman no longer exists, neither does the real man, to whom masculinity belongs. "The emancipated"—no longer woman, no longer man—survive.

The whole series of passages conveying Nietzsche's own personal "truths" about "woman-as-such" is an exercise in knocking down an ideal. The passages censure women's activities in two of the three areas held sacred for them in German culture: *Kinder, Kuche, Kirche* (children, cooking, church); women have failed abysmally in the first two (*BGE* 232, 234), as they are hopeless with children and their cooking is terrible. In the third area, that of religion, Nietzsche—having constantly attributed European decadence to the alliance between Christianity and the eternal feminine—writes that "a woman without piety would . . . be something utterly repellent and ludicrous to a profound and godless man" (*BGE* 239). In these passages, woman is advised to perfect her own proper weapons—to clean up her act as child-rearer and food-preparer, plaything and source of delight to men, pious slave ("as if slavery were a counter-argument and not rather a condition of every higher culture," *BGE* 239) and actress of the eternal feminine. In an interview with Christie McDonald about his book on Nietzsche and woman, Derrida makes the point that "Nietzsche makes a scene before women" ("Choreographies" 69). This is certainly the case in these aphorisms from *Beyond Good and Evil*. Like a child throwing a temper tantrum, Nietzsche calls for attention from women, but those texts on "woman" in which he carries on most spectacularly also draw attention *to* women. When our gaze is focused, the whole show is exposed as a show. Woman, in the guise of the eternal feminine, is stripped of her costume and make-up and then ordered to remain that way. Long live the comedy!

In the passages in which Nietzsche sets out these "truths" about woman-as-such—and in passages on "woman" as a female person from other sources we have considered—Nietzsche undercuts his assertions about woman because he knows how illogical they are, and how distant from reality as he experiences and observes it. He knows they are based on an ideal or metaphysical dualism that does not exist in nature. He knows that they describe a metaphysical essence, an "as such," a "thing-in-itself," that he has been at pains throughout *Beyond Good and Evil* to discredit. Furthermore, as to the "cardinal problem," "man and woman, for example" (*BGE* 231), he takes pains throughout the book to discredit antitheses: "For it may be doubted firstly whether there exist antitheses at all, and secondly whether these popular evaluations and value-antitheses, on which the metaphysicians have set their seal, are not perhaps merely foreground evaluations, merely provisional perspectives" (*BGE* 2).

The texts I have surveyed in this chapter sometimes contain internal contradictions, and sometimes contradict one another, but their individual and collective impact is negative where woman is concerned. In addition, Nietzsche lets us know that if the eternal feminine were to be "knocked down" as an ideal, the eternal masculine would have to follow—thus the rather odd emphasis on "man and woman" at the beginning of the aphorisms on woman. He tells us there that the antithesis "man and woman" is a "cardinal problem." It is a serious problem, even if it is dealt with diabolically, and worth thinking about in the light of his truths about woman-as-such. To show us how unstable, value-laden and desire-driven the problem is, he makes faces, uses ventriloquism, sneers, gloats, goads, uses the *argumentum ad hominem,* collective vituperation, and faulty logic—the whole bag of rhetorical tricks. He "presents" the problem to us by mimicking the contemporary attitudes and voices on the subject, but the very excessiveness of the presentation indicates that there is something wrong—that there is, in fact, a "problem" here, and a "great stupidity."

2

The "Secret Source"

Ancient Greek Woman in Nietzsche's Early Notebooks

IRONICALLY, given his antagonism toward the eternal feminine of his own time, Nietzsche found in a very ancient eternal feminine the characteristics and values that he thought might just help to save and redeem modern humanity. In this chapter I argue that, long before Nietzsche launched his attacks on the modern ideal of woman as something eternally and necessarily different from man, he began thinking about the ancient Greek woman, who develops into his positive feminine and appears, in time, allegorized as Life, Wisdom, Happiness, and Truth. Rudiments of this positive allegorical Woman appear in Nietzsche's early notebooks, where she is constructed as a complex, polyvalent signifier, associated with nature, and also with myth, tragedy, and the rise of the city-state as the very lifeblood of civilization. These early speculations about the nature of an archaic, mythic "eternal feminine" become one of the key legacies of Nietzsche's period as a philologist. As mythologized in the notebooks, the ancient Greek woman becomes a secret source, or a hidden spring, of Nietzsche's story about human possibilities and human limitations.

Nietzsche's professional academic work began with the ancient Greeks, and although he moved away both from the academy and from the philological study of Greek and Roman texts, he never ceased advocating an outlook that he preferred to think of, generally, as implicit in his ancient sources. In the dichotomy he formulated between the ancients and the moderns, he uses the ancients as a stick to beat the moderns. Why study the classics at all, he asks in *On the Uses and Disadvantages of History for Life* (1874), if not as a means of illuminating differences? "I do not know what meaning classical studies could have for our time if they were not untimely— that is to say, acting counter to our time and thereby acting on our time and, let us hope, for the benefit of a time to come," he writes (*UDH*, Foreword). One of the "untimely" thoughts that Nietzsche drew from classical studies as a catalyst for the present is that of an archaic, mythic "eternal feminine."

When he started teaching classical philology at Basel University, Nietzsche also began keeping notebooks, which he used continuously from then until the end of his working life.[1] The notebooks served as both his writer's diaries and his commonplace books, and in them he jotted down quotations, references, random thoughts, titles and chapter outlines for his own imagined books, draft paragraphs, fragments of poetry, and scenarios for plays. He usually noted the year, and at times the month and place, of his entries. When I surveyed the notebooks in order to research the background of *The Birth of Tragedy,* I read through the notes for the years 1869 to 1872 and was surprised to find not a few, but a great many references to *Das Weib,* woman. The references surprised me, because there are almost no references to women of any description in *The Birth of Tragedy,* the book Nietzsche was planning—indeed drafting—from the notes. How do we account for these references, I asked myself? What was happening in Nietzsche's life during this time? What was he reading, and whom was he seeing, that prompted his interest in the ancient woman? What is the connection, if any, between these notes and *The Birth of Tragedy*? How important was this interest in the ancient woman to his overall goal of promoting classical studies as a helpful antithesis or antidote to the present? In order to answer these questions, I turn to texts in the first part of this chapter that I think helped the young Nietzsche understand and articulate something about the importance of the feminine as defined by the ancients, and about the sexual "springs" or sources of human creativity. In the second part, I trace the influence of these sources in the notebooks; however, the importance of the influence only becomes apparent later in Nietzsche's published work, where, I maintain, its effect is precisely the revaluation of values ascribed to the feminine and the redistribution of these values to all of humankind.

Matriarchy and the Unconscious: Bachofen and Hartmann

Among the intellectual sources Nietzsche discovered during his first year in Basel (leaving aside the galvanizing personal acquaintance and then friendship of Richard and Cosima Wagner), two are of particular interest and relevance to my argument: Bachofen's theory of archaic matriarchy and von Hartmann's theory of the unconscious, which, combined with ancient myth, put the subject "woman" on Nietzsche's agenda. Nietzsche was reading these sources—Eduard von Hartmann's *Philosophy of the Unconscious* (published in 1868), and Johann Jacob Bachofen's *An Essay on Mortuary Symbolism* (1859), *Mother Right* (1861), and *The Myth of Tanaquil* (1870)—during the years 1869 to 1872. Each of these writers demonstrates a characteristic nineteenth-century interest in "sources," or origins. By way of example, in *Mother Right* Bachofen claims that "woman was the source of the first civilization, just as she has played a prominent part in every decline and every regeneration" (144). And Hartmann notes that "[Women] stand nearer to the source of the Unconscious [than men]" (238). Both of these thoughts are reproduced, with interesting modifications, in Nietzsche's philosophy.

When the twenty-four-year-old Nietzsche arrived as a professor in the conservative Swiss city of Basel, he made the acquaintance of several older professors, among them the aforementioned Johann Jacob Bachofen (1815–87), a historian of Roman law. Bachofen had become interested in what he thought were traces of vestigial mother-rights in ancient Roman law, had studied Etruscan tombs and ceramics, and combed ancient texts—both Greek and Latin—in search of evidence to support his theory of social development. In both *An Essay on Mortuary Symbolism* and *Mother Right*, his controversial argument holds that human society began in a chaotic state of sexual promiscuity, proceeded to matriarchy, and finally, after a number of bloody battles whose meaning was embodied in the defeat of the Amazons, shifted to patriarchy. His "romantic" approach to history, largely through myth and free interpretation of evidence, ran headlong into the new "scientific" history of the school of Theodore Mommsen, with whom Bachofen waged a heated public debate that finally drove the author of *Mother Right* from the academy.[2]

Nietzsche was a frequent guest at the Bachofen home in Basel from 1869 to 1874; Bachofen's wife later recalled that her husband "liked him and I know that Nietzsche respected him very much; he had often told me so. *The Birth of Tragedy* was published then, and my husband was delighted with it and had high expectations of Nietzsche—but then came his further works, which my husband totally rejected" (Gilman *Conversations* 49–50). The fact that Nietzsche is on record as having borrowed *An Essay on Mortuary Symbolism* from the University of Basel library in 1871 (Silk and Stern 214) is further proof of the relationship. Curt Paul Janz similarly notes that Wagner read *The Myth of Tanaquil* in 1872 at Nietzsche's instigation (314). Perhaps the most significant evidence that Bachofen's ideas gripped Nietzsche, on some level quite profoundly, comes from his declining years. Nietzsche went mad in 1889, and lived until 1900; we have piecemeal information about him during the last ten years of his life, the best of which comes from notes his mother kept of their conversations. In February 1891, she recorded (in paraphrase) this telling observation he offered: "Prof. Dr. Adolf Bastian lived until now in Siberia and is the best expert in ethnology. He stood in correspondence with Prof. Bachofen in Basel; as the former is for ethnology, so Bachofen is the greatest expert on matrilineal societies" (Gilman *Conversations* 155). Adolf Bastian, who was a professor at Berlin University and president of the Berlin Anthropological Society, wrote a letter of "encouraging admiration" to Bachofen in 1870 (Bachofen lii). Not only did Nietzsche know about the correspondence, but in a disastrously fragmented mental state, he remembered it, offering up what appears to be a perfectly lucid observation from those years in Basel in which Bachofen (whom Nietzsche never mentioned in print in his sanity) is central.

Nietzsche does not refer to Bachofen or his theories by name in print, but in the pages of his notebooks and in the fragments of never-completed essays on Greek culture and philosophy, as well as in the published work, we find traces of Bachofen's hypotheses, as Bachofen himself found traces of a lost world of "the mothers" in ancient Roman law, in myth, and in the inscriptions on mortuary urns and tombs. The name of Bachofen does not appear in Nietzsche's notebooks—my inference being that the impression the former's ideas made was strong, and perhaps somewhat shameful or embarrassing, since they were completely out of vogue and had been "mercilessly massacred" in academic journals (Bachofen xl, 3-4). Ironically, Nietzsche's *The Birth of Tragedy* was to share the same fate for the same reasons: it was deemed out of vogue, eccentric, and iconoclastic of academic conventions and of received opinion about Socrates and Plato. It "represented a challenge to the ideals on which German Hellenism had been founded and to which academic circles in general still adhered. As against the classical, the serenely beautiful, Nietzsche was opting for the archaic" (Silk and Stern 37). In short, Nietzsche was following Bachofen from the region of the fathers to the "secret source": the region of the mothers.

Bachofen on the Stages of Human Development

The binary division of the sexes that organizes Bachofen's texts is drawn directly from his ancient sources. Bachofen quotes Homer and Hesiod, the pre-Socratics (especially Pythagoras), the tragedians (especially Aeschylus), Herodotus, Plato and Aristotle, Plutarch, Isocrates, Strabo, and Pausanias. These ancient sources (or the myths they relate) equate femaleness with darkness and the earth, and maleness with the active "awakening" force associated with light. It is on this fundamental distinction that Bachofen, a Hegelian who understands an idea or an institution by reference to its opposite, builds his theory. Thus, for example, the extraordinary emphasis of Greek and Roman patriarchy on the predominance of the male presupposes an antithetical locus of power: "How shall we understand the end [patriar-chy] if the beginnings remain a riddle to us? But where are these beginnings to be found? The answer is not in doubt. In myth, the faithful picture of the oldest era, and nowhere else" (Bachofen 76).

Bachofen has outraged the scholarly community from his own day to the present not merely by treating myth as history, but by arguing deductively from it. In investigating the prehistory of the ancient Greeks, he focused his microscope on shadows, place names, and mythic monsters (Gorgon, Siren, Sphinx), and then depicted the storied fathers of western civiliza-tion as primitive peoples. He made readers consider the ancestors of their togaed heroes in tribal terms, living in a time of violence, fear, and sexual struggle. He described human social and cultural development as a pro-cess whereby humans achieved "higher" cultural goals through the act of opposing, struggling, and overcoming. In order to reach the heights of classical civilization, he claims, humanity overcame the social and political power of women, for Bachofen holds that women founded civilization. Roman legal texts, inscriptions and drawings on funeral urns and ceramic artifacts, and myth all provide Bachofen with evidence of the "one supreme idea" (Bachofen 120) that he considers a universal historical truth: that human life has undergone a five-stage process of development, and that woman is central to the value systems of the first two stages.

Setting forth the particulars of the model, he labels the first stage of human social development, of indeterminate duration, the "tellurian," with the earth as its symbol. From his ancient sources, Bachofen extrapolates their belief that in this stage woman was closely identified with material nature—with fertility, birth, and death: "That which is begotten belongs to the maternal matter which has enclosed it. . . . This mother is always the same: ultimately she is the earth" (128). The "maternal principle" is univer-sal and, "like the life of nature, knows no barriers" (80). Bachofen finds that, if there is a guiding principle in the tellurian phase, it is that of *ius naturale,* the "natural law" of sexual promiscuity, "based on the principle of the domination of the generative womb" (97). He calls this "a stage of Dionysian materiality, so preparing the way for . . . a new flowering of the mother cults" (116).

Bachofen associates Dionysus with potent male sexuality inseparable from the earth, and thus with the first (tellurian) and the second (which he designates matriarchal) stages of existence because written and icono-graphic evidence links the god to woman: "The phallic god [Dionysus] cannot be thought of separately from feminine materiality. Matter, the mother who bore him to the light, now becomes his wife. Bacchus is both the son and husband of Aphrodite. Mother, wife, sister merge into one. Matter takes all of these attributes by turns" (30). This last rather odd formulation, which suggests incest on a grand scale, may be an attempt to describe a time of undifferentiated boundaries and roles and of unrestrained sexuality: "Sexual union is always the fundamental Dionysian law" (30).

The word "bestial" is used several times to describe this period (134). Bachofen similarly calls upon metaphors of plant life or swamp life, or both; in this earliest phase of human existence, "the people's lot is no different from that of the swamp plants which come into being and pass away unwept" (181). For Bachofen, "the law of opposition governs the tellurian world of appearance" (34) and the dominant opposition of this early stage of existence is life and death:

> Everything is restless, eternal motion. The life of tellurian generation suffers no halt. In it everything comes into being and vanishes. Material life moves between two poles. Its realm is not that of being but that of becoming and passing away. . . . Only through the equal mixture of the two is the survival of the material world assured. Without death no rejuvenation is possible. . . . Death is not the opposite but the helper of life, just as the negative pole of magnetism is not the adversary of the positive pole but its necessary complement, without which the positive pole would vanish immediately, and life give way to nothingness. (33–34)

In the life of tellurian generation, where sexual promiscuity is the rule, woman dominates. Her power is represented by "the dark depths of the maternal womb" (123) and her undisputed material connection to the child which remains "a natural truth" (109); woman "takes the place of the earth and continues the primordial motherhood of the earth among mortals" (123); she is likened to sleep (as man is to "awakening power") (124). The symbolic representative of woman in this phase is the Sphinx, half beast and half woman, "the embodiment of tellurian motherhood; she represents the feminine right of the earth in its dark aspect as the inexorable law of death." The Sphinx's riddle (about the stages of human life) suggests to Bachofen the "utter hopelessness" of life at this time: "In the riddle whose solution will put an end to the Sphinx's power, man is considered only in his transient aspect, mortality. . . . Once it is understood, once its utter hopelessness is recognized, this law will be at an end" (181).

This is a cryptic allegorical reading of the myth, upon which Nietzsche will expand. By "solving" the Sphinx's riddle, Oedipus ends the law of nature;

in other words, conscious knowledge of one's own state, mortality (something animals apparently lack, as Nietzsche reminds us at the beginning of his "history" essay [*UDH* 1]), separates thinking humans from purely instinctual natural life. Bachofen argues that the Oedipus myth marks the advance to "a higher stage of existence"; his text inserts Oedipus into his structure as "the last victim" of "the older state of things," an end and a beginning (185).[3]

The next "stage" of social development in Bachofen's scheme is the matriarchal or "Demetrian" (named for Demeter, the Greek goddess of agriculture). The tellurian stage takes the earth as its symbol; the Demetrian is represented by the moon. The "lunar" stage inaugurates civilization, and the women are the ones who accomplish this, rebelling against the chaos of promiscuity and establishing a primitive social order (142). That mother cults followed a period of natural law, that the mothers instituted the first "civilized" structures, the first human law, the first order—the first culture— is the central thesis of *Mother Right*. In his introduction, Bachofen admits that a nineteenth-century CE audience may find it hard to accept this: "The elevation of woman over man arouses our amazement most especially by its contradiction to the relation of physical strength. The law of nature confers the scepter of power on the stronger. If it is torn away from him by feebler hands, other aspects of human nature must have been at work" (85).

The other forces at work, Bachofen argues, are religious. He cites Pythagoras, Strabo, and Plato as authorities on women's special vocation for religion (85), but treats these, like myth, as inscriptions after-the-fact of ancestral memories of real events. He refers to woman as "repository of the first revelation," woman as first prophet. Her powers are paradoxical but nonetheless powerful for that: "Mystery is rooted in her very nature, with its close alliance between the material and the supersensory; mystery springs from her kinship with material nature" (87). Here the text hints that the famous body-spirit split had not yet been celebrated, but that woman's body and spirit were thought of and venerated as a generative and regenerative unity. "Demeter's exclusive bond with Kore leads to the no-less exclusive relation of succession between mother and daughter; and finally, the inner link between the mystery and the chthonian-feminine cults leads to the priesthood of the mother" (87). Because of her special power as "the prophetess who proclaims the *fatum*" (the Delphic Pythia, the Sibyl), woman was regarded as the repository of justice: "She manifests justice unconsciously but with full certainty" (144). The worship of woman as "the embodiment of the higher principle, as the manifestation of the divine commandment" and "the religious primacy of motherhood," leads to a primacy of the mortal woman: "Women now rule over the family and the state" (143).

In time, the fathers rout the mothers and the matriarchal stage gives way to the patriarchal, whose emblem is the sun and Apollo, the sun god: "Once the creative principle is dissociated from earthly matter and joined with the sun, a higher state sets in. Mother right is left to the animals and the human family goes over to father right" (129). In Bachofen's account, the transition to patriarchal authority is bloody. "The rise of father right begins with the war against the Amazons" (154), a war that symbolizes for Bachofen a series of battles in which the males wrest power from the females by force, and then the females give in gracefully—indeed, gratefully. As he notes, Penthesilea, queen of the Amazons, dies in Achilles' arms, for "the woman recognizes the higher strength and beauty of the man and gladly inclines to the victorious hero" (130). In the triumphal tone of trumpet fanfare that marks the description of this phase (now no longer simply a "phase"), Bachofen writes: "The lunar principle is destroyed by the luminous powers, woman's natural vocation is restored to her, and spiritual father right becomes dominant for all time over material motherhood" (154). This stage is similarly marked by the triumph of the Olympian gods over the earthy Titans; Bachofen lyrically praises the principle of "higher justice" symbolized by Apollo radiating, "celestial and luminous, the perfect law of Zeus." The "ultimate sublimation" of "the bloody, dark justice of the first material era" implies its dissolution: "Through liberation from all material admixture, law becomes love. . . . Its perfection transcends even the concept of justice and so becomes the ultimate and complete negation of matter, the resolution of all dissonance" (190).

At the end of *The Birth of Tragedy,* Nietzsche promotes dissonance and the human state as dissonant, protesting by counterpoint Bachofen's happy ending which, classically Hegelian as it is, sounds (like Hegel's own resolutions) a bit forced. This point notwithstanding, Bachofen's overall argument demonstrates that there is nothing natural, eternal, or final about social order, or about the roles of women and men within it.

Hartmann and the Unconscious

Eduard von Hartmann's three-volume *Philosophy of the Unconscious* appeared in 1868 (when Hartmann was 27 and Nietzsche was 24); unlike Bachofen's published writings, the work was popular, running through 12 subsequent editions during Hartmann's lifetime (he died in 1906). It was translated in full into English in 1884 (by contrast, Bachofen's work has never been fully translated) and reissued in 1931 with a preface by C. K. Ogden, who recognizes it as a "pioneer formulation" of the Unconscious (xv). And in contrast to Bachofen's theories, Hartmann's work is cited in Nietzsche's notebooks, discussed in his letters, and critiqued in his published books; as a source for Nietzsche's thinking, it is both evident and important.[4]

Nietzsche is careful to distance himself from Hartmann in his published commentary as well as in his notebooks and private correspondence.[5] By 1874, when he publishes *On the Uses and Disadvantages of History for Life*, Nietzsche has taken up the battle with Hartmann, calling his work a "parody" of world history (*UDH* 9); he polemicizes against Hartmann's "practical pessimism" as something impossible to take seriously: "What Hartmann proclaims to us from the smoky tripod of unconscious irony amounts to this: he tells us it would be quite sufficient, for our time to be exactly as it is, to bring about, eventually, a condition in which people would find this existence intolerable. . . . The rogue illuminates our age with the light of the Last Day" (*UDH* 9).

Interestingly, this focal image—the smoky tripod of unconscious irony— provides a confluence of three tributary sources: Bachofen's interest in the Pythia (who sat on a tripod at Delphi and "administered justice unconsciously but with full certainty"); Hartmann's narrative of the decline of the unconscious; and Nietzsche's own distancing "irony" from each of these. However much distance Nietzsche attains, though, it is not enough to offset the force of Hartmann's narrative, which, like Bachofen's, makes its way with all speed into Nietzsche's thinking—something apparent in the notebook entries—and lodges there. In *On the Uses and Disadvantages of History for Life* (1874), Nietzsche paraphrases, without attribution, a parable from the *Philosophy of the Unconscious* that takes on great significance for him. In a chapter entitled "The Irrationality of Volition and the Misery of Existence" in volume 3, Hartmann (like Schopenhauer before him and Freud after) attributes the will to go on living to unconscious, irrational instincts. He then praises the rationality of preferring death to life, and names those philosophers who have done so—Plato, Kant, Fichte, Schelling. These however, he notes, have been geniuses. He asks us to imagine someone who is no genius, well endowed and happy: "Let us imagine Death to draw nigh this man and say, 'Thy life-period is run out, and at this hour thou art on the brink of annihilation; but it depends on thy present voluntary decision, once again, precisely in the same way, to go through thy now closed life with complete oblivion of all that has passed. Now choose!' I

question whether the man would prefer the repetition of the past performance to non-existence, if his mind be free from fear, and calm" (3:5).

Nietzsche draws this narrative first into the history essay, where he introduces it casually to illustrate the difference between the "historical"
condition, tied to time and "process," and the "suprahistorical" vantage
point, above time and events, whose very remoteness makes it impossible
to "feel any temptation to go on living or to take part in history" (*UDH* 1).
"If you ask your acquaintances if they would like to relive the past ten or
twenty years, you will easily discover which of them is prepared for this
suprahistorical standpoint: they will all answer No, to be sure, but they
will have different reasons for answering No" (*UDH* 1). Eight years later,
Nietzsche repeats Hartmann's proposition in perhaps the most famous
passage in *The Gay Science:* "—What, if some day or night a demon were to
steal after you into your loneliest loneliness and to say to you: 'This life as
you now live it and have lived it, you will have to live it once more and innumerable times more . . . ?'" (*GS* 341). In Hartmann's version, the reader has
a choice: another life, exactly the same, or death. Hartmann insists that it
is rational to choose death. Nietzsche's first account, in the history essay,
gestures in the direction of the "suprahistorical," the position above time
and history, that would lead "his acquaintance" to choose death. In his
second take, Nietzsche has withdrawn the life/death choice and substituted
for it what we might call a gut reaction to the news that we shall relive our
lives. Shall we gnash our teeth and curse the messenger? Or shall we rejoice?
Our response, as Clark argues, tells us whether or not we are affirmers of
eternal recurrence (*Nietzsche on Truth* 281).

For Hartmann, the choice between life (again) or death is determined
largely by the outcome of the struggle between the unconscious life instincts
and conscious rationality. Although gender is not highlighted in his three-
volume work, it is clear that the Unconscious, were Hartmann to have allegorized it, would have been female. The first volume argues that although
humans cannot "know" the Unconscious, they can come close to it through
its best representatives, animals and women. He observes that women
often fall in love suddenly, because they "stand nearer to the source of the
Unconscious" (238). As in Schopenhauer, this source is sexuality—but
where Schopenhauer finds the ceaseless striving of the unconscious will
pointless, Hartmann values it (to a point, as we shall see). The Unconscious,
Hartmann claims, "can really outdo all the performances of conscious reason"; by way of example, he cites not only the amazing instinctual life of
animals, but also "those fortunate [human] natures that possess everything

that others must acquire with toil, who never have a struggle of conscience, because they always spontaneously act correctly and morally in accordance with feeling . . . and live in eternal harmony with themselves, without ever reflecting much what they do. . . . the fairest specimens of these instinctive natures are only seen in women" (2:40). The Unconscious is none other than "the spring of life"; it is creatively productive and inventive, and if man "loses the faculty of hearing the inspirations of the Unconscious, he loses the spring of his life. . . . The Unconscious is therefore *indispensable* for him, and woe to the age which violently suppresses its voice, because in the one-sided overestimate of the conscious-rational it will only give heed to the latter" (2:42).

The unconscious will propels the individual into the future—"In every volition *the change into another state than the present* is willed" (1:118); the goal of the will lies in the future. The goal also provides the idea, the content of the will as its object. The goal may be (and usually is) unconscious; the more unconscious the goal, the easier the action to achieve it—as for example, in reflex actions like jumping or climbing, which are "executed much more easily, more certainly, and even more gracefully, if they are performed without conscious volition. . . . Every intervention of the cerebral consciousness operates only inhibitively and disturbingly. . . . For conscious reflection always brings along with it doubt and hesitation, and thus frequently a fatal tardiness" (1:132–33).

Hartmann suggests three remedies for over-rationality: first, occupation with the arts, "as that in which the Unconscious finds its most immediate expression" (2:43); second, acquaintance with animal life (43); and third (of course), "intercourse" with women—as long as women are "real women":

> One ought to be quite particularly on one's guard against making the female sex too rational, for where the Unconscious must first be reduced to silence, success is only attained at the cost of repulsive caricatures. . . . Woman namely is related to man, as instinctive or unconscious to rational or conscious action; therefore the genuine woman is a piece of Nature, on whose bosom the man estranged from the Unconscious may refresh and recruit himself, and can again acquire respect for the deepest and purest spring of all life. And to preserve this treasure of the eternal womanly, the woman also should be as far as possible shielded by the man from all contact with the rough struggle of life, where it is needful to display conscious force, and should be restrained in the sweet natural bonds of the family. (2:43)

Having ensured that the treasure is closely guarded and kept away from ideas, the man will find in woman's company a delight and an education:

"The eternal womanly will remain for all time an indispensable, complementary, and educating moment for the youth of the male sex. It is not saying too much that for a young man noble female intercourse is far more helpful than male, and in a greater degree the more philosophical the man's bent . . . Lack of male intercourse may be compensated by books, of female never" (2:44).

Passages like these are commonplaces of mid-nineteenth-century knight-errantry: confusion and contradiction. How much "noble intercourse" is possible with one who speaks only the language of the unconscious? The strict binary male/female division is as intact here as it is in Bachofen's Greek examples—no longer as the battle of the sexes, but nonetheless as divided by explicitly delineated boundaries, where male is conscious and rational (and cultural), and female is unconscious and instinctive (and natural). Socially, woman is still in her place at the hearth, instinctively nurturing her offspring (and her husband) as in patriarchal Greece and Rome.

In Hartmann's scenario, the heroine—the Unconscious—has to die, because universal teleology "wills" it. A section of volume 1 entitled "The Unconscious in Bodily Life" places a great deal of emphasis on the creative and recuperative powers of the unconscious. With regard to the latter, Hartmann argues that miracle cures and faith healing can be explained through belief in certain effects: "The art in such cures is then only this: to inspire the belief in success. . . . Of the unconscious Will the word holds literally true: 'the more will, the more power'" (1:183). For Hartmann, the unconscious is present and operative in both mind and body without distinction, as "unconscious will"; he is thus ahead of his time in seeking to overcome the mind/body dualism, and Nietzsche follows him. Hartmann argues that it is the business of the unconscious will to create illusions to keep us living; this is the most important creative function of the unconscious.[6] When, however, illusions are recognized as such, then the unconscious gives way to consciousness and is *"destroyed along with the destruction of these illusions with advancing conscious intelligence.* This inquiry cannot be spared, because all progress has in view the increase of conscious intelligence" (3:10). Progressively, unconscious instincts submit to the control of conscious reason: "Pitiless and cruel is this work of the destruction of illusion, like the rough pressure of the hand that wakes one sweetly dreaming to the torment of reality. But the world must onwards; the goal cannot be approached in dreams. . . . only through pain lies the path to redemption" (3:109–10).

And what is the goal? The answer is stunning: it is total human annihilation. In volume 3, the complementarity of unconscious (female) and conscious (male) gives way to warfare: "The world-process appears as a *per-petual struggle of the logical with the non-logical,* ending with the conquest of the latter" (127). The intellect seems to act negatively, but in fact it serves to further the *"general world-redemption"* (133). Is it possible, Hartmann asks, "to achieve *"universal negation of the will"* (139)? He thinks it is. When the greatest possible evolution of consciousness is attained through the logi-cal principle, then "consciousness suffices to hurl back the total actual volition into nothingness, by which the *process* and the *world ceases,* and ceases indeed without any residuum whatever whereby the process might be continued" (142). This, according to Nietzsche, is the light of the Last Day that illuminates Hartmann's philosophy. Although he calls it uncon-scious parody, he nonetheless finds Hartmann's examples useful, and much of his work stands as a refutation of Hartmann's teleology.

Nietzsche, Bachofen, and Hartmann

Bachofen's and Hartmann's texts share several features. They are progres-sivist and evolutionary, and move toward a teleological resolution of con-tradictions established in the course of the works. The sense of an ending is strong in both Bachofen's five-stage model of human social development and Hartmann's narrative of humanity's struggle for conscious existence. However, neither resolution is synthetic; neither ending involves a "recon-ciliation" of the opposing concepts, a homogenization of the opposing sides of the dichotomies. Rather, one of the two sides gains permanent ascendancy—in both instances the side the texts have allotted to the mas-culine. Both writers equate woman with the nonrational: nature, instinct, the unconscious. Both see a historical progression whereby these qualities are subdued, overcome by superior intellect: the "awakening light," con-scious awareness, the strength of logic, or the scientific principle. Both writers treat myth ("illusion" for Hartmann), dream (and sleep), and the unconscious as equivalents, and for each, the awakening into "reality" is liberating, transcendental, redemptive. Both writers actually use the word "negation" to describe this final liberation. For Bachofen, patriarchy repre-sents "the ultimate and complete negation of [feminine] matter, the reso-lution of all dissonance"; for Hartmann, the "goal of evolution and the significance of consciousness" (the title of his final chapter) is *"universal negation of the will"* (underlined in the original).

Bachofen provides Nietzsche with an image of a violent, brutish, and chaotic past, only subdued with effort—a past in which "woman" played a key and central role, symbolic of those forces of nature which must be overcome. Hartmann, on the other hand, provides an image of a neurotic and nihilistic present, which has arisen because the powers of unconscious creativity, especially observable in animals and in women, have been subdued by the very forces Bachofen praises (and masculinizes): the forces of reason. Caught between these powerful evolutionary interpretations, Nietzsche creatively incorporates parts of both, blending and bending them to fit his own scenario.

The Greek Woman in Nietzsche's Notes

Beginning in 1869 and continuing roughly until 1872, Nietzsche's notes formulate a haphazard but identifiable series of sexualized binary oppositions, placing on one side of the dichotomy the terms nature, the unconscious, music, myth, religion, tragedy, art and woman, with consciousness, language, logic, Euripides, Socrates, and "Wissenschaft" (scientific knowledge) on the other. These summary dichotomies are not equivalent to the conventional nature/culture opposition, for art, tragedy, music, myth, and religion all cluster together with nature, the unconscious, and woman, in opposition to science and logic. The term "man" does not appear opposite the term "woman," yet it is implied, and the pairing is fully sexualized when, as we shall see, the male Oedipus ("symbol of science") overthrows the female "Sphinx of nature." By linking nature and the feminine, Nietzsche is guided by classical sources, as well as the work of Bachofen and Hartmann, and engaging in the ongoing construction of a myth of woman-as-nature. However, he modifies that myth significantly. Following Hartmann, Nietzsche links creativity and the unconscious. The unconscious is already strongly associated with woman for Hartmann, and thus a web of connotations knits together creativity, the unconscious, and woman. When Nietzsche speculates about the nature of art (music, poetry, and tragedy in particular), his associations of art with unconscious body drives or instincts leads him to link art and the body of woman.

He makes these connections, curiously, through the figure of the Sphinx—a creature made-to-order to represent Hartmann's unconscious: half woman, half animal (lion). One of his early notes employs Bachofen's descriptions of the Sphinx as symbol of tellurian life as a point of departure, combining it with Hartmann's theory of the unconscious: "The parricide and incest-living Oedipus is at the same time the riddle-solver of the Sphinx, of nature. The Persian magus was born from incest: it's the same idea. That is, so long as one lives under the rule of nature, she masters us and conceals her secret. The pessimist hurls her into the abyss, as he solves her riddle. Oedipus as symbol of science" (*KSA* 7:141). This passage views the myth of Oedipus allegorically; the Sphinx symbolizes nature, and Oedipus, culture (science). Science destroys nature, but at a heavy cost. In Sophocles' story, the price is Oedipus's eventual fulfillment of the oracle's pronouncement that he will kill his father and marry his mother. Incest, as a law of nature symbolized by the Sphinx, is central to Bachofen's "tellurian phase," and the Sphinx's overthrow by Oedipus inaugurates the beginning of a new historical phase.[7] The links to pessimism and science recall Hartmann's narrative of the overthrow of the unconscious by reason, which begins the plunge down the slippery slope to nihilism.

Another of Nietzsche's notes links beauty, sexuality, and the Sphinx: "What is the beautiful?—a joyful feeling, which conceals from us the essential intentions that the will has in appearance. By what means will the joyful feeling now be excited? Objective: the beautiful is a smile of nature, an excess of strength and pleasure in sensation. . . . It is the virgin body of the sphinx. The purpose of the beautiful is seduction to life. Essentially, what is that smile, that fascination? Negative: the concealment of necessity, the smoothing out of all wrinkles and the serene glance of the soul of things" (*KSA* 7:143-44). The Sphinx as nature, in her aspect as the beautiful seductive virgin, conceals the secret of fate, of necessity: the truth that we are born to die. It is a truth best hidden if sexiness, the excess of strength and pleasure in sensation, is to continue: "The purpose of the beautiful is seduction to life." Art and music also seduce, by reminding us and renewing pleasures of sensation: this idea remains constant for Nietzsche all through his productive life.[8] Art connects us to our "sources" in the material body and its unconscious instincts—to the Sphinx whose beauty conceals her connections to the transitory.

There are only a few scattered references to woman in the 1869 notebook entries. Of these, one is worth noting here: "Music as the mother of tragedy" (*KSA* 7:13). A few pages later, Nietzsche jots down some observations about the nature of music: "What does music do? It elucidates an idea in the will. It contains the universal forms of all states of desire: it is through and through symbolic of the drives, and as such in their simplest forms (beat, rhythm), understandable everywhere to everyone" (*KSA* 7:23). Nietzsche, concerned about tragedy's genealogy, already knows who its mother is. Influenced by Schopenhauer's connection of the desirous will and music, and by Hartmann's pairing of creativity and the physical unconscious, Nietzsche finds that music's basic rhythms correspond to the body (heart beat, breath), and so to the mother, whose body rhythms first nourish and seduce us to life.

In the notes dating from 1870, references to "woman" begin to proliferate, with a flurry of them appearing between September 1870 and January 1871. An early 1870 entry reads: "Greek cleverness in their pupa stage [as in butterflies]. The meaning of woman for the older Hellenes" (*KSA* 7:81). Nietzsche here suggests that the archaic period, whose characteristics are those of Bachofen's tellurian phase, is the pupal stage of Greek culture, when the "Greek genius" is still hidden in the chrysalis. The note serves to remind Nietzsche to write about the meaning of woman during this time. In Bachofen's tellurian stage, woman *is* meaning; as bearer and representative of the natural law of birth and death, woman is truth. The truth is hard, cruel, undesirable. Nietzsche accepts this interpretation. For him, the question is how did Greek art "grow" from this truth?

Nietzsche's draft plan for a book called *Socrates and Instinct* lists "Religion and Mythology" and "Statelore, Law, Popular Education" as chapter headings, with the following list of possible subjects: "The mythological woman. Fate and pessimism of mythology. Era of ugliness in mythology. Dionysus and Apollo. . . . Music as means of statehood. The teacher. The priest. The tragedian and the state. Utopias. Slavery. Woman" (*KSA* 7:80). This list may be taken as a rudimentary chronology, proceeding from "mythological woman" in an era of ugliness (the "pupal stage" of Greek culture)—to "the tragedian and the state" (the high point)—to "utopias" (of which Plato's *Republic* would be representative)—to slavery—and finally, last and least, to woman. As in Bachofen's scenario, the outline suggests that men's power increased as women's declined.

The moment of equilibrium, when power was balanced among rival forces, is, in Nietzsche's outline, that of Dionysus and Apollo (the tragedian and the state). As Nietzsche drafts and redrafts *The Birth of Tragedy*, his desire to develop the related themes of the origins of tragedy and of the Athenian city-state emerges in the notebooks. In autumn 1870 Nietzsche makes this entry: "We ought to shy away from no abyss of contemplation in order to trace tragedy back to its mothers: these mothers are Will, Delusion, Woe."[9] The notes had already named a mother of tragedy: music. Now music has been replaced by the womb of the archaic past as origin, when "woe" prevailed, when nature's terrifying manifestations were given the shape of mythical monsters as "delusions," and when "will" (linked to the unconscious and to music in the notes) meant both sexual procreation

and, following Hartmann, the creation of delusions/illusions. The implication of the notes is that this womb, this chrysalis, gave birth not only to
tragedy, but to all of classical Greek culture. Nietzsche associates woman
with tragedy and identifies her—in her guises as mother, and bringer-forth
of new creations as "delusions," and as representative of the suffering and
misery of existence itself—as its source.

A draft "Preface to Richard Wagner" intended for *The Birth of Tragedy*
again names the abyss of contemplation: "I remember, on a lonely night
with the wounded soldiers lying in the ambulance, and serving as their
nurse, that my thoughts were on the three abysses of tragedy, whose names
sound: 'Delusion, Will, Woe'"(*KSA* 7:354). This assertion tells us explicitly
that the "mothers of tragedy" *are* tragedy's abysses; they (delusion, will, woe)
are *gaps,* holes where the "horror" of life is revealed. Rather than repressing
this horror, as in the psychoanalytic myth, Nietzsche states that the horror
is something tragedy does not shy away from, but rather acknowledges
and looks at.[10]

After the first "mothers" note, the fragments continue to build a theory
of tragedy's origin: "Here [in tragedy] blissfulness shows itself in the
knowledge of the highest *woe.* Therein the *will* triumphs. It looks at its
most *dreadful configuration* as the spring of possibility for existence" [my
emphases] (*KSA* 7:121). Here Nietzsche parts company with Hartmann, for
whom the unconscious will (to live, to create life-empowering illusions)
simply dies when it attains consciousness. For Nietzsche, the will "looks at
its most dreadful configuration," and this glance into the abyss of its own
endless purposelessness is the transformational agent. It is Oedipus's triumphant encounter with the Sphinx nature. The will is empowered and
incited to creativity precisely by the conscious knowledge of its own futility,
which it is able to forget, but which tragedy reawakens.

Empowered? Why? The answer is to be found in Nietzsche's later work,
which develops the germ of this note. Like the Greek "pupal stage," the
note contains the embryonic ideas of self-overcoming and the will to power,
their psychological effect—the feeling of a surcharge of positive energy when
"the most frightful thing" is encountered, and the aesthetic means to
achieve this state of "blissfulness" in tragedy. To paraphrase the entry from
the vantage point of Nietzsche's later works: There is salvation, "blissfulness" in knowledge of the worst, because by confronting it, the will's ener-
gies are aroused, its capacities for command engaged, its transformational
potential released. "What is good?—All that heightens the feeling of power,
the will to power, power itself in man. . . . What is happiness?—The feeling

that power *increases*—that a resistance is overcome" (*A* 2). This note fore-shadows the content of Zarathustra's nightmare-like vision and riddle, where the dreadful serpent is overcome and transformed, from woe to bliss, by the shepherd's act of will.

The notebooks for 1869 and 1870 also indicate that Nietzsche was work-ing toward his theory of the origin of tragedy in the tragic chorus, whose connection with "the Mothers" may be gleaned in his accounts of the ritual madness and sexual wantonness of Dionysian festivals, and in the mysteries and their ritual enactment of Demeter's loss of Persephone. Nietzsche's notes tend to conflate the three events—Dionysian festivals, mysteries, and tragedy. In his notebook for the year 1869, Nietzsche writes of Dionysian rites as the "secret source" of Greek tragedy. The inherent advantage of ancient drama was its proximity to "nature" and to folk festivals—"orgiastic" ecstatic Dionysian rites. It is the misfortune of modern art, he writes, "not to stem from such a secret source" (*KSA* 7:10). Scattered entries from 1870 refer to "the mysteries" together with tragedy, as in the following exam-ples: "The mysteries and the drama born at one time, also their outlooks were afterward related" (*KSA* 7:127); or, "Why shouldn't we attain that standpoint of artistic transfiguration that the Greeks had? The Dionysian festivals were the most solemn of the religion—with the exception of the mysteries, in which however again dramatic performances were staged" (*KSA* 7:121).

The ancient Greek cultic festival known as the Eleusinian mysteries was an annual festival that attracted initiates from the entire Greek-speaking world. The oldest source of our knowledge of the mysteries, a Homeric hymn from the seventh century BCE, explains why Eleusis (outside Athens) is the site of the rites and how the grain goddess Demeter inaugurated them. After relating the story of Demeter and her daughter Kore (the vir-gin) or Persephone, the hymn ends by stating that Demeter's "essential gift to man"—superior even to the fruits of the earth—was "the ceremonies which no one may describe or utter" (in Kerenyi 13). Karl Kerenyi tells the story as follows: The young virgin Persephone is lured to a meadow, where the ground begins "to gape." An abyss is imminent. The meadow is iden-tified as the Nysan Plain, named after the mountain of Nysa, the birth-place of Dionysus (Kerenyi notes that "Dionysus himself had the strange surname of 'the gaping one'" (35)—among many other epithets). Hades drives his horses out of the earth and seizes the girl. The place where this happened was called Erineos, after a wild fig tree there, and since the fig is sacred to Dionysus (not only his *baubon* or wooden phallus but also his mask was cut from its wood on Naxos), there is evidence to link the abduction of Persephone to Dionysus, including a vase that shows Persephone with Dionysus. (Kerenyi claims Dionysus took the form of Hades and ravished the girl himself [35]. In support, he quotes Heraclitus: "Hades is the same as Dionysus" [40].) The connection between Dionysus's name, "the gaping one," the hole in the ground from which he/Hades appeared, and Hades as god of the Underworld of death, reinforces the connection Bachofen found between Dionysus and the nature and spaces attributed to woman—their connection with life as inseparable from or entailed with death.

The story continues: Demeter, missing her daughter, begins searching for her; her grief is inconsolable; she dries up the earth's fertility causing famine; she takes the form of an old woman and sits by a well in Eleusis mourning her kidnapped daughter. Iambe, a "hearty serving maid," cheers her up by means of raillery, jests, and obscene gestures. In the Orphic hymn that relates the Demeter/Persephone story, the part of Iambe is taken by Baubo, who makes the goddess laugh by raising her skirt above her head and showing her "belly."

The reference to Baubo brings us back to Nietzsche, who slips her into his published work by giving her a prominent position at the end of the preface to the second edition of *The Gay Science* (1886), which he then reproduces at the climactic finale of his last book, *Nietzsche contra Wagner* (1889). However, although the position may be prominent, the reference is unexplained, enigmatic, veiled—as per the passage in which it appears, which recommends that truth should—and the ancients demanded that the "mysteries" must—be so. Doubly veiled, enigma wrapped in mystery, the text reads: "Perhaps truth is a woman who has reasons for not letting us see her reasons? Perhaps her name is—to speak Greek—*Baubo*?" (Preface 4).

Baubo goes way back. According to W. K. C. Guthrie *(Orpheus and Greek Religion),* her name means "that which she showed to Demeter"—a veiled allusion to the genitals. (Guthrie euphemizes this as "the female counterpart of the phallic emblem" [135]; Sarah Kofman refers to it by its Greek name, *koilia* ("cavity"), "another of the 'improper words used in Greek to designate the female sex'" ("Baubô" 197). Maurice Olender, in a comprehensive 1990 essay on Baubo texts and contexts, emphasizes the difficulties and complexities of offering interpretations of a figure so ancient (with connections to Anatolian fertility cult goddesses), whose story has lured scholars into attempts to "determine just which sort of 'archaic' ritual found its belated echo in Baubo's gesture [of displaying her genitals]" (Olender 91). What is clear is that Nietzsche was intrigued, and though there is no mention of Baubo in the notebooks of the period that I consider here, there are references to sources for the Demeter and Baubo stories,[11] to the mysteries, and to the smile of Demeter. Baubo and Baubon (her male counterpart) both appeared as puppet figures at the Eleusinian mysteries, where "the female sexual organ is exalted as the symbol of fertility and a guarantee of the regeneration and eternal return of all things" (Kofman "Baubô" 197).

Exactly what Baubo reveals is a matter of dispute; the early Church Fathers Clement and Arnobius each quote the Orphic hymn that tells the tale, but draw from different versions of the text. Each is dramatic. Here is a passage from the Arnobius version: "At these words, Baubo pulls up her garment from the bottom and exposes to sight the objects shaped on her natural parts [*formatas inguinibus res*]." Olender notes that an influential commentator took this to mean "the object drawn," assuming that a child's head had been drawn on her decorated belly. "Below, she agitates them with her hand—the shapes resembled a little child—and she pats it and gently manipulates it." As Arnobius observes: "The goddess' gaze falls on the pubis and feasts on the sight of this extraordinary sort of consolation"; she laughs and relaxes, is at ease, and so, Arnobius remarks, "the obscenity of a lewd act was able to attain what Baubo's modest behavior had long failed to accomplish" (Olender 88). The laughter breaks Demeter's sorrow, the earth is restored to fecundity, and the deal is struck whereby Persephone visits her mother on the earth's surface for two-thirds of the year and stays with her husband in the underworld for the other third. So goes the myth.

Indeed, the central events of the mysteries were mysterious. Once a year the initiates or *epopts* (both men and women) "came in a ritual procession to this festival of 'vision', at which *epopteia,* the state of 'having seen', was attained" (Kerenyi 65). They were sworn to secrecy about what they saw, but Kerenyi relates that Pindar, Sophocles, Isokrates, and even Cicero, who had all been in attendance, reported that the initiates saw a vision of "blessedness" that gave them hope in facing death ("[They] know the end of life and its beginning", Pindar writes [Kerenyi 14-15]). The mythic account of Demeter's loss of Persephone, of her mourning, Persephone's voyage to the Underworld, Baubo's gestures, Demeter's laugh, and fertility restored, has a clear trajectory from death to rebirth. Several sources note that the rites concluded with the birth of a "mystic child" (to represent renewed fertility) whose identity is disputed (Zeitlin 306). Nietzsche's source, the *Souda,* calls the child "Dionysos." The "climax" of the ceremonies "always entailed the experience of a dazzling light" (Zeitlin 308). Kerenyi concludes that "we are confronted with the historical fact that in the Mysteries both men and women seem to envisage the *feminine source of life,* but not in an intellectual way" (xxxiii).

The terms that Nietzsche makes use of in his notebooks to associate religion and tragedy, or to designate the effect of tragedy, "blissfulness" and "transfiguration," are the same ones that ancient writers used to describe the effect of the mysteries. The hope the mysteries engenders in participants, he holds, derives from the same impulse as that which drives participants in the Dionysian orgies. Nietzsche writes that this impulse is a "wisdom" that passes the understanding of Winckelmann, whose characterization of Greek art as embodying "calm simplicity" and "noble dignity" misses the "metaphysical nature of the mysteries, strongly working *in der Tiefe*—in the depths." For "the Greek," Nietzsche maintains, this wisdom of the depths is stronger and surer than that of the Olympian gods, and therefore the desecration of the mysteries is the one cardinal sin (*KSA* 7:176).

What is this powerful wisdom, which is revealed both in the mysteries and in the orgiastic mania? In *Thus Spoke Zarathustra,* Nietzsche names it the eternal return. In his notes, he is clearly groping to express an intuition about the "worldview" and the effect of tragedy as it corresponds with that of the hillside manias and the mysteries. All three of these types of festival involve a ritual sense of loss of self, of beneficial and live-giving self-forgetfulness, as part of a celebration of a greater whole. They share, Nietzsche writes,

> The fundamental knowledge of the oneness of everything in existence, the perception of individuation as the primeval ground of all evil, the beautiful and art as the hope that the ties of individuation will be burst, as the idea of a re-established unity. . . . The whole institution of the mysteries is intended to give this insight in images to those who are ready. . . . In these images however we learn again about the eccentric voices and knowledges that the orgy of the dionysian spring festival almost always aroused: the denial of individuation, the horror over broken unity, the hope for a new world-creation, in short, the feeling of a blissful shudder in which the knot of joy and terror is tied together . . . a guarantee of the rebirth of Dionysus . . . a hope-glance from the ever-sorrowing countenance of Demeter. (*KSA* 7:178–79)

For Nietzsche, these rites affirm the value of sexuality and of life's continuity— not the life of the individual, but of the community as a whole. For him, tragedy—the art form that arises out of a sense of life's sacred value— breaks down the distinction between life and death, or rather, knots them together so artfully that the two cannot be disentangled.

Although *The Birth of Tragedy* articulates this thought, the point is refined and condensed only with its appearance in a late work. The concluding sections of *Twilight of the Idols* announce Nietzsche's countermove, both to Bachofen's proclamation of patriarchy as the highest and final state for humankind and to Hartmann's hypothesis of reason's destruction of the unconscious will to live. Nietzsche, in effect, endorses the psychology (not the historical accuracy) of the first two Bachovian stages:

> I was the first to take seriously that wonderful phenomenon which bears the name Dionysus as a means of understanding the older Hellenic instinct, an instinct still exuberant and even overflowing. . . . It is only in the Dionysian mysteries, in the psychology of the Dionysian condition, that the *fundamental fact* of the Hellenic instinct expresses itself—its "will to life." *What* did the Hellene guarantee to himself with these mysteries? *Eternal* life, the eternal recurrence of life; the future promised and consecrated in the past; the triumphant Yes to life beyond death and change; true life as collective continuation of life through procreation, through the mysteries of sexuality. ("What I Owe to the Ancients" 4)

A bit further on in this passage, Nietzsche emphasizes the femininity of the mysteries: "Every individual detail in the act of procreation, pregnancy, birth, awoke the most exalted and solemn feelings. In the teachings of the mysteries, *pain* is sanctified: the 'pains of childbirth' sanctify pain in general" (*TI* "Ancients" 4). Childbirth, the event that Nietzsche imagined was enacted at Eleusis, becomes a touchstone for the value and renewed promise of earthly life.

The "mysteries" is a topic that shows up in Nietzsche's notebook chapter outlines for *The Birth of Tragedy* in connection with another heading, "the Pythia" or "oracle" (*KSA* 7:136, 146–47). We know that Bachofen counted woman's prophetic powers as the means by which she consolidated her civic ones; Nietzsche also posits a link between the Pythia and the rise of the state. For Nietzsche, woman's fundamental ties to the mysteries are also fundamentally connected to Dionysus and the ritual breakdown of individuation and political order; conversely, her ties to prophecy are connected to Apollo, the individual, and political consolidation. "The position of woman with the Greeks was the right one: from it was engendered reverence for the wisdom of woman: Diotima, Pythia, Sybil, also Antigone. Here we think of the German woman, as Tacitus described her" (*KSA* 7:137–38). In *Germania* (98 CE), Tacitus reports that men of the various German nations revere "most highly" their wives and children, and that German men "believe that there resides in women an element of holiness and a gift of prophecy: and so they do not scorn to ask their advice, or lightly disregard their replies" (108). For Nietzsche, ancient Greek women similarly engendered reverence and helped to guide the state through the powers of prophecy vested in the Pythia.

Though he is aware that ordinary Greek wives in classical Athens were little better than slaves, Nietzsche also acknowledges the presence of an undeniable feminine power in Greek myth and religion, absent in the present day. Women in Periclean Athens had no public power, yet the Greeks stood in "reverence" or awe and fear of the oracular "wisdom" of women; the Greeks respected the mysteries; their goddesses were powerful, their protection was solicited and their propitiation offered as part of everyday life. At one point in the notes, Nietzsche ponders the anomalous position of women and asks what to make of these apparent contradictions: "Why didn't culture become feminine?" (*KSA* 7:146).

His answer to this question (framed in subsequent notes) leads me to think that he took Bachofen's hypothesis seriously. Bachofen's solution to the contradictions about the feminine derived from the anthropological and textual evidence is simply that over time men wrested power from the women by force. There is an entry in the 1870-71 notebooks that suggests a measure of agreement with this solution: "The [Greek] state originates in the most cruel way through subjugation, through the production of a drone sex. Its higher destiny now is to let a culture grow from these drones" (*KSA* 7:142). There are other scattered references to "drones" (as in bees) in Nietzsche's work; an aphorism from *Human, All Too Human* compares nonworking women to drones in a hive, as we have seen (1:412).

In "The Greek State," a draft essay from this period, Nietzsche reflects on war's barbarisms and the Greek instinct that asserts, "Power gives the first right, and there is no right, which at bottom is not presumption, usurpation, violence." In this instance it is "nature," not Greek men, who is cruel: "Here again we see with what pitiless inflexibility Nature, in order to arrive at Society, forges for herself the cruel tool of the State—namely, that conqueror with the iron hand" (*EGP* 10). Nature is Will, let us remember; Will is a Mother; the will to power wants to destroy and to create, and is "pitiless." If indeed culture did not become feminine, it was because a superior power exerted its will; the conqueror's hand was no doubt encased in a masculine iron glove.

According to Bachofen, for whom the conquering is literal, the conquerors also rewrote the script, erasing or writing over cultural signs of women's earlier civic roles. Bachofen's thesis that women were written out of history is taken up more generally and later by Nietzsche in the guise of the will to power as interpretation, and the idea of cruelty as the motor behind the "progress" of civilization was to become a central Nietzschean thought. "Almost everything we call 'higher culture' is based on the spiritualization and intensification of *cruelty*," Nietzsche writes in *Beyond Good and Evil* (229). Clearly, in his notes from the early 1870s, he uses as example the overcoming of women by men.

For Nietzsche this possibility is not necessarily an objection; indeed, as his fragment on "The Greek Woman" demonstrates, he muses on it with a kind of wonder. This text—an unshaped draft ultimately excluded from Nietzsche's published prose (save for scant appearances in later works)—was extracted from the notes and published as a separate pamphlet entitled "The Greek Woman," both in Oscar Levy's edition of Nietzsche's complete works in English translation in 1911 and in a series of "Leaflets to the German Youth" in 1917 (Eugen Diederichs, Jena). As a result, it has been anthologized and quoted, excerpted from an excerpt, as exemplary of Nietzsche's position on ancient woman.[12] "The Greek Woman" constructs (or reconstructs) an ancient ideal of the eternal feminine that it contrasts with the modern ideal, and with the radical suggestion Plato makes in the *Republic* that marriage should be abolished and women trained equally with men. Standing against the attack of Platonic reason and scientificality on the institution of marriage (with its parallel in the movement for women's emancipation in the nineteenth century), Nietzsche's "Greek Woman" defends the Athenian custom of sequestering married women in a strictly private sphere.

With what will become his characteristic reversal of received opinion, Nietzsche asks his readers to consider the position of Hellenic women as *not* "unworthy and repugnant to humanity" (*EGP* 21). The inquiry begins with the question, "Should not the nature and the position of the Hellenic Woman have a *necessary* relation to the goals of the Hellenic Will?" (21). The end-purpose or goal of this will, according to Nietzsche, is the production of genius, to which the women lent the dark peace of their physical sequestration and the eternal Same of their wombs. The text rehearses what Nietzsche takes to be the Athenian ideal of the feminine; it finds in woman's nature "the healing power" and the rest which restores and nourishes—like sleep, like the dark, like plants and animals. This woman is the place where "everything immoderate" and excessive regulates itself. Much of this description echoes the work of Bachofen, who, following classical sources, similarly described woman in the tellurian state as "always the same," as sleep, and as identified with nature, and in the matriarchal state as regulating the excesses of promiscuity. Nietzsche stresses nature over culture in his description of the feminine: "Culture is with her always something external, a something which does not touch the kernel that is eternally faithful to Nature" (*EGP* 23).

Never mind that Athenians revered Athena for wisdom, justice, and military prowess, Hestia for domestic skills, Artemis for forestry and hunting, and Hera for administration and Olympian wheeling and dealing. Nietzsche has his own agenda, for which he is content to claim that the Hellenic "will to power" demanded that women remain firmly linked to nature, *as an ideal,* or as a myth. This myth is the precise opposite of the nineteenth-century ideal of the eternal feminine, which separates woman from nature to the extreme of having her embody not sexuality, but incorporeal virtues and values: moral goodness, selflessness, faith, heavenly salvation. In the Athenian ideal, woman embodies the earth from which new life grows; she is the earth mother. "The Greek Woman" identifies the highest aim of Greek political instinct with "the Hellenic will"—a will that was anti-individualistic and pro-culture [*Kultur*]. The family existed for the benefit, and "as the expedient," of the city-state, and while the *polis* was unified in its aim, possessing a singular collective will, its culture waxed and thrived.

"The Greek Woman" makes the case that there is no real distinction between woman as analogous to nature and woman as goddess or mythic heroine. The reason for the lack of contradiction between the two, and the primary difference between the ancient Greeks and the moderns, is that for the Greeks nature hadn't yet lost its importance and its sacred significance. The Greeks compared woman with sleep—a comparison Nietzsche relays; but sleep itself is positively valued, as dark, quiet, fertile, the place of forgetfulness (Nietzsche quotes "Epicurean wisdom" to this effect [*EGP* 23])[13], the place of dreams, and finally, the font of prophecy. Far from being denigrated in ancient times, the text argues, women were revered and glorified "as never since. The goddesses of Greek mythology are their images: the Pythia and the Sibyl, as well as the Socratic Diotima are the priestesses out of whom divine wisdom speaks" (24).

The text goes on tentatively to support Bachofen's hypothesis of matriarchy, though not explicitly or by name: "As long as the State is still in an embryonic condition [the pupal stage again], woman as *mother* preponderates and determines the grade and the manifestations of Culture: in the same way as woman is destined to complement the disorganized State."

She complements the State in her role as prophetess: "How far this divining power reaches is determined, it seems, by the greater or lesser consolidation of the State; in disorderly or more arbitrary conditions, where the whim or the passion of the individual man carries along with itself whole tribes, then woman suddenly comes forward as the warning prophetess" (*EGP* 25). Thus "above all it is in the *Pythia,* that the power of woman to compensate the State manifested itself so clearly [the phrase is repeated] as it has never done since" (25). Nietzsche's notes state that "woman" was the civic organizer, keeping "the whole tribe" on the path to cultural unity by helping to maintain the collective will, as against the idiosyncratic "passion of the individual man." Here the "herd animals" are the constructive ones; the individuals are dangerous.

In Nietzsche's draft account in the notebooks, as in Bachofen's published assertions, the role of woman was instrumental in the development of Greek culture, and for the same reason: as the human agent considered closer to nature (including animal and plant life) than man, and as the obvious creative vessel, woman retained a connection with the "mysterious" powers of life and death. These powers became anthropomorphized and personified as goddesses and ritualized in cult (as at Eleusis), and woman as prophetess retained her direct access to them, guiding her human community by speaking the truth of god's—Apollo's—voice. Nietzsche's notebook confers on the Pythia the title of "Apollonian preparation"; she represents a step—indeed *the* step—necessary to the development of Greek high culture. In a sequence not excerpted in Levy's edition, the text discusses the Pythia as a manifestation or a signpost on the way to "art": "In her Apollo revealed himself, not yet as god of art, but as the healing, warning state-god, who keeps the state on the path where it must encounter genius" (*KSA* 7:174-75). The Pythia, Delphi's feminine spokesperson, is the first "revelation" of the art god Apollo, and Apollo himself, as symbolic of the "illusion" of art, is also the prophetic god. It is clear that in Nietzsche's accounts, Apollo, like Dionysus, shares a history, if not an identity, with women.

Bachofen's emphasis on women's religious preeminence in their communities during the matriarchal period is reflected, in Nietzsche's notes, by Dionysus's connections with the mysteries and Apollo's with the Pythia. The mothers of tragedy and the Sphinx connect with Bachofen's tellurian phase and also to Hartmann's unconscious will. "The Greek Woman" fragment constructs the Greek ideal of the feminine as the eternal Same [*das ewig Gleiche*], which in German is a play on the eternal feminine [*das ewig Weibliche*] and apparently endorses that ideal. The repetition of the adjective *ewig,* eternal, becomes a bell that tolls for Zarathustra in his "Ewige Wiederkunft des Gleichens" (eternal return of the same) and for his bride "Ewigkeit" (eternity); and there are other traces of the eternal sameness of the Greek Woman scattered throughout later Nietzschean texts.

This sameness is anything but static; it is empowered by its direct connections to nature—to sexuality and childbirth, change, and death—connections not exclusively the property of woman. These are the basic truths of life, and so woman, in Nietzsche's later texts, becomes emblematic of life and truth; of wisdom, or the ability to transform the basic truths into stories we can live by; of happiness, the laugh of Demeter at the vision of the woman enjoying herself; and of eternity, the perpetuation of earthly life in time.

3

The Birth of Tragedy and the Feminine

The Birth of Tragedy's major structural analogy uses heterosexuality to claim that the production of art depends on the interaction of two opposite "art drives," just as the production of new organic life depends on that of the two opposite sexes. Tragedy is "engendered" when the art impulses symbolized by the god Apollo combine with the opposing impulses symbolized by the god Dionysus. The coupling is announced in the text's first sentence: "We shall have gained much for the science of aesthetics, once we perceive not merely by logical inference, but with the immediate certainty of vision, that the continuous development of art is bound up with the *Apollonian* and *Dionysian* duality—just as procreation depends on the duality of the sexes, involving perpetual strife with only periodically intervening reconciliations" (I).[1]

For our purposes, the immediate problem that this analogy poses is that Apollo and Dionysus are mythical Greek gods of the masculine persuasion, whose sexual union for the purposes of procreation is out of the question. The analogy is weak at best. We could leave it at that; many critics have not considered it worthy of attention.[2] I do wonder, however, why Nietzsche used the analogy at all, if the "sexual interest" of the text were nil, and if its ideas could have been stated equally well without recourse to a clumsy figure of speech.

We know that the notebooks that Nietzsche kept as he drafted *The Birth of Tragedy* define "nature," "music," and "myth" in the feminine (nature is a woman; music is a mother; Sphinx is a female virgin, a myth, and a symbol of nature). In his notes he lists "mythological woman," the mysteries, the Pythia, and "woman" as themes or topic headings of interest for his work, and he devotes some time and energy to writing a draft essay on the meaning of woman for the ancient Hellene. We know, too, that he advised himself, by way of a note, to trace tragedy back to its mothers (*KSA* 7:93). And yet in the final product, a book that investigates the origin of tragedy, whose structure depends on the analogy of heterosexual relations—a book carefully crafted, drafted and redrafted—the "mothers" are relegated to the back sections, and the word "woman" hardly appears at all.

Tragedy is the Greek art that supremely "idealizes" woman: it mythologizes her, and puts her on stage. In the surviving plays of Aeschylus, Nietzsche's favorite tragedian, five out of seven choruses are composed entirely of women, and women play leading parts in the onstage drama. In *The Eumenides*, there are *two* choruses of women, one of Furies and one of women of Athens; the Pythia speaks the play's prologue (giving "first place of honor in my prayer / to her who of the gods first prophesied, the Earth" and proceeding to invocations to other female prophets, who preceded Apollo [lines 1–2]). In *The Libation-Bearers*, which Nietzsche taught in 1869 (Janz 342), the chorus is composed of "foreign serving women," and the central roles are those of Electra and Clytemnestra. In Sophocles' *Electra*, which he also taught in 1869–70, the protagonist is a woman, her sister and her mother figure on stage, and the chorus is composed of "women of Mycenae." Of Euripides's plays, 14 out of 19 tragedies feature women in their title roles and have female choruses.

Those critics who have noticed the absence of references to women of any description, mythic or historical, in *The Birth of Tragedy*, have considered it either a wonder ("a striking omission," Silk and Stern 173–74), or a puzzle solved by psychoanalysis ("it ['the almost complete absence of maenads'] qualifies as an instance of repression," Staten 118). Given the attention to "woman" in Nietzsche's notes and in the tragedies themselves, I believe that the omission of a female partner to the "birth" cannot be an oversight or a repression, but is rather the result of a conscious intention. The feminine is in fact overwhelmingly signified in the text, but rarely "as such"—that is, as "woman." It is signified by the figures and images used to connote the concepts nature, will, music, myth, and tragedy, and by the metaphors of the Apollonian and especially, the Dionysian "art drives of nature."

Why did Nietzsche use the analogy of sexual procreation to describe the origin not merely of tragedy but of all art? Could *The Birth of Tragedy* have made its aesthetic points without the analogy? What function does the analogy serve? And if the feminine is present, why is it hidden or disguised by metaphor and symbol, when "nature"—the act of sexual procreation—demands its participation and signification? The answers to these questions may be discovered by analyzing the textual strategies Nietzsche adopted in order to enact his meaning, which, I shall claim, includes the apparent disappearance of values attributed to the feminine in archaic Greek myth and cult, and the possibility of their recovery. I shall argue that Nietzsche, rather than forgetting or ignoring his Greek woman, deliberately dismembered her, as Dionysus was dismembered by the Titans, and scattered her pieces through the text, with the expressed hope that she may be reborn. Rather than slighting the feminine, Nietzsche gives it mythic status.

Those readers who have looked to both *The Birth of Tragedy* and to Nietzsche's notes will notice that he has transferred phrases descriptive of "the Greek woman" from the latter to the former. In "The Greek Woman" (which was discussed at some length in the previous chapter), woman's nature possesses "the healing power," "the beneficial rest," "the eternal Same," the womb wherein "the future generation dreams" (*EGP* 22–23). In *The Birth of Tragedy* 1, we read that the "joyous necessity of the dream experience has been embodied by the Greeks in their Apollo," who also embodies the "deep consciousness of nature, healing and helping in sleep and dreams." Apollo's function as the soothsaying god, of course, also follows from the Pythia, central in the notes as a guiding, warning, prophesying woman. "The Greek Woman" emphasizes the "eternal sameness" of woman and her closeness to nature in comparison with man; *The Birth of Tragedy* 7 describes the chorus of satyrs as "a chorus of natural beings who live ineradicably, as it were, behind all civilization and remain eternally the same, despite the changes of generations and of the history of nations." In this setting, it appears as though women have been metamorphosed into satyrs, close companions of Dionysus. Dionysus is the truly suspicious character, however. His attributes as the Dionysian art impulse of nature are classically feminine—boundless, formless, ecstatic, creative/destructive; he is aligned with the mothers of tragedy, and the text may be an allegory about the loss of the power of the feminine with the demise of tragedy and the rise of Socratic rationality.

At the same time that *The Birth of Tragedy* points in the direction of a story about the feminine, however, it also points to its own storytelling function, in a clear self-reflexive gesture that deprives the narrative of its mythic status even as it seeks to constitute it. This self-reflexivity qualifies the text's truth claims without totally effacing them. In the area of sexuality, the self-reflexivity separates biological sex and gender, de-essentializing woman. This move enables qualities of femininity formulated in the notebooks to float free of their reference to female bodies and to be dispersed widely as active, powerful, and indispensable qualities for all humans, attached, in this case, to male gods. In this manner, the choice of the "tragic culture" (*BT* 18) involves a subtle, but I believe clearly indicated, conceptual disruption of the myths of dimorphic sexual identities. In *The Birth of Tragedy*, Nietzsche makes a radical move toward destabilizing sex-gender paradigms.

The Birth of Tragedy as a Mythic Text

The Birth of Tragedy is about myth, but it also possesses mythic qualities itself. It makes us consider myth in two ways: as truth and as fiction. Mircea Eliade's work approaches myth from the point of view of the tribal believer: "Myth is thought to express the *absolute truth*. . . . Being real and sacred, the myth becomes exemplary, and consequently repeatable" (23). On the level of narrative, *The Birth of Tragedy* views myth from this perspective, as the true and the sacred. When tragedy dies, myth dies—destroyed by reason— for myth, Nietzsche writes, "wants to be experienced vividly as a unique example of a universality and truth that gaze into the infinite" (*BT* 17). "Myth," in the sense of sacred reality, in Nietzsche's view, gave ancient Greece its cohesion.

In defining "myth," Eliade also maps the provenance of its meaning as "that which is not true." "Everyone knows," he writes, "that from the time of Xenophanes (ca. 565–470 BCE—who was first to criticize and reject the 'mythological' expressions of the divinity employed by Homer and Hesiod—the Greeks steadily continued to empty *mythos* of all religious and metaphysical value. Contrasted both with *logos,* and, later, with *historia, mythos* came in the end to denote 'what cannot really exist'" (1–2). Nietzsche— and this is part of the "doubleness" of *The Birth of Tragedy*—uses "myth" to refer both to that which is true, real, and sacred, and to that which is fictitious.

At the time that he was drafting *The Birth of Tragedy,* Nietzsche wrote the phrase "the mythological drive" (or "instinct": German, *Trieb*) in his notebooks, as though it actually had a meaning (*KSA* 7:77). As a drive or instinct this refers to something Nietzsche thinks is both material (of the body) and "irrational"—that is, not controlled by the conscious subject. As material and irrational, the mythological drive falls onto the "feminine" side of the conventional table of binary oppositions that has, for at least two millennia, linked "female" with the formless, dark, and material qualities— and by extension with the unconscious and the irrational, in a repetitive set of associations that is itself mythic. Both Bachofen and Hartmann, as we have seen, perpetuate the associative repetitions and thus prolong the life of the myth. His notebooks suggest that Nietzsche too inclines toward a perpetuation of the myth that links woman and nature, the unconscious, the body, the emotions, and the material world of "coming to be and passing away." Indeed, it appears as though Nietzsche wishes to retrieve these qualities from their subordination to their "masculine" counterparts, inscribed explicitly and approvingly as "patriarchal" in Bachofen's texts: consciousness, and the "higher" life of the mind—law, moral codes, logic.

The "mythological drive" drives *The Birth of Tragedy* in a number of ways. First, it powers the structure of the plot, which moves in a double orbit, from ancient times to the present and back again, and then back to the present once more. The narrative effect is not only that of a double orbit, but also of a double exposure, with ancient and modern times superimposed on each other. This double exposure gives us the two meanings of "myth," as truth (for archaic times) and fiction (for the present). The structure of *The Birth of Tragedy,* which is built upon prominent sets of binary oppositions, exemplifies Lévi-Strauss's formulation of myth. For Lévi-Strauss, "mythical thought always progresses from an awareness of oppositions toward their resolution. . . . Two opposite terms with no intermediary always tend to be replaced by two equivalent terms which admit of a third one as a mediator, then one of the polar terms and the mediator become replaced by a new triad, and so on" (*Structural Anthropology* 1:224). For the structure to be maintained, the center to hold, the myth must undergo a dynamic process admitting of the permeability or even interchangeability of its terms. Thus the contradictions that may well be unresolvable for society are mastered and order is brought out of chaos.

The Birth of Tragedy's story follows this trajectory, for it turns on the nature/culture opposition to show how an art form, Greek tragedy, developed or was "born" from a series of transformations of its major terms, the two primary "art impulses [drives] of nature." This move anthropomorphizes and thus mythologizes nature shamelessly—as though nature had art instincts! But this is precisely Nietzsche's point: nature may be said to have a "reproductive instinct," and the two sorts of productivity, sexual and artistic, are at least analogously related, as Nietzsche implies by contiguity in his first sentence. The initial paragraph goes on to establish his hypotheses—that is, to build its myth—by using Greek mythic thought as its model and tool: "The terms Dionysian and Apollonian we borrow from the Greeks, who disclose to the discerning mind the profound mysteries of their view of art, not, to be sure, in concepts, but in the intensely clear figures of their gods." Not in concepts: this is the key point, since mythic thought is ignorant of abstract language. Lévi-Strauss writes of mythical thought that it "does not seek to give [natural beings] a meaning—it expresses itself through them" (*Structural Anthropology* 1:221). So Nietzsche, using the mythic figures Apollo and Dionysus, seeks to express through them a meaning that he partly explains "in concepts" and partly leaves unexplained as myth.

The Birth of Tragedy is a genetic or genealogical story of origin, and in this it is also mythic, for myth, according to Eliade, is "always an account of a 'creation'; it relates how something was produced, began to *be*" (6). Eric Blondel's book on Nietzsche takes Nietzsche's penchant for genealogy as its starting point, arguing that "genealogical research is an inquiry into the physiological and biological, or more precisely sexual, origins of concepts and knowledge, in other words of culture in general, origins which are normally hidden but which can be inferred through the simple medium of language" (*Nietzsche: Body and Culture* 17). *The Birth of Tragedy* uses a sexual analogy, and sexual imagery throughout, to account for "the continuous development of art." If the "natural" (or sexual) side of the binary "is normally hidden" in genealogical researches, here it is apparent; the sexual origins of cultural forms are exposed from the first sentence. "Paradoxical as it may seem," writes Roland Barthes, "*myth hides nothing:* its function is to distort, not to make disappear" (121). The sexual operation toward which the text gestures, while visible, is certainly distorted, if the union of Apollo and Dionysus furnishes an analogy to the "duality of the sexes"— unless, of course, one of the two is a female masquerading as a male, or we are meant to take seriously the first paragraph's assertion that the productive union of the two "art deities" was a "miracle," rather like the virgin birth. We are, after all, in the realm of myth, where anything is possible.

The book draws on Bachofen's mythic account of cultural origin in the far distant tellurian period, the stage of Dionysian materiality when the "maternal principal" is universal and, like the life of nature, "knows no barriers" (Bachofen 80); where life is chaotic and pointless, and sexuality promiscuous. In *The Birth of Tragedy* Nietzsche takes up the story and tells us that the myths that originate in this period, a time before the Olympic gods dominated the scene, form the basis of tragedy. They represent various expressions of the wisdom of Silenus (the wise satyr who accompanied Dionysus): it is best not to be born; second best, to die soon (*BT* 3), and in the meantime, to suffer. This is tragedy's "profound and pessimistic" view of the world (*BT* 10), and we recognize it as the province of the mothers of tragedy: Will, Delusion, Woe—those three abysses into which tragedy resolutely stares, that lie at the heart of the Olympian "magic mountain." As Nietzsche writes: "The Greek knew and felt the terror and horror of existence. That he might endure this terror at all, he had to interpose between himself and life the radiant dream-birth of the Olympians. That overwhelming dismay in the face of the titanic powers of nature, the Moira enthroned inexorably over all knowledge, the vulture of the great lover of mankind, Prometheus, the terrible fate of the wise Oedipus, the family curse of the Atridae which drove Orestes to matricide"—these "mythic exemplars" of "the original Titanic divine order of terror" precede the "Olympian divine order of joy" and give birth to it (*BT* 3). The earliest myths reflect that which *The Birth of Tragedy* holds for truth: "suffering, primal and eternal, the sole ground of the world" (*BT* 4).

Nietzsche borrowed Bachofen's *An Essay on Mortuary Symbolism* from the University of Basel library in 1871, while he was writing *The Birth of Tragedy* (Silk and Stern 214). Bachofen's essay—taking its departure from the analysis of a mural found in a Roman tomb which shows three eggs on a table, each painted half black and half white—stresses the importance of the "twofold force, creative and destructive," in ancient thought. Bachofen insists on the equal justification of both halves: "Death is the precondition of life, and only in the same measure as destruction proceeds can creation be effective. . . . No other idea holds so large a place in the symbolism and mythology of the ancients" (25–26). The twofold force of birth and death also accounts, he claims, for "the frequency of pairs of brothers [in myth], sometimes represented as forever struggling with one another, sometimes as friendly, and usually as twins"; they are "two opposites joined in a unity" (27). He goes on to mention "the close ties between Dionysus and Apollo" (29), and the importance of the two-colored egg in the Bacchic mysteries: "The two-colored egg at the center of the Dionysian religion shows us the supreme law governing the transient world as a *fatum* inherent in feminine matter" (28). The "feminine materiality" symbolized by the egg and by pairs of brothers locked in contest subsumes both birth and death. Nietzsche's tragedy, I suggest, is the whole (divided) egg—the divisions being the Apollonian and the Dionysian. Late in the text, Nietzsche very nearly quotes Bachofen when he writes, "The intricate relation of the Apollonian and the Dionysian in tragedy may really be symbolized by a fraternal union of the two deities" (*BT* 21); these in turn symbolize the inseparable forces of feminine materiality—life and death—in archaic Greek mythological thought. Bachofen's mythic structure undergirds that of Nietzsche in *The Birth of Tragedy,* from the Dionysian/Apollonian division to the overall narrative line. But Nietzsche reinterprets Bachofen's ending—the triumphant ascendancy of patriarchy—and moves it to the middle of his text.

The Birth of Tragedy plots the beginnings of tragedy in the Dionysian satyr chorus and dithyramb, the middle in the plays of Aeschylus and Sophocles, and the end of its power on the Greek stage with the arrival of Socrates, Euripides, and "reason." In Nietzsche's mythic narrative, when reason arrives, myth goes, and with it goes tragedy ("The demise of tragedy was at the same time the demise of myth" [*BT* 23]). Tragedy has thrived—by this account—on a certain mystery, enigma, incommensurability; when Euripides looks at the drama of Aeschylus and Sophocles, it seems to him the "primeval chaos" from which he is to bring order and intelligibility (*BT* 12). At the midpoint of the text, myth and tragedy are synonymous with religion, and both are vanquished by "'aesthetic Socratism' whose supreme law reads roughly as follows: 'To be beautiful everything must be intelligible'" (*BT* 12). Tragedy has, in fact, committed suicide, out of despair.

At this point, it becomes apparent that *The Birth of Tragedy*'s narrative is not Aristotelian (that is, working from beginning to middle to an end-point authorized by causality); only halfway through the text its subject is dead. A whole new narrative unfolds midbook. But in truth this isn't new; we've heard it before—it plots the birth, rise, and decline of scientific rationalism ("Socratic optimism," "theoretical culture"), bringing the text, and the reader, to the Nietzschean present (1872) when, the story goes, Socratic culture is faltering. Socratic culture in its extremity resembles tragic culture in the Hellenistic, "Alexandrian" period—a time of exhaustion and decadence, of the loss of a binding cultural myth.

From Nietzsche's vantage point, modern Europe is witnessing the same sort of heterogeneous decadence as Alexandrian culture after the death of tragedy; old myths have died out, and there is no consensus about their replacement. However, the contemporary European is awakening to his [*sic*] predicament: "The disaster slumbering in the womb of theoretical culture begins to frighten modern man" (*BT* 18). At the same time, *The Birth of Tragedy* announces that the wheel is now turning backward; modern time is moving "analogically in *reverse* order," passing through the chief epochs of Hellenic genius "backward from the Alexandrian age to the period of tragedy" (*BT* 19). Tragedy, in short, is being reborn—out of the spirit of music, Wagner's music—and a "tragic culture" is being reinaugurated. Dionysus is among us again: "But how suddenly the desert of our exhausted culture . . . is changed when it is touched by the Dionysian magic!" (*BT* 20). So the narrative moves, as the text explains, in a "double orbit" (*BT* 19); its narrative is mythic, not historical.

The "double orbit" of Heraclitus, a Greek pre-Socratic philosopher, also supplied Nietzsche with a mythic structure; like that of Bachofen, this structure unfolds through oppositions, but, in contrast, the whole does not progress toward a resolution. Instead, it moves in a double orbit, growing and declining as opposing movements of the same whole, endlessly. Nietzsche included the pre-Socratic philosophers together with the tragedians in his catalog of fifth-century heroes; their philosophy, the tragedies, and the mysteries all share the quality he calls "tragic wisdom." In the preface to "Philosophy in the Tragic Age of the Greeks," written just after he finished *The Birth of Tragedy,* he writes that the early Greek philosopher appears in the sixth and fifth centuries, "among the enormous dangers and temptations of increasing secularization. . . . We may suspect that he comes, a distinguished warning voice, to express the same purpose to which the tragic drama was born during that century, and of which the Orphic mysteries hint in the grotesque hieroglyphics of their rites" (*PTAG* 33).[3] All of the aforementioned elements—the philosophers, the tragedies, and the mysteries—come "to warn" of the dangers of secularization. Is this not also Nietzsche's purpose as post-Socratic philosopher? The mysteries revert to the archaic myths to tell the story of Demeter; their "grotesque hieroglyphics," including the unveiling of Baubo, serve to return their celebrants to the contemplation of the intimate and necessary connections between sex, birth and death. The tragedies unveil the same connection— as do the pre-Socratic philosophers, in Nietzsche's estimation.

Myth as Truth: The Dionysian

I think there is no doubt that Nietzsche's Dionysus is the chief agent through which those characteristics that the ancients (and Bachofen and Hartmann) classified as feminine are borne into the text. Apart from a few feminine traits, Nietzsche's Apollo is more conventionally masculine by ancient Greek standards, but Dionysus is another story. In the first five sections of *The Birth of Tragedy,* Nietzsche establishes the key distinctions between these godly paradigms. Apollo, the god of sculpture, comes to represent structure itself, the demarcating boundaries and limits of plastic form, image, and concept (what Nietzsche calls "individuation"); Dionysus, boundless, limitless, timeless, de-individuation—in short, imageless, and comparable to the emotional/physical/psychological states induced by music and intoxication—represents the opposite. These dichotomies may be extended, thus: Apollo as static, Dionysus as dynamic; Apollo as the one, Dionysus as the many; Apollo as light (the sun god) and Dionysus as dark (the god of nighttime revel and orgy); Apollo as thought, consciousness and Dionysus as emotion, the unconscious, so closely related to music and the will. Moreover, Apollo is the god of classical Olympus, son of the "sky" god Zeus; Dionysus is his half-brother, but associated with earlier, archaic times, tragedy, and the mysteries. The oppositions amount to a table of masculine versus feminine values and attributes;[4] the partners are apparently bound in a dynamic antithesis whose whole truth lies in their unity. Such a tidy table would be a neat, Hegelian account of the structure of *The Birth of Tragedy*, but it does not hold up, as we shall see.

In the preface he added to the 1886 edition of *The Birth of Tragedy*, Nietzsche admits that his Dionysus may not be the same as the one alluded to in ancient texts, exactly. Of the instinct he invented to oppose Christian morality in *The Birth of Tragedy*, he writes, "As a philologist and man of words I baptized it, not without taking some liberty—for who could claim to know the rightful name of the Antichrist?—in the name of a Greek god: I called it Dionysian" (*BT* "Attempt at a Self-Criticism"). His Dionysus takes as a point of departure what Nietzsche knows about the ancient god, as the early notebooks show. The references to Dionysus in 1869 are historical: to "the orgiastic processions of Dionysus"; to satyrs; to the "phallika" or ritual parading of figurines of phalluses, with (according to the notes) "song and buffoons," naturalistic dialogue, and "ever new occasion for mockery and insult"; to the satyr-dramas; to dithyramb, the choral song in honor of Dionysus; and to the Greater Dionysia, the festivals in which playwrights presented in competition a tragic trilogy and a satyr-play (*KSA* 7:19, 30, 42). Nietzsche's notes link the origin of tragedy to folk festivals honoring Dionysus, apparently as a principle of male fertility. Yet in *The Birth of Tragedy*, the Dionysian is more conventionally feminine than masculine.

In *Dionysus: Myth and Cult*, Walter Otto stresses the contradictions bound up in Dionysian myth and ritual (93), an emphasis that Nietzsche shared (including the attribution of masculine and feminine traits to the god). E. R. Dodds's interpretation of Dionysus emphasizes the god's liberating function: "The joys of Dionysus had an exceedingly wide range. . . . at all levels, he is Lusios, 'the Liberator'—the god who . . . enables you for a short time to *stop being yourself*" (76). Relief from the burden of self (including one's gender) also relieves one of linear time and memory; forgetting, living unhistorically, is necessary for humans to "*live* at all" (*UDH* 1). Forgetting, and its mate remembering, are key elements of the Apollonian-Dionysian partnership. Like Apollo, Dionysus is also a prophet, and "the bacchic revel is filled with the spirit of prophecy" (Otto 97, based on Plutarch's statement that "the ancients credited Dionysus with a role in divination"). He is associated with rampant sexuality and sexual revels, and with suffering and death. The myth of the god as Zagreus, torn apart limb from limb as a child and scattered on the land, to reappear when the new corn sprouts, is an ancient fertility myth analogous to that of Osiris in Egypt.

Where does Dionysus himself stand in relation to the sexual energy he symbolizes? Does he manifest it or merely, as it were, orchestrate and direct it? Jean-Pierre Vernant depicts Dionysus an agent of deconstruction, personifying the presence of the Other, calling the social order into question, assuming "all aspects without confining himself to any one. Like a conjurer, he plays with appearances and blurs the boundaries between the fantastic and the real. . . . he is at once both male and female" (quoted in Henrichs 33); in an essay titled "The Asexuality of Dionysus," Michael Jameson comments that, from evidence of vase paintings in particular, Dionysus seems detached from sex "while representing it" (45). Other scholars have recently considered him bisexual, or discussed his "transcendence of sexuality." By contrast, some ancient Greek sources—notably Euripides' *Bacchae*—refer to his effeminacy; a fragment of a lost Aeschylus play reads: "Where does this woman-man come from?" (Jameson 45). His followers are the maenads, women known in some stories as "the nurses"—because nurses took care of the baby Dionysus after his birth and brought him up—and are thus nursing mothers themselves. Nietzsche picked up on some of these connotations and reproduced them in his subsequent assertion of the central importance of the pain and suffering and the ecstasy of childbirth, which overflow the limits of normal experience. This essentially is what Dionysus in all his manifestations does: he overflows the limits, exceeds and obliterates boundaries.

Much of the imagery of *The Birth of Tragedy* anticipates psychoanalytic accounts of relations between nature (the Dionysian sex instincts in the unconscious) and culture (Apollonian fictions constructed to order the chaotic instincts). Dionysian manifestations of the eruption of the unconscious into *The Birth of Tragedy* include repetitive use of verbs of penetration (*eindringen,* to enter by force or penetrate, and its adjectival form), of consummation *(vollziehen),* and of procreation or "engendering" *(erzeugen);* "the shudder of ecstasy," "paroxysms of intoxication" (*BT* 1), "orgiastic flute tones" (*BT* 6), "the whole excited Dionysian throng" (*BT* 8), "the suddenly swelling Dionysian tide" (*BT* 9). There are references to wombs, to births and "continual rebirths" (*BT* 8), to the sea (water: waves), and to abysses (gaps, chasms, clefts). The Dionysian is said to be the originary "place" of tragedy: the bacchic chorus is "the womb that gave birth to the whole of the so-called dialogue" (*BT* 8).

The terms that Nietzsche uses to describe the Dionysian in *The Birth of Tragedy* are all metonymic substitutions for the primordial mother, the origin: nature, will, and the *Ur-Eine,* the primordial unity. In a single sentence, we read that in the Dionysian, "nature cries to us with its true, undissembled voice: 'Be as I am! Amid the ceaseless flux of phenomena I am the eternally creative primordial mother, eternally impelling to existence, eternally finding satisfaction in this change of phenomena!'" (*BT* 16). In the next paragraph, we learn that nature as Dionysian is "the exuberant fertility of the universal will" exulting in both the creation and the destruction of phenomena (*BT* 17). The Dionysian "breaks the spell of individuation" and "opens the way to the Mothers of Being, to the innermost heart of things" (*BT* 16). Nature is personified thus: "Wild and naked nature beholds with the frank, undissembling [*unverhüllten,* uncovered or unveiled] gaze of truth" (*BT* 10). Nature is cruel (*BT* 7), and brings death as well as life.

The Dionysian celebrates connection, unity with the whole. Its opposite, separation—for which the Apollonian principle of individuation is responsible—provides its own sexual imagery. Separation and division are emphasized in *The Birth of Tragedy* by a number of references to chasms, abysses, or gaps—signifiers of castration in the Freudian/Lacanian myth, the "law of the hole" that separates from and bars return to the mother. The first abyss is "the immense gap [*ungeheuere Kluft*] which separates the *Dionysian Greek* from the Dionysian barbarian" (*BT* 2). A subsequent series of reconciling gestures between Dionysian and Apollonian Greeks cannot disguise their differences: "At bottom, the chasm [*die Kluft*] was not bridged over" (*BT* 2). The Dionysian can eradicate "the gulf [*die Klufte*] between man and man" (*BT* 7); a "chasm [*Kluft*] of oblivion" separates the worlds of everyday reality and of Dionysian reality" (*BT* 7); Dionysian drama is "separated, as by a tremendous chasm [*ungeheuere Kluft*], from the epic" (*BT* 8). With *Oedipus Rex,* the poet gives us a "glance into the abyss" [*einem Blick in dem Abgrund*]; he tells us that "wisdom, and particularly Dionysian wisdom, is an unnatural abomination; that he who by means of his knowledge plunges nature into the abyss of destruction [*den Abgrund der Vernichtung*] must also suffer" (*BT* 9). But these chasms are as nothing compared to the one that opens up with the death of tragedy. "When Greek tragedy died, there arose everywhere the deep sense of an immense void [*Leere*]" (*BT* 11). Abysses, chasms, empty spaces, voids: all are signifiers of the feminine; they are places of "the uncertain, that which could never be illuminated," an "enigmatic depth, indeed an infinitude" inexplicable to Euripides (*BT* 11). It is these spaces that Euripides and Socrates denied and tried to paper over, seamlessly. They did not succeed, and in their failure lies the "turn," or return, in the plot of the text.

We arrive at Richard Wagner. In sections 21 and 22 of *The Birth of Tragedy,* Wagner's *Tristan and Isolde* is the prime example of the Apollonian and Dionysian art drives in action, where the Dionysian "music" is described in such terms as "the highest ecstasies of music" (*Musikorgiasmus,* musical "orgies" or even "orgasms," *KSA* 1:134), and in confessions ("Who would be able to perceive the third act of *Tristan and Isolde,* without any aid of word and image, purely as a tremendous symphonic movement, without expiring in a spasmodic unharnessing of all the wings of the soul?" [*BT* 21]). Where the music is so powerful as to cause an "orgiastic self-annihilation" (*BT* 21), however, word and image come to the rescue and "save us" (so repeated three times in one sentence) from drowning in "longing, for very longing, not dying"—at one with the terrible pain at the heart of the world (*BT* 21).

The Dionysian is clearly feminine in these confessional discussions of *Tristan and Isolde* in *The Birth of Tragedy,* and the images of femininity intensify: music is a language musical people speak "as their mother tongue," with which one has an immediate relationship like a "motherly womb"; it is "flood and excess," "primordial suffering," unconsciousness in the "bosom [*Schoosse,* womb] of the primordially One" (*BT* 22). Such is the Dionysian that is being reborn, with Wagner's music, and will "save" us even as it drowns us. Present-day Socratic culture is enfeebled, decadent—so runs the story of *The Birth of Tragedy*—and there is some evidence that the Dionysian abyss may again be opening. As section 16 begins: "By this elaborate historical example [the birth and death of tragedy in ancient Greece] we have sought to make clear how just as tragedy perishes with the evanescence of the spirit of music, it is only from this spirit that it can be reborn."

Music is Dionysian par excellence, because it symbolizes the will. In Nietzsche's terms, the will is physical (not metaphysical, since its descriptions connect it with the body) and a "mother" of tragedy. "Language can never adequately render the cosmic symbolism of music, because music stands in symbolic relation to the primordial contradiction and primordial pain in the heart of the primal unity" (*BT* 6). Music, Nietzsche tells us, "appears as will," though it can never *be* will, for "will is the unaesthetic-in-itself" (*BT* 6). Nevertheless, in its appearance as will music has the capacity to lead us closer to "the heart of things" than anything else. It possesses all of the qualities we have seen of the Dionysian: it is a womb; it gives birth to myth; it liberates body and mind; it dissolves the self into a spirit of oneness with all that exists.

However, music only "appears" as the will after sound has mated with the Apollonian constructive, ordering principle. Pure Dionysian sound resonates with cacophony—roaring, shrieking, jubilating, howling—the "cry" of the Eleusinian mysteries, the "shrill laugh" of Silenus, "lamentation," "orgiastic flute tones," "the whisper of inclination to the roar of madness," "roaring hymns of joy," and "the mystical triumphant cry of Dionysus." Although these noises express the truth from the heart of nature, they have no form and cannot be called "music" until the moment when the Apollonian and the primordially Dionysian meet and marry—when, as Luce Irigaray puts it, alluding to the argument of *The Birth of Tragedy*, "the eye and the ear alone wish to marry/make merry" (*Marine Lover* 116).

The marriage of Apollo and Dionysus is sensational—of the eye and ear, of sight and sound, and perhaps also of the paternal and maternal principles. Twice the Apollonian is designated as paternal in the text: once as the art impulse that "gave birth" to the entire Olympian world ("and in this sense Apollo is its father" [*BT* 3]), and again explicitly in connection with tragedy. In an explication of the myth of Prometheus, the text tells us that, because of his overwhelming zeal on behalf of mankind, Prometheus is "a Dionysian mask, while in the [play's] profound demand for justice, Aeschylus reveals to the thoughtful his paternal descent from Apollo, god of individuation and of just boundaries" (*BT* 9). No mother is here mentioned, yet the logic of the passage suggests that it is Dionysus.

To follow the way of the Nietzschean myth, let us consider briefly, in proper genealogical fashion, the children of Apollo and Dionysus. Their named exemplars are daughters. The "mysterious union, after many and long precursory struggles, found glorious consummation in this child—at once Antigone and Cassandra" (*BT* 4). This sentence is famous for its mystification and I shall not attempt here to demystify it, but will merely observe that, of all the choices that might have been made, the child of the mysterious union is female. It is even more significant that, as both Apollonian and Dionysian, the composite female offspring has a voice. As tragedy, she is represented, she appears, and she speaks. Her parentage grants her access to Dionysian wisdom, the abyss of woe which is the human *moira*, a destiny from which to appear and then to disappear again; it also gives her the means, the will, to transform this wisdom into "delusions" or illusions, forms that make it bearable or pleasurable, as she pleases. In guaranteeing a speaking role to the "tragic myth," which does not "shy away from" exemplifying the wisdom of Silenus symbolized by the mothers of tragedy, the "ugly and disharmonic" (*BT* 24), Nietzsche's myth salvages and restores principles of the archaic feminine characteristic of Bachofen's tellurian phase.

The text is not sloppy about its gender designations. Section 4 (of 25) so names the offspring of the "glorious consummation" of Apollo and Dionysus as a composite daughter (Antigone and Cassandra are mythic daughters of Oedipus and Jocasta of Thebes, and of Priam and Hecuba of Troy, respectively), and in section 11 the offspring returns, grown up into "tragedy" in its death throes. Before she dies, she mates—the myth's dialectical structure now pairs tragedy, the central mediating term of the mythic structure established by the text, with Socrates or science to form a new triad—and produces New Attic Comedy: "When a new artistic genre blossomed forth after all . . . it was noted with horror that she did indeed bear the features of her mother."

The allegory that Nietzsche constructs might simply derive from the feminine gender of the German word for "tragedy," *die Tragödie*. However, the text personifies tragedy as a "mother," and speaks of the "mothers of being" that lie behind tragedy, in a genealogically matrilineal fashion. Tragedy has "mothers," is a mother, and produces daughters. If there is anything "miraculous" about this genealogy it is the relative absence of males (Apollo being, at times, a "father"). But in a Bachovian cycle, the fathers appear in the next dispensation, the new age of rationalism. New Attic Comedy (with Antigone and Cassandra as its mother and Euripides as its father) is infected with Socratic scientific optimism, and so myth-as-truth disappears along with Apollo, Dionysus, and their children, the female tragedies.

One way to interpret the narrative is to derive allegorical meaning from it, as follows. The Dionysian possesses the feminine characteristics I have noted, and is furthermore the position of truth; the Apollonian has some feminine characteristics, sharing access to the sacred and to the tragic myth with the Dionysian. In tragedy, or *as* tragedy, the feminine speaks. The paradigmatic exchange of places of Apollo and Dionysus has given her a voice, a tragic voice that has been lost since the fifth century BCE but which the text predicts will reappear as the healer of a debilitated modern culture. The modern world needs myth, needs the tragic insight, and in fact may be experiencing its rebirth (in Wagner's musical dramas). The presence of the woman in *The Birth of Tragedy*, symbolized by the various masks of the Dionysian—by the wombs and abysses, clefts and empty spaces, and the dreams and prophesying of the Apollonian—bespeaks the "tragedy" of the missing feminine and of the loss for culture of those feminine aspects that connect it, through the body, with nature and unconscious instincts. This interpretation follows the general argument of Carolyn Merchant's *The Death of Nature* (1980), that "the notion of the natural world as mothered held good until mechanistic philosophies of the 17th century replaced it"; then the female world-soul died, "or more precisely, was *murdered,* by the mechanistic revisioning of nature" (quoted in Bordo 7–8). Less violently, but with the same general configuration, Fiona Jenkins finds that "tragedy represents for Nietzsche the insight of wisdom, a wisdom that becomes lost through the quest for scientifically valid knowledge initiated by Socrates"; this wisdom, unlike that of science and morality, "serves no instrumental ends" (215). With the rebirth of tragedy, the feminine voice of tragic wisdom will again be heard, reminding us of the limits of scientific rationalism, and of the "indestructibility and eternity" of "primordial joy in existence" (*BT* 17).

Toward the end, the text tells us that a tragic culture does not evade or paper over the "wisdom" born of a glance into the abyss, acknowledging (as in the mysteries) that pain and death are necessary parts of the whole, and sex as their prerequisite is both fundamental and without shame. The culture will be stronger for this knowledge, but not meaner or more indifferent; indeed, its "most important characteristic," Nietzsche writes, is that "wisdom takes the place of science as the highest end." In a brief character sketch, Nietzsche asserts that wisdom "turns with unmoved eyes[5] to a comprehensive view of the world, and seeks to grasp, with sympathetic feelings of love, the eternal suffering as its own" (*BT* 18).

Myth as "Illusion" or Fiction: The Apollonian

One of Apollo's epithets is the "Far-darter," for Apollo can shoot an arrow a long way and hit the target. Taking that trait as symbolic of his skill with language, we know that Apollo will hit home with words. In *The Birth of Tragedy,* his goal or target is myth itself. Apollo lets fly a whole series of myths (as is his wont, as god of illusion); he takes aim at them, pierces them with his arrows, brings them down, and continues the process—at least he does so if he is Nietzsche. Reading the text, from time to time we become aware of contradictions, inconsistencies, "gaps," and a monstrous use of tropes, which undercuts the supposed truth of the myth. This awareness, when it comes, is Apollo's arrow.

The key Apollonian disruptive agents of myth are Apollo and Dionysus themselves, the text's major mythical figures. Consider their coupling to produce tragedy, which the text identifies on page one as a "miracle." Then think about the text's definition of myth, which includes miracles: "*Myth* . . . a concentrated image of the world that, as a condensation of phenomena, cannot dispense with miracles" (*BT* 23). It follows then that the text, which asks us to accept miracle, is acting as a myth. By asking us how we respond to miracles "on stage" (*BT* 23), the text also asks for our critical response to its own miracles. It pulls questions directed outward back, always, to itself in a metatextual gesture that asks us to recognize the constructed, textual, mythic nature of what we read.

One of the myths Apollo and Dionysus disrupt is the heterosexual binary division that applies a set of gendered traits to the feminine (and by extension to biological females) and an opposing set to the masculine (biological males). The text refers at least three times to the "fraternal union" that produced tragedy (*BT* 21, 22, 24), but more problematic still than the naming of this pair of brothers as progenitors (something we might accept symbolically) is the gender instability of the binary oppositions established under the Apollonian and the Dionysian, so precarious as to invalidate the consistent alignment of the former with the masculine and the latter with the feminine. This rejection of such tidy associations, and indeed, the tendency of both to cluster on the feminine side of the demarcation, disqualifies the sexual dichotomy as "natural" and points to its character as a construct.

Aside from gender, there is something else rather odd about the description of the coupling of Apollo and Dionysus. The division of the Greek world by the two "art deities" is described as a "tremendous opposition"—an *ungeheuer Gegensatz* (a phrase that is repeated several times). *Ungeheuer* can also be translated as "monstrous," or "huge," and thus the Apollonian/Dionysian opposition is also perceived as monstrous—so huge that the dichotomy, as opposition, forms an abyss or chasm between its terms. Given *The Birth of Tragedy*'s subtextual preoccupation with sex, the monstrous opposition between Apollo and Dionysus foreshadows the telling phrase in *Beyond Good and Evil*, "the most abysmal antagonism" between man and woman (238). Examined closely, just how abysmal is this antagonism, how opposite this opposition? Here are some of their paired characteristics in the text:

Apollonian	Dionysian
Dreams (nature)	Intoxication (nature)
Sculpture (art, culture)	Music (art, culture)
Prophecy (religion)	Mysteries (religion)
Alienation from nature	Oneness with nature

Form	Formlessness
Beauty, illusion	Ecstasy, truth
Limit, "nothing too much"	Excess
Individuation	De-individuation
Consciousness	The unconscious

One thing to note about this set of "binary oppositions" is that many of the horizontal pairs are not oppositions at all but contiguous relations, metonymic rather than antonymic. Scanning for the nature/culture opposition, constructed horizontally or syntagmatically, do we find it? The text emphasizes that *both* gods represent "artistic impulses of nature"; both dream and intoxication are of the body (*BT* 1) and "burst forth from nature herself, *without the mediation of the human artist*" (*BT* 2). This "opposition" tells us that art originates in the body of the artist, and that art's imitation of nature is initiated there during moments when consciousness is disengaged— moments of dreaming and of self-forgetfulness. I hold that the dream/intoxication dichotomy falls along a continuum, and is not an opposition at all. Apollo's ancestry here, as we know, is feminine.

Let us turn to the remainder of the so-called enormous oppositions between our two art deities. The division between sculpture (hard) and music (wavy), both of which are "cultural," suggests a masculine/feminine contrast. Apollonian prophecy and the Dionysian mysteries are both cultural, both religious, both feminine and elaborated symbolically by the female body—indeed, the female genitals. The Pythia sat over a tripod at the crack in the earth from which vapors poured up between her legs as she spoke the oracle (Sissa 3); the female genitalia were unveiled at the mysteries. Both cults have archaic histories, connecting female fertility and divinity, a connection hinted at in references to soothsaying (and its link with art through dreams) and the mysteries in *The Birth of Tragedy*. With respect to their "mythic" or specifically religious characteristics, the two art deities have much in common.

Moving on, we find that individuation/de-individuation and consciousness/the unconscious are similarly not so far apart as to constitute binary oppositions. Freud has argued that consciousness and the unconscious are not distinct entities. Though we feel that our ego is "autonomous and unitary," psychoanalysis has discovered "that such an appearance is deceptive, and that on the contrary the ego is continued inwards, without any sharp delimitation, into an unconscious mental entity which we designate as the id" (*Civilization* 65–66). Nietzsche posits the connection between consciousness and the instinctive, the latter determining the former (*BGE* 3), and his Dionysian state blurs or destroys the boundaries between the ego and the external world, once again suggesting continuity rather than an antithesis between Apollonian and Dionysian.

Let us focus our attention on the opposition of illusion and truth, with which Nietzsche's later texts are concerned. In the first section of *The Birth of Tragedy,* Nietzsche explains, through the analogy with dreams, that illusion gives itself away: "Even when this dream reality is most intense, we still have, glimmering through it, the sensation that it is *mere appearance*" (*BT* 1). He notes that we often have the experience of knowing we are dreaming and saying to ourselves, "in self-encouragement, and not without success, 'It is a dream! I will dream on!'" (*BT* 1). In this instance, which of "us" is Apollonian illusion, and which Dionysian truth? Consciousness piercing the dream aligns with truth in the passage, acknowledging the "illusion" of the dream. Yet the text takes pains to align consciousness with the Apollonian, and the Apollonian with illusion. If both the dream illusion (i.e., the dream images) and consciousness are Apollonian, then the latter is itself split (as is the Dionysian will, or primordial unity). Categories divide and subdivide throughout the text. "Dream illusion" becomes analogous with ordinary waking "empirical reality." Like sailors in small boats on the sea (here Nietzsche quotes Schopenhauer), we are borne up by our faith in our rational ability to behold and understand the world as unified individual selves. But if occasionally the "principle of sufficient reason" that keeps us afloat on a sea of chaotic Will "suffers an exception," then we are terrified and are simultaneously filled with "blissful ecstasy" "at the collapse of the *principium individuationis*" (*BT* 1). Nietzsche asserts that we are ecstatic because for a moment we feel ourselves once again part of the "whole," unalienated, relieved of our burden of self-consciousness. Our bliss is mixed with terror, but the emotions are irreducibly true.

However, Apollonian illusion can "appear" and, most of the time, feel true. It deceives us into believing that we possess unified autonomous egos, and that we see clear outlines. If, from the Dionysian perspective, we are alienated from nature, most of the time we don't know it. This is the function of necessary "forgetfulness," the ability to drift along, oblivious to the "illusory" nature of the "dream reality" in which we mostly live. Apollonian forgetfulness is different from Dionysian "self-forgetfulness." Self-awareness is an Apollonian illusion, whereby I forget I am a fragmented stranger to myself. The experience of Dionysian self-forgetfulness shows me the full illusory character of my normal consciousness.

Nietzsche's description of the compositional process of the lyric poet Archilochus (a contemporary of Homer) demonstrates the complexity of Apollo's tie to illusion. In this instance, and through a number of other examples, Nietzsche tries to elucidate his intuition about the production of art in the "coupling" of the Apollonian and the Dionysian. He asserts that in order to write lyric poetry—a genre dominated by the "I" of the speaker-poet's most personal account of love, sorrow, and the like—the poet has to undergo a metamorphosis, a Dionysian process whereby the poet's normal conscious self, the one that says "I," is "surrendered." The poet now identifies with "the primordial contradiction and primordial pain, together with the primordial pleasure, of mere appearance." Through the surrender of self-conscious ego and identification with the primal reality, however we imagine it, the poet is able to transform "mere appearance" [*Schein*] and give it depth, and thus stamp the "dream images" of the Apollonian with the Dionysian eternal. Thus "the 'I' of the lyrist sounds from the depth of being: its 'subjectivity,' in the sense of modern aestheticians is a fiction" (*BT* 5). Referring to this section of *The Birth of Tragedy*, Jenkins argues that "art is only truly of aesthetic value when it appears as a response to insight into reality"—as a response to life, "an openness to the experience of life" and not "the imposition of meaning on life" (213). Apollonian "illusion" can become "truth," crossing the tremendous chasm, when it lets its defensive barriers down and waits for life to speak first. Then, as a respondent, it "acts," paints, and sings without subjectivity, and at the same time without concealment, having attained a state of receptivity to the world where the subject/object dichotomy simply dissolves. As Nietzsche puts it, "The whole opposition between the subjective and objective . . . is altogether irrelevant in aesthetics" (*BT* 6). Paul de Man notes that "this exchange of attributes [between the Dionysian and the Apollonian] involving the categories of truth and appearance deprives the two poles of their authority" (*Allegories of Reading* 72). Nietzsche begins by linking Apollo to some characteristics and Dionysus to others, but finds that it is impossible to keep them in place. The oppositions tend to vanish into thin air, monstrous as they are, the poles to lose their authority.

The only set of paired terms in the table that remains a genuine opposition is form/formlessness, which subsumes sculpture/music. As sculpture and music are the particular property of the two gods, perhaps this is the one irreducible difference in the text. It is the one dichotomy that aligns, on the level of "dream interpretation," with masculinity (hard, connected with vision) and femininity (soft, watery or wavy, connected with sound).

And yet, so unstable are the poles, and so much transformation is carried out in the process of reading, that this settling into a meaning won't do either. Other gender references must be taken into account. In the second half of *The Birth of Tragedy*, we at last encounter—twice—the mysterious "mothers of being." They have taken the place of the "mothers of tragedy" from the notebooks, but are recognizably the same three fatal ladies. We first meet them here during one of the recapitulations of the main theme. Apollo has once again been named as "the transfiguring genius of the *principium individuationis;* while by the mystical triumphant cry of Dionysus the spell of individuation is broken, and the way lies open to the Mothers of Being, to the innermost heart of things" (*BT* 16). Here are mothers-as-origin, clearly cited, the way to whom lies with Dionysus. In the second instance, the mothers reappear as a distant song: "Tragedy is seated amid this excess of life, suffering, and pleasure, in sublime ecstasy, listening to a distant melancholy song that tells of the mothers of being whose names are: Delusion, Will, Woe" (*BT* 20). As we have seen, delusion—*Wahn*—constitutes the images created by the will to attach us firmly to life. In the binary sexual scheme, "Delusion," as image, is Apollonian and thus masculine. "Will" is Dionysian and thus feminine, while "Woe" is an interpretation of the context, life, provided in the text by Silenus ("the wisdom of Silenus cried 'Woe! 'woe!' to the serene Olympians," *BT* 4), who as the teacher of the satyrs and companion to Dionysus is also Dionysian, and thus feminine. Yet this wisdom is an interpretation, and therefore Apollonian and masculine. And so the "mothers" do not align neatly under Dionysus, as we might expect if we want Dionysus, or indeed the mothers themselves, to be feminine.

Nietzsche points out that his antitheses do not stay in line; for example, having told us emphatically that, following the demise of tragedy, the "new opposition" is Socratic optimism versus Dionysian pessimism, he asks whether, on reflection, "there is *necessarily* only an antipodal relation between Socratism and art" (*BT* 14). This sentence supports Lynne Tirrell's observation that "Nietzsche's strategy for disarming the dualist is to claim that the distinction in question is not a distinction in *kind,* but only in degree. One value is not the opposite of the other, but only its *refinement*" (163). I believe that this refinement informs the whole of *The Birth of Tragedy.* Nietzsche moves on to describe Socrates' "instinct" for logic in Dionysian terms. "The logical urge" [*Trieb,* instinct] in Socrates, "in its unbridled flood displays a natural power such as we encounter to our awed amazement only in the very greatest instinctive forces" (*BT* 13). Socrates will be the founder of a new, powerful, unchallenged myth: the myth of scientific rationalism, the basis of our own "theoretical culture." This is a major stumbling block to an interpretation that determines to find tragedy feminine and science masculine. At its midpoint, the text describes theoretical culture itself as a womb; it too is maternal. In addition, it harbors something, possibly, quite nasty: "The disaster slumbering in the womb of theoretical culture gradually begins to frighten modern man" (*BT* 18). Of course we do know, but have forgotten, that the will fosters both growth and decline, and thus that the maternal egg represents both creation and destruction.

In Nietzsche's estimation, modern man is beginning to question the verities of logical positivism, and if he succeeds in piercing them with Apollo's arrows, then their truth value as *myth* will disappear; science too will suffer the fate of tragedy and be demystified, its verities under suspicion. When the scientists "see to their horror how logic coils up at these boundaries [the limits of the currently knowable] and finally bites its own tail—suddenly the new form of insight breaks through, *tragic insight* which, merely to be endured, needs art as a protection and remedy" (*BT* 15). It is here that Nietzsche parts company with Hartmann, for whom the limit of logic is the end of the will ("Consciousness suffices to hurl back the total actual volition into nothingness" [3:142]). For Nietzsche, logic reaches its limit and recoils on itself, turning to art, in myth, for new insight; myth reaches its limit and becomes history, science, and logic. The Heraclitian wheel keeps turning. Nietzsche alludes to this in the last section, when he offers his final word on the Apollonian-Dionysian relationship: "Of this foundation of existence—the Dionysian basic ground of the world—not one whit more may enter the consciousness of the human individual than can be overcome again by this Apollonian power of transfiguration. Thus these two art drives must unfold their powers in strict proportion, according to the law of eternal justice" (*BT* 25).

Although the text appears to give Dionysus priority as foundational, the movement between the pairs of terms in the table, with "art"—or specifically "tragedy"—as mediator, reveals that the two gods are mutually entailed. If Apollo is illusion to Dionysus's mute truth, then they belong together: Dionysus is truth, but cannot speak or appear; Apollo can speak and appear, but without passion, without "body" and without spirit, until roused to full creativity and truth by Dionysus. At the glorious moment of their consummated union, they exchange characteristics, each denying their proper identity and taking on the identity of the other. This exchange of properties is fully mythic, in the Lévi-Straussian sense; opposites, described as monstrous, are shown to be harmless or even useless, reconciled, with the social anxieties about differences allayed.

The Sexual Analogy and the Gender Dichotomy

Were we ever very anxious about the differences between the *Apollonian* and the *Dionysian*? It is impossible to believe so. However, "we" were, and have been, and are, anxious about sex. Why did Nietzsche use the analogy of sexual procreation to describe the origin of art? Could *The Birth of Tragedy* have made its aesthetic points without it? What function does the analogy serve? And why is the feminine half of the procreative couple hidden or disguised by metaphors? In order at last to answer these questions, I will first consider one more example that Nietzsche employs in *The Birth of Tragedy* to help us understand the sexual aspect of the Apollonian-Dionysian relationship.

Nietzsche's discussion of Wagner's opera *Tristan and Isolde,* which he uses to demonstrate the interconnections between the Apollonian tragic myth and Dionysian music, is this last example. For Nietzsche, the opera performs the trick of complicating the Dionysian/Apollonian opposition to the point where it "denies itself" as an opposition altogether. The two terms of the dichotomy simply refuse to stay separate—including, I suggest, the masculine/feminine opposition. This is Wagner's sleight of hand, not Nietzsche's, but Nietzsche provides the commentary. Toward the end of act 3 of the opera—the act Nietzsche refers to as producing "orgiastic self-annihilation" for the listener (as well as for the characters [*BT* 21])—Tristan, wounded for a fatal third time, is waiting for Isolde's ship to arrive. He is "longing, longing, in death still longing, for very longing, not dying" (as Kaufmann translates the Wagner text via Nietzsche [*BT* 21]). The ship's appearance is announced, and Isolde sighted; Tristan, dying, rips the bandages from his wound in an ecstasy, "Joy without measure / Blissful madness"; he staggers forward singing, "She who will close / my wound forever / comes to me like a hero, / to save me. / Let the world pass away / as I hasten to her in joy!" (Wagner *Tristan und Isolde* 91). At this point, though Tristan has been identified throughout as the "hero," now, *in extremis,* he exchanges gender roles with Isolde. Temporarily the two are on opposite sides of the binary gender grid: Isolde plays the masculine active savior-hero, Tristan the feminine source of bloody pathos. This lasts only a moment, however; in the end they both collapse in Dionysian self-forgetfulness—he in death, she in a death-like swoon.

It is with the description of this scene that Nietzsche reaches the climax of *The Birth of Tragedy*. The Dionysian music of the opera has threatened time and again to overwhelm the individual actors and the dialogue, but the "healing magic" (an allusion to Isolde the sorceress) of Apollo "can even create the illusion that the Dionysian is really in the service of the Apollonian" (*BT* 21). This though would be an illusion: "At the most essential point this Apollonian illusion is broken and annihilated." The real Dionysian effect is so powerful "that it ends by forcing the Apollonian drama itself into a sphere where it begins to speak with Dionysian wisdom and even denies itself and its Apollonian visibility. Thus the intricate relation of the Apollonian and the Dionysian in tragedy may really be symbolized by a fraternal union of the two deities: Dionysus speaks the language of Apollo; and Apollo, finally, the language of Dionysus; and so the highest goal of tragedy and of all art is attained" (*BT* 21.)

When Apollo and Dionysus change places, Nietzsche claims, the goal of all art is achieved. This goal, which has been prophesied in the text, is the sense of "oneness" with existence, the awareness that barriers have fallen. The moment is both joyful and painful; the Apollonian boundaries of identity have given meaning to the world, and when they fall we glimpse the abyss of meaning, its loss. Thus the goal of art, like everything else to which the text ascribes value, is divided in its unity. Reaching the moment of climax produces a cry in which joy and woe are mixed "in strict proportion, according to the law of eternal justice."

In the climactic passage where Apollo speaks with the voice of Dionysus and vice versa, Nietzsche draws our attention to the fact that they are mythic males and their exchange of characteristics is, well, fraternal. They do not undergo a change of sex. It is interesting that, at the moment when tragedy reaches its "most essential point" and "highest goal," Nietzsche chooses to underline the central characters' masculinity, when he is taking such pains to show the collapse of the monstrous opposition. In fact, there is no sexual opposition at all. Heterosexuality as biological or essentialist has been a metaphoric ruse throughout and has been revealed as myth.

Discussing the importance he ascribes to moderation in erotic matters for artists in one of his later notebook entries, Nietzsche writes: "The force that one expends in artistic conception is the same as that expended in the sexual act: there is only one kind of force" (*WP* 815). The sexual analogy in *The Birth of Tragedy* is an early version of that idea. Artistic conception, like its sexual counterpart, depends on difference; but with art, the differences are internal to the artist. The sexual analogy serves several functions:

First, it makes the point that Nietzsche's later note makes explicit: there is only one kind of force, whether its purpose is biological or artistic. The sexual analogy in *The Birth of Tragedy* grounds the practice of art, as artist or as spectator, in that physical force, and demonstrates the close connections between art and sexuality. If you are a creative artist you draw on your sexuality, all of it. When you listen to music, or look at a painting or read or watch a film, your sexuality is engaged, not your gender identity. The Dionysian, with its orgies, its satyrs, and its orgiastic flute tones, is sexual, and its sexuality overflows the boundaries of such concepts as "man" and "woman."

Second, the analogy reminds us that our sexuality is more than a question of masculinity or femininity. The whole of *The Birth of Tragedy* works toward breaking down distinctions, but the key and central distinction that is so reduced is the masculine/feminine dichotomy. Society is not concerned about reconciling the differences between Apollo and Dionysus, but it is concerned about sexual difference. The text tells us that sexual difference *seems* like a monstrous opposition, but in fact it isn't, or needn't be. If you are an artist or a spectator, or both at the same time, you are bound to find both the feminine characteristics and the masculine ones that Nietzsche outlines—in yourself. When you experience a Dionysian engagement with fiction or music, you surrender your individuality and enter into "another body, another character." The "magic of this transformation" (*BT* 8) includes, possibly, a change of sex, or a visit to a state of undifferentiated polymorphous pleasure.

Third, the sexual analogy mystifies; it is one of the warning arrows Apollo shoots to let us know that something unusual is occurring. The first sentence of *The Birth of Tragedy* is a prime example of this mystification. How can we know, either by logic or by "the immediate certainty of vision," that the development of art is bound up with the Apollonian and the Dionysian duality? If we were inclined to gloss over this absurdity, the sexual analogy would serve to pull us up short. We might then be more inclined to investigate the text's points about sexuality, modernity, and tragedy.

Fourth, and finally, the analogy serves the purpose of shock value. Nietzsche wanted very much to define himself apart from his solidly middle-class Lutheran background and from its strict sexual codes. Dionysus was not an exemplar; by anybody's definition he's a rebel. The freedom Dionysus offers is subversive, and though his orgies are fleetingly described in the text, they nevertheless permit and legitimate sexual license, and with this the blurring of boundary lines and distinctions. By offering him as a central figure, Nietzsche is being risqué.

Since Nietzsche did use the analogy, why did he veil the feminine half of the procreative couple in metaphors? He did so, I believe, for two reasons. The first is to underscore his point about the disappearance of tragedy and myth. By aligning these genres with the feminine (as I have asserted in this chapter), he calls attention to the loss of the qualities they represent. That they are *feminine* qualities may not be apparent at first glance, unless a reader asks about the sexual analogy. It is with this that the interpretation I set forth in my discussion of myth as truth begins to unfold.

This is qualified by the second reason that Nietzsche veiled the feminine: the "feminine," as the Dionysian link to loss of self, including to the unconscious and to death, isn't really lost. It is present *in men,* as well as in women. Women represent the feminine in archaic times, as a formidable social power in Bachofen's texts, and as various monsters and goddesses, and as the Pythia, with strong links to nature, in Greek myth. Nietzsche discovers this powerful feminine and, by eliminating its connections with real women, "liberates" it under the sign of Dionysus the Liberator, and his attendant satyrs, for use by men—and in the process he demonstrates that the gendered binary distinction is itself a myth. This move relieves real women of the burden of signifying, *ad nauseam,* the qualities of the Dionysian, with its links to the unconscious, passion, nature, and death. These qualities, the text tells us, belong to Dionysus and so to men; they are the province of artists and "the aesthetic listener" (*BT* 22). The move no more cancels women than it cancels men, however; rather, it breaks down the sex-gender dichotomy, liberating people, as Dionysus is said to, from its narrow prescriptions.

4

"Yes, Life Is a Woman"
Irony, Metaphor, and "Woman"
in *The Gay Science*

In *The Gay Science* (1882), still bearing the values of Apollo and Dionysus and of a tragic culture, Nietzsche's ancient Greek feminine emerges as a metaphorical "Woman." Now the feminine and its linguistic signifier constitute a couple, and make a public appearance as a metaphor for poetry, art, and life itself. At the same time, *The Gay Science* proceeds with the demolition of the modern eternal feminine. Thus the book provides a clear example of Nietzsche engaged in both knocking down the current feminine ideal and erecting a new one based on associations with the ancient world. To do this business persuasively, drawing on the reader's own powers of interpretation, Nietzsche uses figures of speech—especially irony and metaphor, both of which destabilize fixed meanings and confound identifications.

Irony and Woman

In his Basel lectures on language and rhetoric, Nietzsche defines irony narrowly, as the trope whereby "the words say exactly the opposite of what they seem to say" (*RL* 63). This definition distinguishes irony from metaphor; indeed, Nietzsche goes on to observe that the latter "does not produce new words, but gives a new meaning to them" (*RL* 23). Metaphor extends language's capacities, whereas irony reverses meanings. For Nietzsche, irony is connected to negation, but in keeping with Hegel he sees negation as part of a process moving toward affirmation.

In *Zarathustra*'s "Three Metamorphoses of the Spirit," the first stage or metamorphosis is represented by the camel as the tradition-bearing status quo. The second, the phase of negation, is represented metaphorically by the lion: "To create new values—even the lion is incapable of that: but to create itself freedom for new creation—that the might of the lion can do. To create freedom for itself and a sacred No even to duty: the lion is needed for that, my brothers" (*TSZ* 1). The third is represented by the child, who, freed by the lion from the burden of the camel, is the creator of new values.

Irony clears the way for new creation by saying No to outworn values—of which (as chapter 1 argues) nineteenth-century gender roles are for Nietzsche exemplary.

Irony is inherently dramatic, for it presents a conflict of perspectives. Even in its simplest form, when a thing said means the opposite, irony presents two points of view. When the lion roars "a sacred NO, even to duty" in ironic formulation, he is both articulating that duty from the perspective of those who believe in it, as well as negating it. Irony is thus well suited to signify internal as well as external conflict. Although Nietzsche employs a narrow definition of irony—saying one thing and meaning the opposite— in fact he uses it expansively and dialectically, so that it becomes the means or instrument fashioning his perspectivism, or clash of viewpoints.

In the great nineteenth-century work on irony, *The Concept of Irony, with Constant Reference to Socrates,* Kierkegaard asserts a connection between negativity and subjective freedom. As he notes: "It is by means of irony that the subject emancipates himself from the constraints imposed upon him by the continuity of life, whence it may be said of the ironist that he 'cuts loose'" (273). His purpose is "merely to feel free"; "the concern of the ironist is merely to seem other than he actually is. As he therefore conceals his jest in seriousness and his seriousness in jest, so it may occur to him to seem evil though he is good" (273). Nietzsche informs us that this is his practice as well; he disguises his honesty with devilry (*BGE* 227, 230) and seems something other than he actually is by wearing masks, playing parts, and standing above his creations like the ironist he often is. "As the ironist does not have the new within his power," observes Kierkegaarde, "it might be asked how he destroys the old, and to this it must be answered: he destroys the given actuality by the given actuality itself" (279). In this way, the ironist "has advanced beyond the reach of his age and opened a front against it" (278).

For Nietzsche, the philosopher must be such an ironist: "It seems to me more and more that the philosopher, being *necessarily* a man of tomorrow and the day after tomorrow, has always found himself and *had* to find himself in contradiction to his today: his enemy has always been the ideal of today" (*BGE* 212). Irony is the tool that helps Nietzsche to reveal the hollow character of today's ideals—recall our survey in chapter 1 of its results in the critique of the ideal of the eternal feminine. I take up that critique again here by focusing on the ways in which Nietzsche's irony works to destroy what Kierkegaarde calls "the given actuality"—in this context, the attitudes of modern men and women regarding "man and woman" that idealize woman—by turning the given actuality against itself and thus "cutting loose."

Aphorisms 59 to 75 in book 2 of *The Gay Science* take "woman" as their subject and treat her ironically. Key among these is aphorism 68, "Will and willingness" (already discussed in chapter 1), in which the sage posits as the "law of the sexes" the principle that "will is the manner of men" (man creates the image of woman) and "willingness that of women" (who form themselves according to this image). That woman is part of man's framework of self-reference is a point made by this and by many of the other aphorisms.

Book 2 of *The Gay Science* opens with two aphorisms that introduce themes exemplified in the discussions of aspects of woman that follow. The first, aphorism 57, is directed "To the realists"—those who "feel well armed against passion and fantasies" and believe that they are observing reality, including themselves, "unveiled." These realists believe they have discovered all of life's secrets. The aphorism's speaker advises them that they have not; all of their estimations are colored by the human past and are anthropomorphic, and he tells them that it is impossible to separate anything from "your descent, your past, your training." Distance—pure, scientific objectification—is out of the question, for the observer's own subjectivity is always mixed up in even the most dispassionate view, which "still contains a secret and inextinguishable drunkenness" (*GS* 57). As more or less subjective, all views are colored by the Dionysian—emotion, instability, the unconscious.

Aphorism 58, "Only as creators!," approaches reality from the perspective of language, and maintains that "what things *are called* is incomparably more important than what they are." Language, which carries meanings from past to present, becomes part of the descent and the training from which the realist cannot escape in aphorism 57. Over time, we forget that the first word for something was arbitrary and begin to believe that it captures something essential: "The reputation, name, and appearance, the usual measure and weight of a thing, what it counts for—originally almost always wrong and arbitrary, thrown over things like a dress and altogether foreign to their nature and even to their skin—all this grows from generation unto generation, merely because people believe in it, until it gradually grows to be part of the thing and turns into its very body." We cannot simply unlearn generations of belief; we cannot "point out this origin and this misty shroud of delusion in order to *destroy* the world that counts for real, so-called *'reality.'* We can destroy only as creators." For Nietzsche, presumably as the speaker of this aphorism, language has such power that, in thrall to

it as we are, "it is enough to create new names and estimations and probabilities in order to create in the long run new 'things.'" We start at the
surface and retrain ourselves to accept a new word; eventually that word
acquires body and "reality."

The discussion of "woman" follows next, and surely the juxtapostion of
woman with themes of reality, subjectivity, and language's tyranny and
creativity is not an accident. "Woman" itself is only a word, but it has
acquired over time the sort of reality to which aphorism 58 refers. Feminists who have worked on removing sexist bias from the language certainly
believe that the substitution of "letter carrier" for "mailman," for example,
will eventually eliminate a gender bias and promote the notion that postal
workers are first and foremost human beings. Aphorism 58 continues the
argument 57, by maintaining that human "reality" is mostly human
dream, human creation, human artistry.

Aphorism 59—which is entitled "We artists," so announcing its speaking position—has generated a great deal of feminist hostility. The aphorism begins thus: "*We artists.*—When we love a woman, we easily conceive a
hatred for nature on account of all the repulsive natural functions to
which every woman is subject. We prefer not to think of all this; but when
our soul touches on these matters for once, it shrugs as it were and looks
contemptuously at nature: we feel insulted; nature seems to encroach on
our possessions, and with the profanest hands at that. . . . 'The human being
under the skin' is for all lovers a horror and unthinkable, a blasphemy
against God and love."

Readers have assumed that Nietzsche's position here is the same as the
artist's. "Nietzsche fears the body," Kelly Oliver asserts, arguing that men
have always hidden, by art, or psychologically by repression, the natural
female bodily functions out of repulsion and horror ("Who is Nietzsche's
Woman?" 203). Even if we were to read the first paragraph of the aphorism
this way, the second makes this approach hard to sustain. It creates an
analogy between the lover of woman and the worshipper of God: "Well, as
lovers still feel about nature and natural functions, every worshipper of
God and his 'holy omnipotence' formerly felt: everything said about nature
by astronomers, geologists, physiologists, or physicians, struck him as an
encroachment into his precious possessions and hence as an attack—and a
shameless one at that."

In *A Rhetoric of Irony,* Wayne Booth lists the steps through which readers
may reconstruct an ironic text with meanings different from those on the
surface. First, he writes, readers must reject the literal meaning, because

they are "unable to escape recognizing either some incongruity among the words or between the words and something else that [they know]" (10). Considering aphorism 59, we know, from our wider reading of his work, that Nietzsche does not exactly approve of God and his "holy omnipotence." In fact, even if we were not aware of this, the quotation marks around "holy omnipotence" would alert us to the possible presence of another meaning. I think it clear that if Nietzsche displays religion's attitude to science for our disapproval, so too by analogy he exposes the artist-lover's attitude to woman. By comparing woman and God, he sets them both up as ideals whose "reality" men will defend against the precepts of their senses, for example. Nietzsche suggests that men have always hidden women's natural bodily functions out of the sort of fear that Oliver herself attributes to Nietzsche. We "live in a dream" with our eyes wide open; "we somnambulists of the day! We artists! We ignore what is natural. . . . We wander, still as death, unwearied, on heights that we do not see as heights but as plains, as our safety."

The irony of this sentence, with which aphorism 59 concludes, becomes more apparent when we consider number 60, "Women and their action at a distance." The text of this aphorism attacks man's ideal of woman by imaging it as a serene sailing vessel moving "like an immense butterfly over the dark sea" which the speaker observes while standing in the pounding surf on the rocky shore. He describes the noise of the wind and crashing waves as "howling, threats, screaming, roaring coming at me"—a description of unmelodic Dionysian sound—when "suddenly" there appears "a large sailboat, gliding along as silently as a ghost. Oh, what ghostly beauty! How magically it touches me! . . . Does my happiness itself sit in this quiet place—my happier ego, my second, departed self? Not to be dead and yet no longer alive?" The sailboat, in contrast to the explicitly Dionysian noise, is explicitly Apollonian: it is an effect of sight; it is dreamlike; it is a boat (recalling the quotation from Schopenhauer at the beginning of *The Birth of Tragedy*, which compares individual consciousness to being afloat in a "frail bark" on the "howling" sea of the Dionysian will); and it appears in response to, in compensation for, or in competition with, the confusion of the unstructured noise from Dionysian wind and waves.

The speaker then collects himself and explains his own metaphors. "All great noise leads us to move happiness into some quiet distance;" the sailboat, he notes, is a woman, and the man "almost thinks that his better self dwells there among the women, and that in these quiet regions even the loudest surf turns into deathly quiet, and life itself into a dream about life." Another voice interjects—"Yet! Yet! Noble enthusiast, even on the most beautiful sailboat there is a lot of noise"—and concludes by asserting that "the magic and the most powerful effect of women is, in philosophical language, action at a distance . . . but this requires first of all and above all—*distance.*"

Metaphor and irony work together in this aphorism to discredit the enthusiast's ideal and to show it up for what it is: his own "fantasy" ("It seems as if the noise here had led me into fantasies") and dream vision. There is no reality at all about the ghostly sailboat woman; there *is* no woman. The enthusiast is alone with his noise and his deathly quiet. The latter recalls that of the artist in aphorism 59, who loves a woman and wanders, "still as death," in his dream world. Both 59 and 60 hint that such ideals (that of woman separated from bodily functions, or of woman as offering seclusion, peace, and calm in the midst of life's turmoil—classic forms of the nineteenth-century eternal feminine) are deadening.

In aphorism 60, the speaker admits that the sailing ship is a masculine fantasy and—insofar as it matches the conventional nineteeth-century image of woman as offering peace and seclusion to the man of the world—a normal one at that, built on the dichotomies man/noise/life versus woman/quiet/death. The speaker's separation from the ship leads him to associate that distance and quiet with death (or with a "dream of life" rather than life itself). The obvious fallacy of the fantasy is pointed out by the second speaker, who observes that there is "much small and petty noise" on the good ship woman. If the enthusiast wants to maintain his dream, he must hold his distance and keep his ideal of woman as peace, seclusion, and his own "better self." (In other words, "woman" is really man after all.)

The enthusiast's fantasy maintains the sexual dichotomy as normative sexual difference. Distance, which preserves the ideal of woman as something separate from and opposite to man, is needed to sustain this normalcy. The presence of the second speaker gives us an additional viewpoint that clashes with that of the enthusiast and makes an implicit ironic comment: If you want to foster the status quo, which has some affinities with death, or with a dream of life and not life itself, go on and maintain the distance (the "sexual difference") between men and women, which is based entirely on men's defensive fantasies and not on the way things are or on real differences. Distance—Nietzsche writes, ironically, at the end of aphorism 59—keeps the artist "safe" in his dream world.

The motifs of artists spinning fantasies as ideals that are "still as death," that keep the artist safe (in his identity as a masculine lover, as a whole self), that depend on distance from the "natural" or on finding nature disgusting or frightening, are similar in the two aphorisms. Both of these expose the ideal as such, and laugh at the artist-enthusiast who cherishes his fantasy of the woman who doesn't exist "under the skin," or in the noise of the surf of life's action. The artist and the enthusiast are simply doing what human beings have always done: behaving metaphysically and mythically. The metaphysics and the myths are now exhausted; God may be dead, but as aphorism 109 asks, "When will all these shadows of God cease to darken our minds? When will we complete our de-deification of nature? When may we begin to *'naturalize'* humanity in terms of a pure, newly discovered, newly redeemed nature?"

The four aphorisms that begin book 2 of *The Gay Science* suggest that the way to de-deify nature involves acknowledging at the start the extent to which we have already "scribbled" over and covered it with our human interpretations (*BGE* 230). The aphorisms share a common focus on the "constructed" nature of human reality. Once we realize that we have dreamed our world, we can go on to comprehend that we can change it: "It is enough to create new names and estimations and probabilities in order to create in the long run new 'things'" (*GS* 58). It is true that Nietzsche appears generally to favor artists' constructions of the world, but he is not indiscriminate about this preference. The four aphorisms I have looked at here use irony to expose irony itself as distance that may obscure as much as it reveals, that may "keep safe" that which should be put at risk—the stable identity of the creating subject.[1]

The aphorisms concerning woman in book 2 all make the case, I suggest (in accord with Kathleen Higgins, who has noted the same thing), that what feminists call "gender roles" need to be examined and brought more in line with actuality (see Higgins *Comic Relief* 73ff.). One of these aphorisms suggests that gender roles might be reversed: "*Women who master the masters.*—A deep and powerful alto voice of the kind one sometimes hears in the theatre can suddenly raise the curtain upon possibilities in which we usually do not believe. All at once we believe that somewhere in the world there could be women with lofty, heroic, and royal souls. . . , capable of and ready for rule over men because in them the best elements of man apart from his sex have become an incarnate ideal" (*GS* 70). In *The Birth of Tragedy,* Nietzsche detached feminine characteristics from women and redistributed them to gods and men; here, he reverses that procedure by imagining a redistribution of masculine traits to women, admitting the possibility of playing with gender performance.

However, role reversal—interesting and thought-provoking as it may be—maintains the two-sex story which, I argue, Nietzsche's texts ultimately dismantle. The last aphorism concerning woman at the beginning of book 2 is interesting and curious. In its entirety, it reads: *"The third sex.*—'A small man is a paradox but still a man; but small females seem to me to belong to another sex than tall women,' said an old dancing master. A small woman is never beautiful—said old Aristotle" (*GS* 75). Walter Kaufmann's note on this aphorism tells us that "Aristotle actually says: 'Greatness of soul implies greatness, as beauty implies a good-sized body, and small people may be neat and well-proportioned but cannot be beautiful.'" Kaufmann adds, "With this absurd aphorism the pages on women reach their nadir and end" (*GS* p. 130n). Kaufmann's observation notwithstanding, I believe that, with this aphorism, Nietzsche's pages on women in The *Gay Science* reach rather their peak and climax. Consider that aphorisms 57 to 75, beginning with "To the realists" (who think they "know" what nature is) and ending with "The third sex" (whose title alone breaks down the male/female binary divide), are all intent on making us reconsider our habitual ideas about sex-gender. They suggest that

(1) we (men) invent fictions about reality (*GS* 57, 58, 59, 60);
(2) we (men) idealize women as an escape from nature (*GS* 59, 60);
(3) woman forms herself in the image man has created for her (*GS* 68);
(4) "upper class women" are kept from knowledge of "nature" (sex) until their wedding nights, at which point they lose their idealism at one blow and become skeptics forever more (*GS* 71) (and old women are more skeptical than any man, and no longer mistake surface for depth; there is no depth [*GS* 64]—that is, there is no binary opposition);
(5) women "could" combine man's best qualities with her own and so "rule over" men (*GS* 70); and
(6) there could be a third sex (*GS* 75).

Writing about aphorism 75, Higgins notes that Aristotle takes the male to be the paradigmatic human, and a large-sized male at that. Nietzsche may here be drawing attention to Aristotle's "height" and gender prejudices and to the perspectivity involved in Aristotle's judgment: "What is more perspectival than height?" (Higgins *Comic Relief* 87). Higgins also notes the connection between this aphorism and number 208, which reads: "*Great man.*—From the fact that somebody is a 'big man' we cannot infer that he is a man; perhaps he is merely a boy, or a chameleon of all the ages of life, or a bewitched little female." "In other words," Higgins writes, "the scale of body demanded by Aristotle is far from 'essential' to the matter of having a great soul. . . . The 'big man' might be a child, or a woman, or perhaps a member of the third sex" (87–88).

In aphorism 75 Nietzsche is undoubtedly pointing out Aristotle's prejudices by introducing women (where Aristotle generalized to humanity from man), and is certainly using "perspectivism"—that is, the fact that every view springs from a specific set of prejudices—to make us think here about professed knowledge having to do with beauty and gender. The aphorism also parodies the system of classification upon which logical categories are based.

The application of "perspectivism" here is ironic, for it implies more than one point of view. In this instance, there are two voices (an old dancing master and old Aristotle) and three points of view. Ostensibly, the whole aphorism develops the absurd claim that because a small woman is not a woman, she must belong to a third sex. The irony begins, however, in the first phrase: "A small man is a paradox but still a man." A paradox is a contradiction and a contradiction in terms cannot be classified (except as a paradox). Thus at the first the dancing master, the initial "old man" speaker, is in logical trouble. Rather than create a fourth category for "small men," however, he allows them to stay classified as "man." With women, he is once more illogical. Rather than divide the class "woman" into small and tall women, he allows tall women to be women, but creates another class, a "third sex," for small women. The comment offered by the second voice, "old Aristotle," introduces a non sequitur to the discussion, and a blatant prejudice: "A small woman is never beautiful." The third voice belongs to the narrator, who makes the editorial decision to give the aphorism the title "The third sex." The discussion is expanded, as Higgins points out, in the "big man" aphorism—where Nietzsche disconnects language and reference again at Aristotle's expense (and to the benefit of my argument). Of what matter is the size, the age, or the sex of a person who is "great" of soul? If Aristotle was consistent, a great soul might be housed in a small female body. Nietzsche's irony leads us, once more, to look at our categories and to ask how rational they are.

Aphorism 363, which appears in book 5 of *The Gay Science,* similarly exposes human illogic through irony: "How each sex has its own prejudice about love." This aphorism is based on a clear and clean dichotomy between man and woman, and their distinctive modes of loving. Its summary thesis reads, "Woman gives herself away, man acquires more." We have heard this before, from "the sage" in aphorism 68 ("Will and willingness"). The sage

declares as "the law of the sexes" that "will is the manner of men; willingness that of women" (*GS* 68), but his assertion is undercut by three other
viewpoints and by internal inconsistencies in his own position. It is interesting to note that Nietzsche later returns to the same position and again
hedges around it with ironies and inconsistencies. This time I think he
outright undermines it—although on the surface the aphorism appears to
be an uncontroversial essentialist statement.

Leaving to one side the fact that Nietzsche doubts and overcomes essen-
tialism (the attribution of fixed universal properties to beings or things),
and taking up aphorism 363 as a self-contained text, we find that it is riddled
with problems. It begins with the negative statement that the speaker, the
"I" of the text, denies the possibility of "*equal* rights in love" for the simple
reason that "these do not exist." From the start we are in a quagmire—the
whole discussion of equality and equal rights—but this is cut short by the
tautologous negative assertion. The assertions are then supported by a
number of other prejudiced claims, which remind us of the aphorism's title,
"How each sex has its own prejudice about love." All of these—title and
assertions alike—hint to us that we are being asked to assess prejudices.
Prejudices are based on social convention; they are "herd" instincts, incul-
cated among groups of people by stories, rituals, habitual phrases, art, and
other cultural practices. That conventions of love are among the most
tenacious of prejudices is perhaps a point that Nietzsche seeks to make
with this aphorism. The speaker declares that "a woman" loves with "total
devotion (not mere surrender) with soul and body, without any consideration or reserve, rather with shame and horror at the thought of a devotion that might be subject to special clauses and conditions." And a man,
he continues, "wants precisely this love from her and is thus himself as far
as can be from the presupposition of feminine love."

The argument the speaker presses—and his verbal repetition makes his
insistence clear—is that "woman wants to be taken and accepted as a possession, wants to be absorbed into the concept of possession, possessed."
We get it. Why the insistence on possession? Does it mirror itself as a fairly
hysterical prejudice? The speaker goes on, stressing (like the sage in the
earlier aphorism) the "naturalness" of the prejudice:

> Consequently, she wants someone who *takes,* who does not give himself or give
> himself away; on the contrary, he is supposed to become richer in "himself"—
> through the accretion of strength, happiness and faith given him by the woman
> who gives herself. Woman gives herself away, man acquires more—I do not see
> how one can get around this natural opposition by means of social contracts

or with the best will in the world to be just, desirable as it may be not to remind oneself constantly how harsh, terrible, enigmatic, and immoral this antagonism is. For love, thought of in its entirety as great and full, is nature, and being nature it is in all eternity something "immoral."

This sounds like a passionate statement of belief on the part of the speaker, and most critics take it as Nietzsche's own word on love. The speaker has summoned to his aid the good will of culture and its wish to be just, but confesses that in this case nature is stronger than culture. We humans would like to be moral, but love is nature, and nature is immoral—and that, folks, is the way it is.

Is it only my own prejudices that incline me not to accept this statement as Nietzsche's view? I admit that these give me my propensities, but the passage conspires with them because, like the series of aphorisms on "woman as such" in *Beyond Good and Evil* (see chapter 1), it is overstated. It is also full of internal contradictions and pointed repetitions that call attention to themselves (another of Booth's tips for recognizing irony). I mentioned the repetition of "possession"; note also the repeated appearance of the phrase "this natural opposition" and "this antagonism" (between woman and man). *What* antagonism, and what opposition? As the speaker describes it, the antagonism vanishes the minute love appears; the man simply absorbs the woman, possesses her fully, and becomes more as she gives herself away, thus eliminating the antagonism. End of story.

The speaker is aware of this ending, and adds a couple of paragraphs to explain its implications. Because a woman gives herself away, following the dictates of "immoral" love, she therefore remains faithful: "*Faithfulness* is accordingly included in woman's love; it follows from the definition. . . . [Man's] love consists of wanting to *have* and not of renunciation and giving away; but *wanting* to have always comes to an end with *having*." Hence if a man is faithful, it is almost an aberration of nature. Have we wandered into the script of *Don Giovanni*? The speaker gives us a set of operatic and novelistic clichés, as much a masculine fantasy, prejudice, and illusion as anything Nietzsche sets up and exposes in the aphorisms on woman in book 2.

What finally exposes the aphorism as a deliberate mockery of "this natural opposition" between the sexes (apart from the fact that the dichotomy falls apart immediately) is its middle paragraphs, which disassemble the opposition so that it is twice displaced. Having asserted that man wants unconditional love from woman, the speaker admits that maybe, just maybe, a man might want to *give* love rather than take it: "Supposing, however, that there should also be men to whom the desire for total devotion is not alien; well, then they simply are—not men." Reading this statement tonally, or expressively, and recalling that for Nietzsche every word, every punctuation mark, is a gesture, we'd have to give weight to the "well," and to the dash separating "are" from "not." The speaker has caught himself in a logical fallacy, and to remain strictly logical he has to assert that men who love like women are not men. They are not exactly women, either. Our speaker needs to have recourse to a third sex, but as he is conventional he can only say that they are slaves. Thus, logically, women who love like women are slaves, but here the speaker avoids that outcome by relying on the solecism that "a woman who loves like a woman becomes *a more perfect woman*."

Having waded into these dangerous waters, where logic is floundering, the speaker nonetheless presses on to a logical conclusion: "A woman's passion in its unconditional renunciation of rights of her own presupposes precisely that on the other side there is no equal pathos, no equal will to renunciation; for if both partners felt impelled by love to renounce themselves, we should then get—I do not know what; perhaps an empty space?" For the speaker, who is full of the normal prejudices and clichés about love that characterize his time and culture, the question appears to be how to maintain one's identity if one is a man in love. (This is a man's concern, and though the aphorism gives us something of what the speaker assumes is the "woman's" prejudice, the real questions, as in this instance, are the province of men.)

In this context, the man is also asked to renounce, but his renunciation is of pathos itself, the emotion of love that seeks to give. To "be a man," a man must only desire to receive—and conversely, a woman, only to give.[2] If both renounce themselves, then from the speaker's vantage point there would be trouble; rather than only the woman disappearing, which is normal, both man and woman would disappear, which for the speaker is impossible and unthinkable. What is impossible is for man to cease to be himself, to lose his self-identity or to have it threatened. What makes man's position ironic is, among other things, his failure to see that the disappearance of the woman might be a problem for them both. But since he has told himself from the outset that there can be no question of "equality" between them, he can justify and even applaud her disappearance as she gives herself away.

In fact, the woman in this aphorism is Zarathustra's Übermensch, the one who puts her identity at risk and "goes under." Nietzsche may be suggesting that this act of putting one's sex-gender identity at risk is difficult for men especially, but it is not, as the speaker of aphorism 363 maintains, impossible. In fact, the "equal will to renunciation" deplored by this speaker is a source of astonished admiration in *Daybreak* 532, "Love makes the same." This is the very proposition against which the speaker of aphorism 363 fulminates, and *Daybreak* 532 too looks at it skeptically. Love "is constantly deceiving and feigning a sameness which in reality does not exist." However, the text goes on to note: "There is no more confused or impenetrable spectacle than that which arises when both parties are passionately in love with one another and both consequently abandon themselves and want to be the same as one another: in the end neither knows what he is supposed to be, what dissimulating, what pretending to be. The beautiful madness of this spectacle is too good for this world and too subtle for human eyes."

Daybreak 532 describes the sort of union where love "makes the same" as a "miracle"—which recalls the miracle of the Hellenic will that united the Dionysian and Apollonian art drives in *The Birth of Tragedy*. Losing one's identity and becoming the "same" as the "other" is what creativity entails. The impossible "empty space," which is for aphorism 363's speaker a "*horror vacui,* the nausea of spilling into a void" (as Staten [166] puts it), is only so for a certain type of male individual, the appropriator. As Henry Staten points out, "appropriation undoes itself" (164), for by taking into itself the other, it becomes the other. "Love makes the same"; passion dissolves boundaries, gender rules and identities; and the empty space, for those who love, is that of possibility and futurity.

Woman as Metaphor

The Gay Science establishes major precedents; it is here that Nietzsche first writes "God is dead," first mentions the eternal return, and first uses "woman" metaphorically. These subjects are interrelated; to borrow a trope from kinship,[3] I suppose that "God is dead" is the mother of eternal return and of the revaluation of woman. Rhetorically, "God is dead" employs a form of metaphorical transfer, known as personification, which typically shifts attributes of sentient beings—in this case, life itself in its inversion—to inanimate, non-sentient, abstract, or ideal entities (or indeed, in this instance, to all of these). That "God" is a fiction is a point Nietzsche makes implicitly through the unexpected figure.[4] (He is explicit on this point in *Thus Spoke Zarathustra*, having Zarathustra say, "Ah, brothers, this God which I created was human work and human madness, like all gods" [1 "Of the Afterworldsmen"].) With the old God out of the way, the "horizon is open" for a new valuation, a new ideal, a new metaphor; into the space steps Woman as metaphor for life, and the eternal return of life.

"Woman"—the concept-sign, or her iconic form, her body—has been used, principally by male artists, to "add value" to other concept-signs throughout human history. Woman's form has symbolized truth, wisdom, love, justice, the theological virtues, the seven liberal arts, the artistic muses, victory, liberty, communism, and nation states. Advertising has seized on it to sell products from toothpaste to cars. Ancient poets, Hesiod among them, equated woman and nature, and especially woman and birth; Bachofen asserted that this equivalence dominated the earliest epochs of human life on earth, giving women the more important roles in human communities, until women's political power faded and her symbolic power rose.

In *Monuments and Maidens: The Allegory of the Female Form*, Marina Warner attributes the existence of woman's symbolic power to her position as *fons et origo*, or "origin of life," a position so significant that, according to the ancient myths, the female "was perceived to be a vehicle of attributed meaning at the very beginning of the world" (225) and her shape or name was given to other valued objects. This attribution was made possible by the conventions of metaphor and allegory—conventions that enable the sending and receiving of double meanings. According to Longinus's third-century definition in *The Art of Rhetoric*, allegory "adorns speech by changing expression and signifying the same thing through a fresher expression of a different kind"; it is a means of persuasion, a "weapon of delight and of art" (quoted in Warner xx). As bearer of metaphysical value, and as a weapon that persuades through the delight of her form—her body—woman is an enduring and durable metaphor. Nietzsche's attribution to woman of the values of life, truth, wisdom, conscience, sensuality, happiness, and eternity (mostly in *Zarathustra*) belongs to this ancient and enduring tradition. Woman is hardly a novel metaphor, hardly an effort of poetic creativity on Nietzsche's part. She comes ready-made.

Using the form of woman to signify life's important values is a tradition that has drawn the ire of many feminists. As Warner comments, woman may represent Liberty, but this representation does not mean that women are free. Rather, woman as Liberty affirms nature within culture itself, thus "recapitulating the ancient and damaging equivalences between male and culture, female and nature" (292–93). For Luce Irigaray, woman is "stifled beneath all those eulogistic or denigratory metaphors," "hemmed in, cathected by tropes," "rolled up in metaphors" (*Speculum* 142–44). The problem with metaphor, for Irigaray and other scholars, is that it draws into a unity two unequal terms, eliminating one of them in the process and collapsing difference into identity. "Life is a woman," for example, assimilates the "woman" to Life, and substitutes life for woman, leaving her with no existence, no nature, no reference of her own. It "dissolves" woman, according to this critique. But *does* metaphor collapse difference into "the same," into—as Irigaray puts it—the masculine "one"?

The answer depends on how we think about metaphor. If we see it as the *substitution* of one word for another, then the qualities of the defining term pass over to the term to be defined; in the phrase "Life is a woman," woman's qualities are used to define life, and woman disappears. If, however, we view metaphor as the *interaction* between two terms, then, according to Ricoeur, the resemblance between the them becomes a "transaction between contexts" (*Rule of Metaphor* 80). I will follow Max Black's interactive theory, which holds that metaphor can be understood under certain conditions to "generate insight about 'how things are' in reality" (Black 39)—that is, insight about truth. I believe that this theory most closely agrees with Nietzsche's ideas of the powers of metaphor. Nietzsche thought that metaphor could redescribe reality, bringing it closer than could existing concepts to a poet's "powerful present intuition" (*PT* 90). Following Aristotle, but imposing his own value judgments, Nietzsche notes, "Logic is merely slavery within the fetters of language. But language includes within itself an illogical element: metaphor, etc." (*PT* 94). This "illogical element" highlights a tension between identity and difference; two terms are compared, and shown to be both alike, and different, at the same time.

For Black, the two terms or subjects of a metaphor "interact" in the following way (which I illustrate by using "life is a woman" as an exemplary metaphorical statement): "(a) The presence of the primary subject [e.g. "life"] incites the hearer to select some of the secondary subject's [e.g. "woman's"] properties; and (b) invites him to construct a parallel implication-complex that can fit the primary subject; and (c) reciprocally induces parallel changes in the secondary subject" (28). The listeners or the readers select, organize, and project the properties of both subjects of a metaphor; the interaction between "subjects" thus takes place in the mind. Metaphorical statements demand *uptake,* a creative response from a competent reader (Black 28). This very nearly explains Nietzsche's extensive use of metaphor: it throws the responsibility for interpretation back to the reader.

Nietzsche sets great store by the invention of new metaphors. Since "woman" has been metaphorically done to death through the ages, why does he continue to use her? In aphorism 92, woman, in her divine aspect, personifies poetry. She faces off against masculine prose in a sexual analogy similar to that of *The Birth of Tragedy:* "Good prose is written only face to face with poetry. . . . Everything abstract wants to be read as a prank against poetry and as with a mocking voice; everything dry and cool is meant to drive the lovely goddess into lovely despair." With these words, Nietzsche invites us to think of poetry as a lovely goddess who is driven into "lovely despair" when confronted with dry, cool, and abstract language, which is personified as a masculine tease. The metaphor foregrounds its own interaction. Prose is a *prank* against poetry and cannot be fully understood as prose unless we take its relationship to poetry into account. As in *The Birth of Tragedy,* where the Apollonian and the Dionysian are locked in "perpetual strife with only periodically intervening reconciliations" (*BT* 1), so too in this aphorism "often there are *rapprochements,* reconciliations for a moment" between masculine prose (the "prose-men") and feminine poetry.

The aphorism attributes "opposite" genders to the genres, but begins by mingling the two within the one writer: "Great masters of prose have almost always been poets, too—if not publicly, then at least secretly, in the 'closet.'" This image suggests that the prose-writer's revelation of a poetic capacity is analogous to coming out of the closet and revealing his femininity. When good prose is written, poetry is always implied, according to Nietzsche; present in absence, poetry motivates the forms of good prose. As he observes: "All of its attractions depend on the way in which poetry is continually avoided and contradicted." Because Nietzsche here genders the genres, we are invited to think metaphorically about gender. The aphorism sustains the alliance formulated in *The Birth of Tragedy* and the early notebooks between poetry (with its musical properties—especially rhythm, which echoes the mother's heart beat) and the feminine. Here too, Nietzsche claims those poetic feminine qualities for the "good prose writer," who is "masculine." The aphorism makes the point that what constitutes a genre, or a gender, are conventions or rules of the game, and then goes on to justify the existence of those rules, as adding sexual interest to writing. Poetry as feminine is present, though hidden, or veiled, by prose as masculine; nonetheless, Nietzsche's aphorism doesn't quite hide her. He does not keep his poetic stance in the closet, but lets her appear as a metaphor, a goddess. As Sarah Kofman writes, "Nietzsche inaugurates a type of philosophy which deliberately uses metaphors, at the risk of being confused with poetry" (*Nietzsche and Metaphor* 17). Aphorism 92 implies that the risk of genre confusion parallels and is analogous to the risk of gender confusion, and that both are risks worth taking.

The goddess returns with the last aphorism in book 2 of *The Gay Science,* number 107 (entitled "Our ultimate gratitude to art"), which builds on the poetry/prose distinction, as well as that of truth/illusion in *The Birth of Tragedy,* and uses a gendered metaphor once again to bring together concepts that are ordinarily, logically, kept apart. Without art, Nietzsche writes, our *"honesty"* (Dionysian truth) would lead us to nausea and suicide, but "the good will to appearances" (Apollonian illusion) saves us. He continues: "We do not always keep our eyes from rounding off something and, as it were, finishing the poem; and then it is no longer eternal imperfection that we carry across the river of becoming—then we have the sense of carrying a *goddess,* and feel proud and childlike as we perform this service." Nietzsche suggests that we can't help it when we "round off something." Humans want and need wholeness and closure, and so, from the imperfection of the world, they create whole, complete, and perfect things—art in the very broad sense of artifact—out of the "eternal imperfection" of their condition. Aphorism 107 suggests that our ordinary course of action is to carry eternal imperfection across the river of becoming, but when we "round off something" and create a whole thing, we carry a *goddess* rather than imperfection with us.

The act of carrying across, or carrying over, is, metaphorically speaking, that of metaphor—the figure of speech that carries connotations across from one subject to another to make us "see as." Like paradox and irony, metaphor breaks down logical distinctions. Aristotle's "law of non-contradiction," which for him is "the most indisputable of all principles," states that "it is impossible for anything at the same time to be and not to be" (*Metaphysics,* IV, 3–4, 1588). This principle solidifies individuation and is the active force behind conceptualization. Metaphor, as opposed to logic, posits that something is something else; categories collapse, boundaries fade, and "being" slides into "becoming."

When Nietzsche writes in *The Gay Science* that we normally carry our own imperfection across the river of becoming, *we* are the bridge. "Man is a bridge, and not a goal," says Zarathustra (Z Prologue 4). Like a bridge, metaphor, too, establishes connections; it is above all relational. Logic separates; metaphor connects—without, however, eradicating differences. Metaphor leaves a space for the differences and the similarities between its terms to interact, to cross back and forth. Consider Zarathustra's metaphor "man is a bridge." By "man," context tells us that Zarathustra means "humankind"; the word "is" carries human qualities across the metaphorical span to the concept "bridge," thus animating and anthropomorphizing it; at the same time, interactively, it carries qualities of the bridge, principally those of connection, across to humankind. Bridges typically connect two bodies of land across a body of water or of air that lies between them (note how "naturally" we have come to metaphorize the human body). What two "bodies" does the human bridge span?

In the essay "On Truth and Lies in a Nonmoral Sense," Nietzsche asserts that the human bridge connects the external world, which supplies nerve stimuli, to the body that receives and transforms them. Conversely, the body sends stimuli to the external world. As human beings, our lives consist of crossing over from one bank to the other. We personify "bridgeness," or metaphoricity; we bring opposites into relation in ourselves. In George Lakoff and Mark Johnson's terms (25), this is an "ontological" metaphor, one that describes the state of being human. We connect externally and internally, and our nervous system is something akin to a tissue of bridges, or synapses, carrying impulses back and forth.

Expanding the metaphor, Zarathustra explains that "man is a rope, fastened between animal and Übermensch—a rope over an abyss" (Prologue 4). Here the two "bodies" between which the human bridge is suspended are animal and Übermensch. As humans, we connect with the animals and with our future capacities, whatever they may be. The crossing is difficult and dangerous, with the abyss yawning beneath. One way to perceive the image equates the abyss with the loss of meaning, and thus the human rope is our fragile, difficult, and necessary capacity to make connections and create meaning. We see each other and ourselves *as* something: as selves, as whole, as women, as men, as citizens, as a number of concept-metaphors that delimit us and our roles. By contrast, we do not see ourselves as chains of nerve impulses, or if we do (as Nietzsche thinks Hamlet did [*BT* 7]), we fall prey to vertigo and cannot function. As metaphors, and by using metaphors, we forget ourselves as "eternal imperfection," and perhaps even carry a goddess or two across the river.

"A complete thing" or a "perfect" thing is often metaphorized as woman in Nietzsche's texts, and sometimes as divine woman; "poetry," for instance, is a goddess. An aphorism in volume 2 of *Human, All Too Human* establishes the gendered complete/incomplete contrast. Its title is "Woman fulfills, man promises": "Through the woman, nature shows the point it has by now reached in its work on the image of mankind; through the man it shows what it had to overcome in attaining to this point, but also what its *intentions* are with respect to mankind.—The complete [also "perfect"—*volkommene*] woman of every era is the idleness of the creator on that seventh day in the creation of culture, the repose of the artist in his work" (*HAH* 2:274). Woman is that thing that has been "rounded off," whereas man still has rough edges, gaps, room for pregnancy and future creation. At the start of the aphorism, both woman and man are treated as aesthetic objects, creations of nature; toward the end, the aphorism seems to fall back into the conventional gender pattern, with woman as the creation (the art work) and man (or God) the artist. However, the metaphors break down the logical pattern of binary oppositions. "The complete woman" is finished, like the poem, or the world on the seventh day, but in Nietzsche's analogy she is not an aesthetic object, separate from her creator. Rather, she is "the idleness of the creator" after the work is done; she is "the repose of the artist in his work"; she is what is "complete" and "perfect" in the creator. As in *The Birth of Tragedy,* the feminine and the masculine come together in the artist to produce an offspring, the "complete" work of art, but it is the feminine in the artist that "is" this perfection.

Let us return to aphorism 107 of *The Gay Science,* where the "complete woman," as the creator's idle pause on the seventh day, is the "goddess" that human creators carry across the river of becoming. The metaphor breaks down the conceptual divisions between man and woman by transforming the presumably masculine artist into a feminine divinity, a goddess. Drawing upon new combinations of metaphors, this figure tells us what the act of artistic creation *feels like* for a man (that is, for Nietzsche). The artist senses that he is performing a service, one that he is glad, happy, and proud to perform; he feels heroic, or even manly. He also feels "childlike"—a state that Zarathustra compares to that of the creator. Yet, as the one who is "crossing over," he is also the goddess, rather than his ordinary self. The artist-creator in the man, the aphorism implies, becomes a divine woman.

Nietzsche's essay "On Truth and Lies" distinguishes between those exhausted and ordinary metaphors that have lost their transformative power and been reduced to concepts and the fresh metaphors that break down the "prison" walls and liberate the intellect. "The drive toward the formation of metaphors is the fundamental human drive, which one cannot for a single instant dispense with in thought, for one would thereby dispense with man himself" (*PT* 88–89). Under the aegis of this drive, the intellect produces conceptual metaphors, joins them together in linguistic systems, and thereby constructs "a regular and rigid new world . . . as its prison."

From then on, "to be truthful means to employ the usual metaphors . . . to lie according to a fixed convention" (*PT* 84). Normally, humans carry the weight of tradition, of past connotations attached to concepts by repeated and habitual use over time. The benefits that accrue from this use are "repose, security, and consistency" (*PT* 86), all of which are necessary to human life. However, when the intellect tires of this repose, when security becomes a prison, then it breaks out: "That master of deception, the intellect, is free; it is released from its former slavery and celebrates its Saturnalia. With creative pleasure it throws metaphors into confusion and displaces the boundary stones of abstractions" (*PT* 90). So liberated, it invents, following its intuitions, and by throwing the conceptual framework into confusion it "puts it back together in an ironic fashion, pairing the most alien things and separating the closest," creating another "illusion," this one closer to its "powerful present intuition" (*PT* 90).

The metaphor of carrying a goddess across the river of becoming conveys an intuition about the experience of creativity, and, self-reflexively, it demonstrates how a good "new" metaphor works in breaking down conceptual barriers. Goddess and human male, two separate categories, have been fused in one—or rather, the barriers, those prison walls confining the two in separate quarters, have fallen. In this instance Nietzsche has most certainly "appropriated" the feminine as a metaphor to describe the male artist's creative pride and joy in his work. By doing so, he has taken the ready-made "woman" and given her a new setting, a new context. Since she is a goddess, his models for this undertaking are the ancient epics of Homer and Virgil, where goddesses (Athena, especially) simply take over a hero's body during a crucial time in order to "inspire" him. Through the creative process, the aphorism implies, an artist is thus taken over—and yet he remains in charge; he is carrying the goddess, not the reverse. The obvious analogy here is to woman's role as child bearer.

The aphorism maintains the distinction between imperfection and perfection, however. Ordinary language does not perform a "divine" service; only "making it new" does that. Putting old things together in new ways exercises our intellects, by making us see "new meaning" (*RL* 65). Thus, crossing the river is made bearable: "As an aesthetic phenomenon existence is still *bearable* for us, and art furnishes us with eyes and hands and above all the good conscience to be *able* to turn ourselves into such a phenomenon" (*GS* 107). This sentence reveals much: when we make art, we transform ourselves; we *bear* and give birth to ourselves as our work; we are both artist and work of art simultaneously, and this gives us the "goddess" feeling. Those who carry a goddess across the river become "new, unique, incomparable, [they] give themselves laws, [they] create themselves" (GS 335).

The "service" we perform as artists carrying a goddess across the river is simply to make life bearable. I don't think we should read the line, "as an aesthetic phenomenon existence is still bearable," as a statement that justifies life as art in the narrow or effete sense; rather, I think it would be better taken as a good example of punning understatement. As we have seen, "bearing" a goddess across the river of becoming means finding interest, enjoyment, and pride in one's work, and thus in oneself. Being an artist in the widest sense has, in fact, a moral implication as much as an aesthetic one; it means taking responsibility for making life "bearable" by striving to forge new connections, new relations, new metaphors—finding the goddess or the god, or both, in oneself and in other people, sometimes forgetting the old boundary markers or even throwing them about.

Being an artist may also mean learning to love. Aphorism 334 of *The Gay Science* suggests that new music, like other new, strange, and unaccustomed things, has to be experienced awhile before we can learn to tolerate and finally to love it. This is another way of carrying a goddess: it implies passivity and receptivity rather than active striving, but it is nonetheless effective as a means to grow. As the aphorism notes: "But that is what happens to us not only in music. That is how we have *learned to love* all things that we now love. In the end we are always rewarded for our good will, our patience, fairmindedness, and gentleness with what is strange: gradually, it sheds its veil and turns out to be a new and indescribable beauty. That is its *thanks* for our hospitality. Even those who love themselves will have learned it in this way: for there is no other way. Love, too, has to be learned" (GS 334).

Aphorism 334 sheds light on what is to my mind the most puzzling and revealing of *The Gay Science*'s aphorisms, number 339, entitled "Vita femina." Here the bridge that "man is" becomes a "veil" that woman is, and that veil is life ("Yes, Life is a woman"). Like aphorism 334 on learning to love, aphorism 339 is also about unveiling, but its terms are purely metaphorical. It explicitly connects woman and metaphor. Here the metamorphoses, the loss of identity, and the play of differences of metaphor itself are all on display. It is an upbeat, dramatic text centered on sexuality.

The Latin tag that serves as its title carries connotations of the classical, ancient, and scholarly, attributing the conjunction of life and the feminine to ancient tradition (indeed, perhaps very ancient, recollecting Nietzsche's regard for the Eleusinian mysteries). The metaphoric equation of life and woman, where characteristics pass from woman to animate life in a certain way, relies on connotations carried by the word "woman" for its interpreta-tion. Woman brings forth new life from her body and in so doing is also connected antithetically with death. In *The Birth of Tragedy,* Nietzsche holds that the primordial mother creates and destroys with equal relish (*BT* 16). These contextual associations may color our view of an aphorism whose first words are *vita femina.*

This presumption notwithstanding, the text begins by directing our thoughts toward the aesthetic: "For seeing the ultimate beauties of a work, no knowledge or good will is sufficient; this requires the rarest of lucky accidents" (*GS* 339). The difference between seeing the ultimate beauties of a work, and the process of learning to love set forth in aphorism 334, is that we can accomplish the latter through patience and good will; for the former those qualities will not suffice. Here instead we must partly depend on chance. Then comes the first metaphor: "The clouds that veil these peaks ["the ultimate beauties of a work"] have to lift for once so that we see them glowing in the sun." The text sets forth the conditions necessary for the unlikely unveiling to occur: "Not only do we have to stand in precisely the right spot in order to see this, but the unveiling must have been accom-plished by our own soul because it needed some external expression and parable, as if it were a matter of having something to hold on to and retain control of itself" (*GS* 339).

The aphorism extends this metaphor of mountain peaks to describe how arduous and rare the process is wherein we see the cloud cover lift. We have to be in "precisely" the right spot when the sun breaks through and the peaks are revealed. Although the process of getting to the mountains may involve some effort, once we are there we are passive observers of a rev-elation that proceeds without our assistance, through forces of nature or circumstances beyond our control. We do not know where precisely the right spot will be, or when, if at all, the sun will break through the clouds. These external forces must be matched, nonetheless, by our own need. The soul becomes the actor, and accomplishes the unveiling itself. The moun-tain peaks (if we ever see them) are an "external expression and parable" that act *like* a handhold and means of self-control for the soul. The insight or revelation, though sought and indeed effected by our very own soul, comes when it will, not when "I" will (as Nietzsche summarily describes a thought's independence from will in aphorism 17 of *Beyond Good and Evil*). Aphorism 339 sets forth two conditions under which the uncommon unveiling of the mountain peaks (the flash of insight, the intuition, the revelation) may occur. First, we have to be in the mountains—that is, in a place propitious of thought. (For Nietzsche, the mountains are such a place.[5]) Second, our soul—that which is most ourselves—has to want the insight and then, as in learning to love, must be patient.

The text continues: "But it is so rare for all of this to coincide that I am inclined to believe that the highest peaks of everything good, whether it be a work, a deed, humanity, or nature, have so far remained concealed and veiled from the great majority and even from the best human beings." This statement expands the object of the revelation from the ultimate beauties of a work to "the highest peaks of everything good," and highlights the extraordinary rarity of this almost impossible disclosure. Then the drama intensifies; if we get this lucky break, we get it only once: "But what does unveil itself for us, *unveils itself for us once only.*" What "unveils," finally, is a moment in time:

> The Greeks, to be sure, prayed: "Everything beautiful twice and even three times!" They implored the gods with good reason, for ungodly reality gives us the beautiful either not at all or once only. I mean to say that the world is over-full of beautiful things but nevertheless poor, very poor when it comes to beautiful moments and the unveiling of these things. But perhaps this is the most powerful magic of life: it is covered by a veil interwoven with gold, a veil of beautiful possibilities, sparkling with promise, resistance, bashfulness, mockery, pity, and seduction. Yes, life is a woman. (GS 339)

The golden veil of appearance that Life wears is *maya,* illusion, metaphor, the Apollonian: Life seems beautiful and, like art, or the Sphinx from Nietzsche's early notebook entry, seduces us to go on living. The seduction "conceals" necessity and smooths out all wrinkles (*KSA* 7:143–44); it promises us wonderful things, sparkling possibilities, and it veils our necessary decay and death. Anything that reminds us of our strength and *Lustgefuhl*—our lusty feelings, our pleasure in sensation—binds us to life and throws a veil of forgetfulness over "necessity." In the unveiling, is the aphorism referring to the "necessity" that is the Sphinx's secret?

Nietzsche introduces sex-gender into the discussion by naming this crucial aphorism *vita femina*. In so doing, he addresses his words to a male audience, and by attributing sparkling promise, resistance, bashfulness, mockery, pity, and seduction to Life, he sets up a masculine relationship of flirtatiousness with "woman." As prose depends on its hidden poetry, the effect of the entire aphorism hangs on the sexual flirtation which the speaker, the subject, the narrator, carries on with Life, the woman, the object of his attentions. As it is unlikely that a woman would compare her feeling of joy in creation to "carrying a goddess across the river," so too is it unlikely that a woman would flirt with Life as a woman—provided she is heterosexual. (As we have seen, Nietzsche tends to maintain the heterosexual conventions so that he may subvert them.)

In "Nietzsche: Life as Metaphor," Eric Blondel argues that the *vita femina* metaphor, and metaphor in general in Nietzsche's texts, is used "to designate the separation between body and thought, a kind of displacement that has structured the development of culture since its very inception" (151). For Blondel, the veil of Life is Apollonian, cultural, and feminine; what is veiled is the repressed body of the father. The metaphorical operation displaces the body and the instincts, and indicates a "split between the conscious and the unconscious" (163). Blondel argues that for Nietzsche, the metaphorical veil of life, in displacing and disarming the instincts, seduces us into forgetting the body, and that "appearance and appearing are the only reality of the *vita femina* when this is taken as the metaphor of meta-phor." From this perspective, there is no truth beyond or beneath appearance; there is nothing to unveil (157).

Yet the *vita femina* aphorism strongly suggests that there are "ultimate beauties" behind the veil and that we can in fact catch them, once, if we are lucky. Life is not just any woman, but a striptease artist, most proficient in her profession. If Blondel is right, then that which the veil covers is the naked body (which makes sense), but if Life the woman finally strips off and reveals the body of the father, then we have a most Nietzschean identity crisis on our hands. As I see it, this crisis is the very point of the aphorism.

Following Blondel's suggestion that what is veiled is the body of the father, we might take the mountain peaks as phallic symbols, standing in for an instinctual sexuality normally covered over with the metaphoric veils of language and thus forgotten. However, when we seek a *Gleichniss*—an image or parable to hold onto and give us back the feeling of power—in our ultimate need, if luck is with us the peaks are revealed as our own "ultimate beauties," the power we obtain from our bodies, or more specifically from our phalluses, our generative capacities. Blondel uses Freudian terminology when he writes of the repressed body of the father, but he does not analyze the metaphors in the aphorism, nor does he undertake a Freudian reading. If we "see" these highest peaks, they are objectified, distanced, metaphorized—as dream symbols are also veils. (In Freudian terms, they are defenses.) That the peaks appear in the plural would seem to indicate that the dreamer, Nietzsche, is warding off castration by imagining a number of phallic objects; if this is the case, then the peaks are defensive constructions against the "ultimate" unveiling, that of the naked body of the woman.

However, a Freudian reading does not take account of all the elements present in the text. As with *The Birth of Tragedy,* this aphorism precedes the rise of psychoanalysis, and though his ideas are very close to those of Freud, Nietzsche produces an interpretation that affirms the naked body of the woman or the mother. That which unveils, according to the text, is life's "ultimate beauties" or "highest peaks" (in the plural). Like clouds blowing off the mountain tops, the unveiling happens in time, creating "beautiful moments." Life is a woman, and it is her beauties that are revealed. There is no doubt at all that this revelation is something uniquely marvelous, a "lucky accident" brought about by a combination of chance and our desire for "something to hold onto," something that provides us with confidence and power. There is also no doubt that these "peaks" or "summits" are our own, made manifest to us through a lucky accident. In other words, the mountains that are ordinarily veiled are our own "highest" moments—they are both external to us (as metaphor, the appearance of things), as well as internal (as reality: emotion, sensation, knowledge).

Sometimes (so seldom that it may happen only once, if at all, according to Nietzsche), everything "comes together," including chance or fate (being in the right spot at the right time) and our needy desire. At such a time we may be "given" a perfect moment of Dionysian "resurrection," the unity of the fragments, the wholeness of being (thought, emotion, instinct, and sensation as one) that is pure joy. Nietzsche calls this "ungodly reality," a moment when the transcendental ideal, or the metaphoric construct that subsumes the linguistic concept, disappears like clouds in the sunshine, and we are "here." Unlike the realist of aphorism 57, we have no illusions about experiencing reality unveiled, because illusion has fallen away. Unlike the artist of aphorism 59, or the enthusiast of aphorism 60, we are not in love with the veil at the expense of what it hides. We experience a moment of perfection; it is a passing moment, a moment in time, and furthermore we are permitted to "see" it, to be conscious of it. For the sake of this one moment, Zarathustra holds all of life worth living, not once, but over and over again: "Did you ever say Yes to one joy: O my friends, then you said Yes to *all* woe as well. All things are chained and entwined together, all things are in love. . . . If you ever wanted one moment twice . . . then you wanted *everything* to return!" (4 "The Intoxicated Song"). The only way to experience a uniquely beautiful moment more than once is to will the eternal return of all things.

Thus in aphorism 339 Nietzsche introduces the total affirmation of the eternal return and what makes it possible: an almost impossibly sublime moment. In such an instant, or for its sake, we will the return of everything, including pain and death. We have in fact "learned to love" life, in its strangeness and its differences, and now it gives us "*thanks* for our hospitality" (GS 334). With this, all barriers have truly fallen—we are one with everything—and our experience is *like* seeing the mountain peaks emerging from clouds, glorious, and glowing radiantly in the sun. Mountain peaks are not transcendental, but of the earth, elemental.[6] The image is that of health, strength, magnificence, permanence; it is as close to an image of eternity as any earthly scene comes. At the moment of unveiling, the moment when language ceases to hold its power over our lives, the moment when Apollo and Dionysus exchange characteristics, "man" and "woman" cease to exist as such. If "life is a woman," and I am a man, and it is *my* life, then I too am a woman—though at this instant, with the veils off, the distinction breaks down and I am left with reality as unfamiliar as it is splendid and unique.

Does the metaphor "Life is a woman" eliminate the woman? After all, there are actual women to whom the term "woman" refers. Actual women lend their presence-in-absence, their various attributes, to the abstract concept "life" that the text seeks to characterize. As Marina Warner writes, "A symbolized female presence both gives and takes value and meaning in relation to actual women, and contains the potential for affirmation not only of women themselves, but of the general good they might represent and in which as half of humanity they are deeply implicated" (xx). That "woman" or her iconic form signifies important human values does not prevent her from *also* signifying actual women. Indeed, the structure of metaphor, considered not as substitution but as interaction, makes this polysemantic signification not only possible, but inevitable. And although the *vita femina* aphorism keeps the genders apart, we are given to understand that the separate Apollonian constructs by which Life has practiced her seduction collapse at the moment of unveiling, when opposites are "seen," and understood, to be part of the same whole. They do not have to be cast as "illusions" to Life's unveiled "truth"; that opposition also collapses, at the moment of insight, into "ungodly reality."

And what of Nietzsche's female readers? The aphorism's flirtatiousness with Life leaves us several choices. First, we can identify with our masculine colleagues and think that the revelation, the unveiling, the beautiful moment is similarly ours. After all, we have our highest moments, we are mortal, we need reassurance about our deaths and the value of our lives— in short, we are part of the reality into which the oppositions collapse. Second, we can accept, and celebrate, as women, that Life is indeed a woman, a marvelous woman according to Nietzsche, and unveiled she is neither terrifying nor horrible, but more beautiful than men can dream; she is self-justifying. Third, we can invert the sexual symbolism, and practice saying "Yes! Life is a man!" Here we find the phrase fails the commutation test. Life is not a man; we know this, just as we know that death is not a man.[7] That we are ill at ease with the metaphor "life is a man" shows us how deeply our connotations of life and woman are associated—connections that Bachofen began to recover in hypothetical terms with his assertions about humanity's archaic past. Is this one of the linguistic traditions that Nietzsche is exposing? Once we understand that, regardless of the depth of our sentimental attachment to the connection between "life" and "woman," it is after all only an invention, only a metaphor, will our attachment to it be weakened? Returning to the notion that the *vita femina* metaphor is old as the hills, or mountains, and perhaps worn out, let us finally consider that Nietzsche's irony is unobtrusively at work here, too. Do we wish to reaffirm, we women readers, our faith that "Life is a Woman"? And what of his humor: Life the Woman unveils and reveals phallic mountain peaks— though now I think of it, the snowcapped mountains of Wyoming, the Grand Tetons, are breasts, and the highest peak in the Alps, the Jungfrau, is a female virgin. There is no end to thinking about this aphorism.

Irony, Metaphor, and Life as a Woman

Nietzsche's irony casts suspicion on ideals, providing distance so that readers can see them as constructs, while his use of metaphor establishes new ways of perceiving old things or imagining totally new ones. Woman, one of his prime Apollonian artifacts, is hauled off her pedestal and shown to be a masculine fantasy, but is as quickly reinstated as a figure for life, with Apollonian veils that draw us nearer to her, and to the possibility of knowing her Dionysian eternities as well.

The empty space left when a woman and a man in love both give themselves away, losing their separate identities, is not really an empty space at all; it just seems so to the prejudiced man of aphorism 363. For others, the space is filled with a new, ungodly reality that may be like that which offers itself when Life unveils. Analogous to the "space" left free after the dismantling of the ideal pairing of "man and woman," and to the "immense void" that resulted when tragedy died (*BT* 11), is that with which *The Gay Science* is chiefly concerned: the space left when God disappears. The madman jumps into the marketplace and accuses the people of having murdered God: "'Whither is God?' he cried; 'I will tell you. *We have killed him*— you and I. All of us are his murderers. But how did we do this? How could we drink up the sea? Who gave us the sponge to wipe away the entire horizon?" (*GS* 125). The first aphorism in book 5 declares that the horizon is still there, but, as a consequence of God's death, it is now open: "At long last the horizon appears free to us ["we philosophers and 'free spirits'"] again, even if it should not be bright; . . . the sea, *our* sea, lies open again; perhaps there has never yet been such an 'open sea'—" (*GS* 343).

An empty space, an open sea, life who is a woman, gender conventions under suspicion, a chance for a new art—these key images and themes of *The Gay Science* come together very subtly in what was originally the penultimate aphorism of the work: "The greatest weight" (*GS* 341). This aphorism introduces a demon who asks, hypothetically, how you would respond if you were told that you will relive your life exactly as it is? "What, if some day or night a demon were to steal after you into your loneliest loneliness and say to you: 'This life as you now live it and have lived it, you will have to live once more and innumerable times more . . .' Would you not throw yourself down and gnash your teeth and curse the demon who spoke thus? Or have you once experienced a tremendous moment when you would have answered him: 'You are a god and never have I heard anything more divine.'" If it "gains possession of you," the aphorism concludes, this question would change or perhaps crush you. "How well disposed would you have to become to yourself and to life *to crave nothing more fervently* than this ultimate eternal confirmation and seal?"

Book 4's final aphorism, which marked the original ending of *The Gay Science* prior to the addition of book 5 in the second edition, prefigures Nietzsche's next work, *Thus Spoke Zarathustra*, whose purpose largely seems to me to elaborate the hypothesis proposed by the demon, that of the eternal return. As in *The Gay Science*, in *Zarathustra* life is a woman. Why would Nietzsche, if he were a misogynist, cast life as a remarkable and loveable woman, and in both of these key works? Why would he distribute her qualities to men? Apart from an obvious answer—that he liked and even loved real women, a suggestion that I will take up in the next chapter—I find myself drawn, as Nietzsche was, to another of his thoughts: that for the ancient Greeks, life justified itself. Humans did not need a carrot—a potential happy ending in heaven—to keep them going. They revered life, and its symbol, according to Nietzsche, was a woman in childbirth, pain and joy inextricably linked to faith in the future and in the earth, and to an acceptance of death. To this Greek feminine as a new ideal called Life, Nietzsche, standing in for Life, wishes to seduce us, and his seduction is nowhere as strange as in his own favorite among his works, *Thus Spoke Zarathustra.*

5

Zarathustra's Whip
Disciplining Readers

PEOPLE who don't know anything else about Nietzsche often know that he "said": "Are you visiting women? Don't forget your whip!" This saying occurs in *Thus Spoke Zarathustra,* and it has always drawn flack. In her 1897 biography of her brother, Elisabeth Förster-Nietzsche writes: "How did it come about that my brother is generally considered a misogynist? I believe it is due to a little remark from Zarathustra: 'You are going to women? Do not forget the whip!' For that is the only thing which a hundred thousand women know about Nietzsche" (in Gilman *Conversations* 123). Not only women; another story is told by one Sebastian Hausmann, who writes of being in Sils-Maria (Nietzsche's summer Alpine retreat) in the 1880s after *Zarathustra* was published. He runs into Nietzsche without recognizing him and, though he hasn't read any of his books, tells him that he "doesn't like" Nietzsche's work. When his interlocutor asks for "an example" that causes him "difficulty," Hausmann realizes that he is speaking with Nietzsche himself:

> Frantically I searched my memory . . . suddenly I thought of a statement that my circle of friends had discussed in detail: "Don't forget the whip, when you go to a woman!" or something similar. When I cited this example, he looked at me in astonishment: "But, I beg you, surely that cannot cause you any difficulty! I mean, it is clear and understandable that this is only a joke, an exaggerated, symbolic mode of expression. . . ." He also told me, moreover, that the much discussed and much misunderstood phrase had its origin in a personal memory. (in Gilman *Conversations* 135)

Nothing Nietzsche can say will get him out of the mess the whip continues to get him into with readers. "It's only a joke" won't cut much ice; beating women ceased to make for hilarity in the theater a while back, and it never served the comic turn in real life. As for its being "an exaggerated and symbolic mode of expression," fine, but it doesn't then follow that the line is "clear and understandable." Finally, that the saying about the whip is based on a personal memory legitimates a roman-à-clef approach to the text that uncovers biography but leaves the whip—as a textual joke, or symbol, or image, or rhetorical exaggeration—unexplained.

Given the subject of my discussion, I am not indifferent to the line about the whip. I find it significant that it sticks, and has always stuck, in people's minds and craws when they think about Nietzsche. At the very minimum, it gives people who want to dislike and dismiss a disturbing thinker all the more reason to do so. However, the line is disturbing, and it sticks. I hope to show that there are good reasons for its being memorable. The whip belongs to the chapter on "woman" in *Thus Spoke Zarathustra* that contains the statement "Everything about woman is a riddle." I shall argue that the advice about the whip is also a riddle, that it is central to an understanding of the operation of sex-gender in *Zarathustra,* and that issues of sex-gender are fundamental to Zarathustra's major prophecies, the Übermensch and the eternal return.

How should we take the line about the whip? Is it a joke? Is it serious? Can it be both? This last prospect will be our point of departure. Here, as with Nietzsche's other works, the interpretive focus shifts from author to reader, and as the one at the end of the line, the line about the whip, the reader becomes the provisional power broker of the text's signs. The whip, in short, ends up in the reader's hand. Most readers use the whip on Nietzsche, understandably; they become disciplinarians, cracking the word "misogynist," lashing Nietzsche with accusations of foul play and violence against women. In the text, when Zarathustra threatens her with the whip, Life says, "O Zarathustra! Do not crack your whip so terribly! You surely know: noise kills thought—" (Z 3 "The Second Dance Song" 2). For her, the whip is the agent and symbol of "noise"; as noise it is purely Dionysian, an inarticulate, compelling expression of emotion. Its violence extends beyond the object of its lash, and "kills thought."

Lashing out verbally with the whip that the text has placed in their hands may bring readers a certain emotional satisfaction, not to be gain-said; after all, the whip is lying there, provocatively, asking to be used. I can't help thinking, however, that the noise of the accusations kills the thought of the whip. To get some interpretive leverage on the riddle that it poses, I shall take up the hints Nietzsche supplied in his comeback to Hausmann in Sils-Maria, and begin, in this chapter, by examining the whip's contexts—biographical, generic, and narrative.

Zarathustrian Contexts I: Dionysus (Sex)

Zarathustra's references to woman, both positive and negative, can be approached by reference to ascertainable facts of Nietzsche's biography, though to use these facts to "solve" the text's riddles is to eliminate both the pleasure of the text and the possibility of finding good answers to the riddles. Yet to ignore the life of the author and the ways in which we know that the life impinged on the text is also counterproductive to finding good answers to the riddles, particularly as Nietzsche's reply to Hausmann intermixes his personal life—emotional, passional, sexual, Dionysian—and his text.

Psychoanalytic textual criticism holds that there is a textual unconscious that is manifested in an author's work. For Lacanians, language and thus writing necessarily depend on repression of the "other," the body of the mother, which can sometimes still be glimpsed through gaps in the text, figures of speech, or certain poetic tonal and rhythmic patterns. However, Nietzsche's first psychological critic (apart from himself) was unaware of Lacan, and was instead initiated through her discussions with Nietzsche. She is Lou Andreas-Salomé, who plays a starring role in Nietzsche's biography and is central to a biographical consideration of "woman" in *Thus Spoke Zarathustra,* as well as in all of Nietzsche's work after *Zarathustra.* It was Salomé, after all, who in 1882 was photographed sitting in a small cart holding a very small whip, with two sheepish philosophers—one of them Nietzsche himself—standing in the cart's traces.

In 1894, in Vienna, Lou Salomé published *Friedrich Nietzsche in seinen Werken* (Friedrich Nietzsche in his Works), one of the first full-length studies of Nietszche's philosophy (and, by extension, of the philosopher himself, who was at the time fifty years old, mad, and living in the care of his mother and sister in his childhood home in Naumburg). Nietzsche's European reputation was just beginning to build, so Salomé's well-received book was timely. In addition to inaugurating Nietzsche studies, the book also established at least one specific subgenre: psychological criticism of his work.[1] Anna Freud is reported to have observed that it "anticipated psychoanalysis" (Martin 93). It also anticipated gender criticism of Nietzsche's writings; according to Janet Lungstrum, it "effectively set the stage for current critical discourse on the Nietzschean 'feminine'" (150).

Lou Salomé was born in 1861 and raised in an emigré German family in Saint Petersburg during the liberalizing decade of the 1860s. She was indulged by her upper-class parents and, like other intellectually gifted women of her class, was sent abroad at age twenty to study at Zürich University, where she was allowed to audit courses. She published her first book, a novel, under a male pseudonym at age twenty-five; her second, a study of women in Ibsen's plays, at age thirty; and her third, *Friedrich Nietzsche in seinen Werken,* three years later. Six more novels appeared between 1894 and 1902;

these were followed by *Die Erotik,* (four psychoanalytic studies on eroticism) in 1910, then by five more works of fiction, a 1928 study of Rainer Maria Rilke, and a book on Freudian theory, published in 1931 when she was seventy years old. Her vitae lists some 119 articles, and she left four unpublished manuscripts when she died in 1937. In 1951 her literary executor brought out Salomé's memoirs, which she wrote between 1931 and 1936. This is not a conventional dossier of a *femme fatale,* and yet it was as a fatally dangerous woman that Salomé was best known in her own time.

The features of that more vivid portrait appear in the *ad feminam* nastiness with which Salomé's work was often greeted. They are etched in the account of an admiring biographer who writes, "So great was her personal charm that her presence aroused powerful creative forces in the men who were in love with her. As one of her admirers put it, 'Lou would form a passionate attachment to a man and nine months later the man gave birth to a book!'" (Peters 13).[2] The first of these literary births was Nietzsche's; exactly nine months after meeting Lou Salomé, he produced part 1 of *Thus Spoke Zarathustra.*

Thirty-eight-year-old Nietzsche met Salomé, a beautiful, charming, intellectual, and free-spirited twenty-one-year-old woman, through his close friend Paul Rée.[3] Both philosophers fell for her, without admitting it to each other, and agreed to a study threesome (a classic recipe for disaster, complicated by whatever amorous feelings, if any, existed between Nietzsche and Rée[4]). Nietzsche at first kept Salomé a secret from friends and especially, family. He advised her in a letter (dated June 7, 1882) to be circumspect about their plans to study together the following winter: nobody "need break their heads and hearts over things that we, we, we alone are and shall be up to, whereas they may strike others as dangerous fantasies" (in Binyon 63).

A number of episodes from their relationship—which lasted from spring to fall 1882, the period in which Nietzsche edited the first four books of *The Gay Science*—surface, transformed, in *Thus Spoke Zarathustra.* In May 1882, the traveling parties accompanying Salomé and Nietzsche tailgated each other north through Italy, merging at Orta where Nietzsche and Salomé climbed Monte Sacro together. On the sacred mountain, Nietzsche explained to Salomé his thoughts about the eternal return; in Lucerne, by her account, he arranged for a photograph to be taken to commemorate the occasion of the reunion of their Trinity (Salomé-Nietzsche-Rée). This is the famous photograph of Salomé, seated in a small cart and holding a tiny whip that Nietzsche decorated with a sprig of lilac, with Nietzsche and Rée in the shafts (Andreas-Salomé *Looking Back* 48). Nietzsche stage-managed the shot, possibly as a parody of a medieval story about Alexander the Great, his lover Phyllis, and their humiliation of Aristotle, who was Alexander's tutor. As a ruse in that tale, Phyllis mounted Aristotle's back, "carrying [a] flowering branch as a whip" (Allison 156). Nietzsche revisits this parody in the infamous line about the whip in *Zarathustra,* to which we shall return at the end of this chapter.

Salomé and Nietzsche met again in August, when they spent three weeks together walking in the Thuringian countryside near Tautenburg, discussing philosophy; their conversations are well documented as each kept a notebook during this period and exchanged frequent letters, between themselves and the absent member of the threesome, Paul Rée. During this time, Salomé made notes for a "character sketch" of Nietzsche, who, according to Rudolph Binyon (83), she determined to make the subject of her first full-scale work, rather than pursuing her original idea of doing a book on "woman as such." This is an interesting substitution of topic and indeed an interesting situation altogether: "woman" becomes "Nietzsche," as the woman writer takes the man as object. The two met again in Leipzig in October, where Salomé showed Nietzsche the draft of the "character sketch," which he approved, thus authorizing her work.

The period in Tautenberg was immensely fruitful for both Salomé and Nietzsche. "Tautenburg Notes for Lou von Salomé" heads up several pages of Nietzsche's notebooks for August 1882. His letters to friends during and just after Tautenburg find him enthusiastic about her; "She is the most intelligent of all women," he writes to Peter Gast, and his correspondence to Franz Overbeck describes their talks as the "most profitable occupation" of the summer. "Our mentalities and tastes are most deeply akin— and yet there are so many contrasts too that we are for each other the most instructive of subjects. . . . I should like to know whether there has ever before been such philosophical openness as between the two of us" (quoted in Binyon 81–82). Judging from the notebooks—and from a letter in which Elisabeth Nietzsche describes for a friend the details of a fight she had with Salomé and the distress that the relationship between Salomé and her brother caused her—the conversations in Tautenburg were indeed frank. Elisabeth's account of these philosophical discussions fulminates as follows: "What horrid talk the two carried on together! What was a lie? Nothing! What was breach of confidence? Nothing! What was doing one's duty? Silliness. What was the most derisive talk about true friends? Right judgment. What was compassion? Contemptible. Never have I seen my brother together with his philosophy so mean, so paltry! . . . [Lou] is really

... my brother's philosophy personified ... Fritz has changed, he is just like his books!" (in Binyon 82, 84).

Elisabeth's thumbnail sketch of those candid philosophical discussions caricatures Nietzsche's complex ethical arguments from the perspective of "Naumburg virtue"—a perspective that is usually discernable in the background, if not in the foreground, of his work—and in so doing allows us hear its fascinated resentment. All the evidence suggests that Elisabeth and her mother stood in formidable alliance against Lou Salomé, an act that eventually caused Nietzsche's break with her, with them, and with Paul Rée, and sent him into virtual solitude.

The notebooks take up questions of morality, God, and religion, along the lines indicated by Elisabeth, and sex-gender, in terms that seem open indeed; the pair took pleasure in being outrageously free-spirited, no doubt. An early note in the series, written for Lou, establishes one of Nietzsche's fondest principles, under the rubric of materialism: the overthrow of the binary oppositions of dualist thought. He tells her that we tend to overlook the very fine "stuff" that things are made of, and to speak of the "immaterial," but this is a false distinction, just as we typically separate "dead and living, logical and illogical, etc. To unlearn our oppositions—this is the task" (*KSA* 10:10).

One of the major concerns of the Tautenburg notebook is the examination of cultural presuppositions about the "opposite" sexes. For example, Zarathustra's "solution" to the riddle of woman, pregnancy (Z 1 "Of Old and Young Women"), is treated with some anthropological nuance here: "Pregnancy as the cardinal state, which gradually, over the centuries, fixed the nature of woman. Relation of all woman's thought and behavior patterns to this" (*KSA* 10:42). In this note we find Nietzsche and Salomé constructing a genealogical account of "the nature of woman," conditioned by millennia of pregnancy. And this item appears in a list of possible topics for thought and exposition on an earlier page: "Sexual love as means to the ideal (to strive to perish in its opposition)" (*KSA* 10:21). As in *The Birth of Tragedy,* and aphorism 532 of *Daybreak* ("Love makes the same," which we considered in the last chapter), in these notes Nietzsche is exploring the notion of sexual passion as a means of "losing" the self. He implies that sexual love is for him a means of "going under," perishing as the man Nietzsche, in order to create an ideal, an Übermensch, with resentment and "oppositions" similarly dispatched.

In *Friedrich Nietzsche in seinen Werken,* Salomé interprets Nietzsche's philosophy as self-agonistic and self-confessional, prompting an intellectual understanding of inner conflict that becomes increasingly productive for her as she develops her theory of the feminine. In her study she quotes an aphorism from *Beyond Good and Evil:* "There are two kinds of genius: above all, one which begets and another which will gladly allow itself to become fertile and will give birth." To this she comments: "Undoubtedly, he belonged to the latter. In Nietzsche's spiritual nature was something, in heightened dimension, that was feminine" (29). Perceiving this feminine receptivity in Nietzsche led Salomé to speculate, in subsequent articles, that each human is constituted of masculine and feminine impulses or drives (Martin 5 and passim).

The substance of other gender aphorisms in the Tautenburg notebooks turns up later in Nietzsche's published work: "The tremendous expectation in regard to sexual love spoils the eye of women for all broader perspectives" (*KSA* 10:32) is only slightly modified in aphorism 114 of *Beyond Good and Evil*, and the observation, "Behind all his feelings for woman, man always has contempt for the female sex" (*KSA* 10:23) becomes "Behind all their personal vanity women themselves always have their impersonal contempt—for 'woman'—" (*BGE* 86). The sex change here enables Nietzsche on one level to intensify his point; contempt for "woman" is generic and not limited to men alone—even women themselves feel it. On another level, the two versions differ substantially. The original attributes the contempt man feels for woman to "the female sex"; biological concerns arise, as in aphorism 59 of *The Gay Science* ("We artists"). The published version draws a distinction between "women" and "woman"—set off by dashes—to indicate the difference between culturally-constructed myths of "woman," of which real women are rightly contemptuous, and real women. We might also note the praise for contempt that Zarathustra offers in his prologue: "What is the greatest thing you can experience? It is the hour of the great contempt" (3)—that time when old values are burned away by one's own self-contempt. The sex change, from "the man's" contempt for the woman, to women's, redirects the focus and the implicit address to women.

This redirection of focus to women happens in the Tautenburg notebooks several times, because for once Nietzsche has a genuine female interlocutor, and because he holds to his own stylistic principle—written for her—that writing should address "one quite definite person to whom you [*du*, second person familiar] wish to communicate: Law of Double Relation."[5] The essay on woman that Salomé apparently wrote, for example, is drafted, or redrafted, by Nietzsche,[6] with an opening paragraph that explicitly focuses on women as originators of ideas. Salomé wishes to examine the topic of woman as "the weaker sex." Nietzsche writes, or rewrites: "'Yes, a weak sex!'—men say this about women, and women also say it about themselves, but who believes that they think the same thing when they use the same words? Let's leave the men to think what they want, for once; what does a woman usually mean, when she speaks of the weakness of her sex?" (*KSA* 10:39).

The caveat "for once" indicates that the collaborators are aware that men "usually" write and publish what they think, even about what women think, while women do not. Here they enjoin—let women think, and speak, for themselves, for once! As the basis for a beginning, the draft works well. It calls attention to the person of the speaker; it denies the notion of the universal speaking subject; it particularizes according to gender, implying that knowledge is perspectival. The rest of the fragmentary essay explains women's legendary weakness as a process whereby belief in weakness is self-fulfilling. Because woman believes she needs a support or prop to lean on outside of herself, she deceives herself "gladly" about the strength of others and she "will not ask, whether the railing that goes over the flood to her, really supports her, because she believes in her weakness and fear."[7]

The need for strength beyond herself, the fragment maintains, has cultural implications, in that it has created both gods and men-as-gods. "The weakest woman will make a god of every man," Salomé and Nietzsche write, and "it is very obvious that for the origin of religion, the weaker sex is more important than the stronger" (*KSA* 10:40). In diagnosing the cultural consequences of women's supposed weakness, the fragment provides a psychological counterpart to Bachofen's "historical" argument that woman initiated religion. It also makes evident the psychological motor that is the relation between men and women, which circa 1882 encourages women's continuing weakness (since women's weakness continues to make men feel strong and godlike). To return to the opening paragraph—men then speak of women as the weak sex and feel stronger, while women speak of women as the weak sex and feel weaker.

In this draft, Salomé and Nietzsche uphold the heterosexual opposition, but in doing so they suggest several things about "the weaker sex," and about the opposition itself. They imply that woman likes her position; that woman's weakness has had remarkable effects in the production of "supports" in moral laws and religious myths, including the creation of gods; that woman's lack of self-confidence in effect acts as a support to men's; and that "as women go," heterosexual relations will continue as they are, unless women themselves make a change. Men have no reason to challenge a status quo that makes them gods for half of the human race.

These ideas, jotted down in a summer notebook after (or during) conversations between two extraordinary people, have become a staple of feminist critiques of the position of women in modern society. That Nietzsche understood their future import is not, I think, in doubt. The direction his thought would turn; the manner in which he would treat "the weak woman" in his own writing after his "Lou experience"; the way in which the implications of Salomé's analysis fit with his already strong commitment to values of "the feminine" as represented by the body, emotions, the unconscious, and "nature"—these are questions that are addressed in his work starting in January, 1883, when, in a burst of inspiration, he wrote the part 1 of *Thus Spoke Zarathustra* in ten days.

After the meeting of Salomé and Nietzsche in Leipzig October 1882, relations soured among the three friends. Elisabeth Nietzsche continued to inveigh against Salomé; plans for the study threesome were abandoned; letters of accusation flew back and forth. There are draft letters by Nietzsche which document his rage, offended pride, disappointment, and grief—at himself, Rée, Salomé, his sister, and the whole fundamentally banal situation. Relations with his sister never completely mended and Nietzsche finally broke with her over her marriage to Bernard Förster, an anti-Semite. His attitude to Salomé remains ambivalent in the correspondence from late 1882—and perhaps evermore.

In one setting, he is the proud teacher of a promising pupil; for example, Binyon reports Salomé's confession to her diary after a few days at Tautenburg that Nietzsche "has given up on being my teacher; he says I should never have such a prop." Binyon notes that this means, "on their terms, never be a woman" (82). This seems most likely if by "woman" Binyon means a weakling; Nietzsche wants Salomé to grow, to "become who she is," to be strong. He is clearly very impressed by her and not a little infatuated.

By the final round of letters he is hostile, vengeful, and vicious, wielding the verbal whip. According to Binyon, Nietzsche sent "three or four" letters to Salomé before the end of 1882, but he drafted many more, both to and about her. The language and the tone of these letters and drafts, familiar as they are to readers of Nietzsche's published works, is worth consideration. It is the voice of resentment toward women. "How stunted your humanity looks," he tells her; he notes that she is perverting her impulse to "sacred self-seeking" into "the predatory pleasure-lust of a cat"—"a cat's character: that of a beast of prey posing as a domestic animal. . . . strong will, but with no great object; without diligence or cleanliness, without civil probity; cruelly misplaced sensuality." And again, "My dear Lou, I must write you a nasty little note. For heaven's sake, what do these little girls of twenty think who have pleasant feelings of love and nothing to do but be sick now and again and lie in bed? Ought one perhaps to run after these little girls to chase away the boredom and the flies?" And on, "Formerly I was inclined to take you for a vision, for the earthly apparition of my ideal. Observe: I have poor eyes." And then, "But Lou, what letters you write! Little vengeful schoolgirls write that way: what use have I for such paltry stuff? Do understand: I want you to raise yourself before me, not lower yourself still further. . . . I wanted the sky clear between us, but you are a little gallows-bird." And finally, "Adieu, my dear Lou . . . I did not create the world and Lou, I wish I had—then I could bear the guilt alone for its having come to this between us" (in Binyon 99–101). The relationship ended in October, after only five months, and a note Salomé wrote during the stay in Tautenburg provides an epitaph: "Only because we are so kindred could he take the difference between us, or what seemed to him such, so violently and painfully" (in Martin 79).

Giving Birth to Zarathustra

Commentators have had fun assigning mother/father roles to the genesis and production of *Thus Spoke Zarathustra*. They take their cue from Nietzsche, who noted in a letter to Gast (dated April, 1883, after *Zarathustra* I was published), "I am a soldier—and this soldier, in the end, did become the father of Zarathustra! This paternity was his hope" (L 211). In *Ecce Homo*, by contrast, paternity becomes maternity, and Nietzsche dates the conception from the moment when the thought of eternal recurrence was "penned" in August, 1881, so calculating the time of gestation to be 18 months, a period that "might suggest, at least to Buddhists, that I am really a female elephant" ("Thus Spoke Zarathustra" 1). Salomé describes Zarathustra as Nietzsche's "son": together she and Nietzsche "laid plans for his son Zarathustra. 'We shall yet see him the prophet of a new religion,'" Salomé wrote in her diary (Binyon 81). For Binyon, however, Salomé is the father; he writes of the "delivery" of part I of *Thus Spoke Zarathustra*, Nietzsche's "son by Lou," which owed her his begetting (102).

Informed by Nietzsche's reference to Salomé in *Ecce Homo*, Gary Shapiro similarly asserts that she should be considered the father of the work; Nietzsche writes that he received a poem entitled "Hymn to Life" during his extended period of gestation, the "amazing inspiration of a young Russian woman who was my friend at the time, Miss Lou von Salomé." He describes why he likes the poem so much ("Pain is not considered an objection to life") and observes that the poem was "a scarcely trivial symptom of my condition during that year when the yes-saying pathos . . . was alive in me to the highest degree" (*EH* "Zarathustra"). Shapiro suggests that Nietzsche included the two paragraphs about the poem which tell of birth and pain, male and female, and its author, Salomé, "to make sure that we do not misunderstand how these are associated with the genesis of *Zarathustra*" (*Alcyone* 128). That the genesis of *Zarathustra* involved Lou Salomé and the exhilarating and humiliating experiences of 1882 is clear to anyone who takes a biographical approach to the text.[8]

Nietzsche gave birth to *Thus Spoke Zarathustra* by fits and starts, more like a cat than an elephant, and the birth was multiple—eventually four parts appeared. As deliveries go, the first three of these came not only easily and quickly, but painlessly and euphorically, according to Nietzsche's account in *Ecce Homo*. The labor before each birth, however, as documented in letters Nietzsche sent to friends Overbeck and Gast, was protracted and difficult. The images of the letters occasionally turns up in *Zarathustra,* and their central motif, that of self-overcoming, is central also to the text. As Nietzsche wrote to Overbeck, on December 25, 1882: "This last morsel of life was the hardest I have yet had to chew, and it is still possible that I shall choke on it. I have suffered from the humiliating and tormenting memories of this summer as from a bout of madness. . . . Unless I discover the alchemical trick of turning this—muck into gold, I am lost" (*L* 198–99). After this, in January 1883, part 1 of *Zarathustra* streamed forth in ten days ("ten absolutely serene and fresh January days," he notes to Gast [*L* 208]). Nietzsche was then beset once more with a month of pain; to Overbeck he confided, in February, 1883, "I will not conceal it from you, I am in a bad way. It is night all around me again . . . I think I shall inevitably go to pieces" (*L* 206). In July 1883, part 2 of *Zarathustra* was written, again in ten euphoric days; this was followed by a relapse, exacerbated by his sister's successful attempts to stoke Nietzsche's hostilities toward Salomé and Rée.

Elisabeth persuaded her brother to write a letter of complaint about Salomé to Lou's mother, which he immediately regretted; afterward he told his sister, "It is only now that I feel truly humiliated" (*L* 215). He echoes this in a letter to Overbeck: "Every contemptuous word that is written against Rée or Frl. Salomé makes my heart bleed; it seems I am not made to be anyone's enemy (whereas my sister recently wrote that I should be in good spirits, that this was a 'brisk and jolly war')" (*L* 215). In August, 1883, he goes on to write to his friend: "I am still the incarnate wrestling match, so that your dear wife's recent requests made me feel as if someone were asking old Laocoön to set about it and vanquish his serpents. . . . The danger is extreme. My nature is all too concentrated, and whatever strikes me moves straight to my center" (*L* 214–15).

Part 3 of *Zarathustra* emerged out of this struggle with serpents in January, 1884. On January 26, Overbeck received this expression of thanksgiving: "The last two weeks have been the happiest ones in my life: I have never sailed with such sails across such a sea, and the terrific, exuberant daring of the whole mariner's tale, which has been going on for as long as you have known me, since 1870, reached its climax" (*L* 220). With the completion of parts 1 through 3 of *Zarathustra*, Nietzsche feels he has finished the work he started in Basel, the work begun in the early notes and drafts for *The Birth of Tragedy*. He confessed to Overbeck, after the part 1 was printed, that he poured "himself" into *Zarathustra*, noting that the work "contains an image of myself in the sharpest focus, as I am, once I have thrown off my whole burden. It is poetry, not a collection of aphorisms" (*L* 206–7). And his professed hopes, on the publication of *Beyond Good and Evil*, are that this latest work "will have the effect of shedding a few rays of light on my *Zarathustra*, which is an unintelligible book, because it is based on experiences which I share with nobody" (*L* 254). He urges Overbeck to read his earlier works as introductions ("It is a fact that I did the commentary before writing the text" [*L* 223]), and his later works as "afterwords," to *Zarathustra*.

In the preface to the second volume of *Human, All Too Human*, written in 1886, Nietzsche turns to the subject of his own work as autobiography: "My writings speak only of my overcomings. . . . But it has always required time, recovery, distancing, before the desire awoke within me to skin, exploit, expose, 'exhibit,' (or whatever one wants to call it) for the sake of knowledge something I had experienced and survived, some fact or fate of my life. To this extent, all my writings, with a single though admittedly substantial exception, are to be dated back—they always speak of something 'behind me'" (209). (The next sentence admits that *The Birth of Tragedy* is the exception, written while Nietzsche was still passionate about Wagner.) This profession sounds very much like Salomé's analysis of the cycles from experience to knowledge through which Nietzsche typically passes (as set forth in her study of his work). Although she must have been perfectly aware of it, she does not mention that the "experience riddle" Nietzsche puts behind him, beginning with *Zarathustra*, has to do with her. She becomes part of the "knowledge riddle" on which he has been fixed since 1870; as Life, as Wisdom, as Truth, and as Sensuality, she embodies it.

Knowing that Nietzsche found one captivating and intelligent woman, flesh and blood rather than figurative, with whom he drafted aphorisms on "woman," helps to throw some light on the disparagement and the praise of women that occurs in *Thus Spoke Zarathustra*. But the light is dappled—it is twilight—it plays tricks on the eyes. Biography is useful here; if we read the agreeable letters that Nietzsche wrote Salomé, the poems inspired by her, the notes that both of them took during their encounters, and especially the anger and pain of the work that followed their breakup, we simply cannot dismiss Nietzsche out of hand as a misogynist. As a particularly private and vulnerable person, he hid the deepest things, love first and foremost. He tells us as much over and over again. "This spiritual, silent haughtiness of the sufferer . . . finds all forms of disguise necessary to protect itself" (*BGE* 270), he writes; "does one not write books precisely to conceal what lies within us? . . . Every philosophy also conceals a philosophy; every opinion is also a hiding-place, every word also a mask" (*BGE* 289). Caroline Picart (1999) argues that the mask of his writing hides a resentment of women so deep that it poisons Nietzsche's life and ultimately his philosophy. I would assert rather that the resentment is the mask; it is there, on the surface, for all to see and hear. This is particularly evident with regard to the whip, which as symbol of violent emotion is hard to ignore. In *Daybreak*, Nietzsche writes: "Whenever a person reveals something, one can ask: what is it supposed to conceal? From what is it supposed to divert the eyes? What prejudice is it supposed to arouse?" (523). That Nietzsche's textual resentment of women arouses some readers' prejudice is clear; from what, we might ask, does this divert their eyes? I think the mask of resentment, and the noise of the whip, both conceal and reveal the *reality* of love, which is a complex combination of contradictory emotions and psychological needs. The reality includes both negative and positive charges— both of which are capable of creating art—but in *Zarathustra*, the positive, affirming aspects of love, including gratitude and joy, overcome the negative power of resentment (although it is a close call).

Zarathustrian Contexts 2: Apollo (Text)

The "instincts" that Nietzsche is persuaded guide the pen of every philosopher can be understood as the textual unconscious, appearing as images and symbols, verbal repetitions, distortions and other dream phenomena, and silences, all of which indicate Dionysus at work "in the depths," providing the affective energy that powers the formal elements of the text. The passions of loss, sexual desire, anger, shame, jealousy—all these affects of the summer's madness combined with Nietzsche's persistent ill health—effect for him a state of being resembling "woe", a mother of tragedy. This state of woe in turn inspires the creative will (itself a mother of tragedy), enabling Nietzsche to use the affects creatively—to turn, as he puts it, "all the muck into gold."

This artistic alchemy is accomplished through the tricks of Apollo, the conventions of formal technique. In *Thus Spoke Zarathustra,* Nietzsche uses so many different conventions, and alludes to so many different texts, that one critic describes the work as "an exemplary postmodern philosophical tale in which are inscribed an encyclopedic variety of the narrative functions of the West" (Shapiro *Nietzschean Narratives* 35). Readers have heard many echoes in *Zarathustra:* of the Bible; of the writings of Martin Luther, Plato, the pre-Socratics (especially Heraclitus), and Apuleius; of romantic poetry (Goethe's "Faust," Shelley's "Prometheus"), Wagnerian librettos (especially *The Ring of the Nibelungen*), and "orientalism," and even an early nineteenth-century book of adventure stories.[9]

A number of commentators have deplored what they take to be the rhetorical excesses of *Zarathustra*'s style. Thomas Mann, for example, a great admirer of Nietzsche's writing, made an exception for this book and its eponymous hero: "Zarathustra is rhetoric, excited word play, tortured voice and doubtful prophecy, a model of helpless grandezza, often moving and almost always embarrassing—a non-figure staggering at the borderline of the ridiculous" (340). One of *Zarathustra*'s English translators, R. J. Hollingdale, begins his introduction to the text by emphasizing its style or manner, observing that "the book's worst fault is excess" (*Z* p. 11). And Hans-Georg Gadamer summarizes his take on *Zarathustra* with these words: "The style of this book is not to everyone's taste, in any event not to mine nor that of my generation! . . . The form of speech in these discourses is far removed from us" (221, 223).

I think that these comments—that the style approaches the borderline of the ridiculous, or is excessive, or is far removed from us—give us a clue to understanding the genre of *Zarathustra.* Nietzsche's own insistence on the possibilities of parody, and of modernity's need for comedy; his wish that Wagner had written *Parsifal* as parody or a satyr play, because a great tragedian "only arrives at the pinnacle of his greatness when he comes to see himself and his art beneath him—when he knows how to laugh at himself" (*GM* 3:3); his own hints about the wickedness and fun of *Zarathustra*—all of these lead me to hypothesize that the book is a parody on ancient lines, something like Menippean satire.[10]

It is easy to assert that *Zarathustra* is a late—a very late—example of Menippean satire, and impossible to prove it, because we have no examples of the model genre. What we have are a very few ancient imitations and a lot of speculation about what constituted the genre. We do know that it is named for Menippus, a Cynic philosopher of the third century BC, and although nothing by him survives, "there is no reason to doubt that, in keeping with the general Cynic tradition, both quotation and parody had a prominent role" (*Oxford Classical Dictionary* 959–60). The Cynics wrote in every genre, but were especially celebrated for their use of anecdote, diatribe, literary parody, soliloquy, satiric spirit, and seriocomic discourse. We learn something of Menippus from the work of Diogenes Laertius, and from that of Varro in first-century (BCE) Rome, who wrote *Saturae Menippeae* in 150 books, of which 90 titles and 600 fragments survive. The *Satyrica* of Petronius (Petronius Arbiter, who died in 66 CE) draws on Varro and contains many elements of Menippean satire; parodying both literary and social conventions, it includes travesties of Plato, speeches by a disreputable vagabond, long extracts in verse, tragic scenarios, a mock dinner party, emphasis on the "lower" bodily functions, and lots of sex, both straight and gay (with emphasis on the latter). The idea of "mixtures and misalliances of all kinds" typifies Menippean satire (Branham and Kinney xvii).

As an undergraduate at Leipzig, Nietzsche studied this tradition; in his final year, he spoke at the Classical Society on "Varro's Satires and the Cynic Menippus." Just before moving to Basel to take up his university position, he wrote his friend Erwin Rohde that, with his hands at last free to do what he liked, "it will feel like being a bridegroom, joy and vexation mingled, humor . . . Menippus!" (*L* 36–37). Nietzsche's juxtaposition of the theme of the commencement of his life's work (the serious) with the simile of the bridegroom, suggesting possible confusions and embarrassments of sexual inexperience (the salacious, or the ridiculous), performs a small Menippean satire in itself.

Beyond these student references, Nietzsche remains interested in this generic form, considering it both "liberating" and decadent.[11] He praises Petronius, both as a model and as a tool for overcoming biblical heaviness, in a discarded fragment of *Ecce Homo*, where he calls the satire "exuberant," "liberating," and "Dionysian," and applauds its good spirits (*EH* Appendix 1). These are terms that Nietzsche uses in *Ecce Homo* to describe his own work as well, particularly *Thus Spoke Zarathustra*. And with an earlier aphorism in *Human, All Too Human,* he praises another practitioner of this capacious genre, the English novelist Laurence Sterne:

The most liberated writer . . . Sterne is the great master of ambiguity—this word taken in a far wider sense than is usually done when it is accorded only a sexual signification. The reader who demands to know exactly what Sterne really thinks of a thing, whether he is making a serious or a laughing face, must be given up for lost: for he knows how to encompass both in a single facial expression; he . . . even wants to be in the right and in the wrong at the same time, to knot together profundity and farce. (*HAH* 2:113)

When Nietzsche writes "ambiguity," the first association that comes to his mind is "sexual"; after that, the ambiguity of genre is key. The two sorts of ambiguity, sexual and textual, are knotted together in *Zarathustra*, which, like *Tristram Shandy*, also knots together profundity and farce.

On completing part 1 of *Zarathustra*, Nietzsche writes Gast that this work is "the most liberated of all my productions" (*L* 208). According to his later description, the book practically wrote itself, as if from inspired dictation: "One hears, one does not seek; one accepts, one does not ask who gives; like lightning, a thought flashes up, with necessity, without hesitation regarding its form—I never had any choice" (*EH* "Zarathustra" 3). Yet this very compulsion was freedom. Working under strong emotional pressure, Nietzsche found that the words he had gathered over the years in his memory (and in his letters, books, and notebooks) suddenly became available. I do not think that Nietzsche had a choice about genre, either. He began the text intending to write a tragedy, but he couldn't bring it off; he couldn't keep a serious face and make Zarathustra die, which by rights he should have done, to be consistent with the opening narrative motif ("Thus began Zarathustra's down-going"—*Untergang*, or "perishing") and with the scenarios in the notebooks.[12]

The "liberating" genre—ironic, parodic—was the one he had to use. Parody enabled him to pour "himself" into the text and so "confess" in a therapeutic orgy, while at the same time transforming himself according to the demands of the genres he parodied. It freed him from himself—by the very act of mirroring, or parodying, himself. An ironic, parodic genre allowed him to steal and patch together, reinvent and elaborate, familiar material from three incompatible traditions: ancient, Christian, and modern romantic. Themes, narrative plots, images, even actual words from works in these traditions—together with his own words and those of friends and foes in his personal life—served to formalize Nietzsche's rage, pain, humiliation, and triumph in this text, and reworked traditional discourses in order to present them for readers' reappraisal.

Russian Formalist M. M. Bakhtin revived an interest in Menippean satire as a theoretical subject. In his writings, he argues that the ancient parodic-travestying forms provided "the corrective of reality that is always richer, more fundamental and most importantly too contradictory and hetero-glot to fit into a high and straight-forward genre" (55). Bakhtin asserts that the experimentation of Menippean satire led to the development of the novel because it "liberated" the writer from the idea that language and reality were one (60), and celebrates the alienating move that Nietzsche on one level deplores in *The Birth of Tragedy,* the move that hastens the down-fall of religion by inserting the liberating "space" of irony into discourse. Bakhtin is interested in the ways in which "the carnivalesque" genres, through their mocking irreverence, and the clash of subject perspectives (which he called "the dialogic") were able to subvert the more authoritarian "monologic" discourses of the single addresser and point of view.[13]

Carnivals are festive community celebrations stemming from remotest times. In their European manifestations they authorize the subversion of authority, the enactment of a topsy-turvy world "in which fish fly and birds swim, in which foxes and rabbits chase hunters, bishops behave crazily and fools are crowned." In the space of the carnival, "we are liberated from the fear imposed by the existence of the rule" (Eco 2). From Mardi Gras to Gay Pride parades, from ancient times to the present, the subversion of gender roles, the mocking of gender conventions that regulate social behavior (Eco 15), has been a key feature of carnival. In carnivalesque, Menippean discourse, we similarly find a subversion of the laws of gender, as with the laws of genre. If Petronius's *Satyrica* at least partly exemplifies Menippean satire, then all of these, genders and genres, are shown to be polymorphous, multiple, ambiguous.

Thus Spoke Zarathustra is an example of this ancient motley; full to over-flowing, it is "pregnant" discourse, the type that conceives and gives birth to the excesses and the contradictions of a most duplicitous text. Like ancient parodistic genres, *Zarathustra* is a serious/humorous philosophical fable. The humor lies principally in the parodies of the Bible and the clas-sics that mark Zarathustra's "discourses"; the seriousness is found in the satire on modernity, and the veiled suggestions of the ways in which a sick society may be healed. For what is it that Nietzsche is "sending up," or par-odying, in *Thus Spoke Zarathustra?* It is the whole, motley culture—men, women, and children, with Nietzsche included, and their lack of purpose, responsibility, generosity, and love for each other and the earth—as well as its lack of sustaining cultural myths and of the tragic understanding of life. *Zarathustra* undertakes a rereading of past traditions of the West, and in our very act of working through the text, it similarly submits itself to a rereading, by quoting earlier passages in a kind of musical recapitulation of various themes. The text thus obliges its audience to perform a double reading—of the traditions, and of Zarathustra's story. The repetition piles present upon past with the result that we relate to both, and neither. We float, unconnected, free to evaluate.

As we do so, we may notice the relative absence of references to women in the text. Its narrator, central character, narratees, and all of its parodic models are masculine. When women do appear, it is as objects of passing negative comments. This absence of women characters is remarkable and it calls attention to itself. If *Thus Spoke Zarathustra* satirizes the whole of Western civilization and its wisest teachings, by this omission it effectively points to the very great "gender imbalance" of this tradition, and to the scorn with which, on the whole, it has treated women discursively. In *The Birth of Tragedy,* women are invisible. Zarathustra introduces a panoply of professions—tightrope walkers, buffoons, "wise men" with their academic chairs, criminals, warriors, politicians, "great men," journalists, priests, "sublime men," scholars, poets, prophets—yet women are still invisible on the public stage. They are good for one thing only, adept at one job: pregnancy and childbirth. Thus spoke Zarathustra, mimicking and calling attention to our cultural genealogy.

Thus Spoke Zarathustra: Reading as an Erotic Contest

To whom does the text of *Zarathustra* address itself—internally to what cast of narratees, and externally to what sort of implied readers? These questions and their answers are as important in discussing Zarathustra's whip and the Woman Question as are biography and genre—and perhaps more so, because readers determine a text's interpretation. After all, the whip is in the reader's hand. Nietzsche always kept one of his several eyes cocked in the direction of his readers, those of the present and especially, of the future.

Readers are connected to narratives through the formal devices of narration. *Zarathustra* is narrated either in the first person, by Zarathustra, or in the third person "indirect" mode, where the point of view is Zarathustra's.[14] Even though Zarathustra directs the narration of the text, it is clear that he does not speak from a "monological" position; he is himself a battleground of conflicting opinions and desires, whose "voices" appear in the text as parody of other texts, as dreams and visions, as half-spoken thoughts, and as the array of allegorized figures with whom he speaks.

Zarathustra's narratees—the characters to whom the text is directed inside the narrative (that is, apart from the allegorical figures who are extensions of Zarathustra himself)—may be varied, but they are nearly all men or boys. The single exception is the little old woman who hands Zarathustra the symbolic whip to use when he visits women. Most of Zarathustra's discourses are addressed to "My brothers," or occasionally to "a young man" or "the wisest men." The characters who appear in part 4—the Higher Men—are all male. The exclusion of women narratees is especially significant in a text that, by parodying its models, presumes to offer a message of high moral import; readers identify with narratees, who are in this case almost all men. Is it part of the text's strategy of the mimicry of its religious and philosophical prototypes that women are so excluded? Consciously or unconsciously, was Nietzsche taking revenge on Salomé and his sister for the emotional tangle they landed him in, by using men only as Zarathustra's audience? Are there other explanations for the virtual absence of women from the text's narrative structure?

I take my cue here from *The Birth of Tragedy,* where women's absence is actually highlighted by the anomaly of two male gods metaphorically conceiving a child. In that text, the feminine is largely appropriated by Dionysus and the Dionysian outlook, and spliced with the Apollonian to create the artist, presumably a male. "Feminine" characteristics are inscribed as masculine throughout the work, in order to describe the art—tragedy—that brings its audience face to face with the unconscious, with suffering, and with death (all traditionally associated with the feminine). I hold that something similar occurs in *Thus Spoke Zarathustra,* and that the text's very blatant "masculinity"—including Zarathustra's repeated injunction to the disciples and the Higher Men to "become hard"—masks a further, additional, hidden imperative: to become feminine. Indeed, one of Nietzsche's prescriptions for addressing the sickness of late nineteenth-century European manliness is an explicit exhortation to men to be less—and an implicit one to be more—like women. If this is so, then *Zarathustra* is carnivalesque, in terms of both genre and gender.

The narration's subjectivity and Zarathustra's voluntary social isolation in parts 2 and 3 are consistent with Nietzsche's response to one of the ethical questions of the text—namely, how do we create healthy autonomous individuals, those so complete that they can survive and thrive without God? Such persons must contain "multitudes," as Walt Whitman put it ("I am large; I contain multitudes"), and the multitudes must possess characteristics of both genders. Nietzsche, as a male, speaks in *Zarathustra* through a masculine character to masculine listeners, but he does not presume to speak for all other males; as wisdom literature, this book deviates from its models by not prescribing a set of rules as The Way. As the text observes: "This—is now my way: where is yours? Thus I answered those who asked me 'the way.' For *the* way—does not exist!" (3 "Of the Spirit of Gravity"). In the next chapter, I examine the ways in which I think the text preaches the feminine, indirectly but surely, to a masculine audience. Here I want to speculate on how the exclusion of women as narratees (with the single noted significant exception) may affect readers and their interpretations of *Zarathustra*.

As readers, women are not explicitly forbidden the gate to *Zarathustra*, but the narrative does not address them, and they are not part of the social world of Zarathustra's adventures, and thus for the moment I want to treat them as excluded readers. In her analysis of narrative in general, Marie Maclean points out that the excluded woman reader is in some ways in an enviable position with regard to the text. She may find herself in an ironic relation to the text; "the excluded reader can play a very positive role by bringing a new and frequently ironic perspective to bear on performances designed for others" (38). Whether the response is emotional or intellectual, or a combination perhaps, the excluded reader, through her absence, plays an important role in the narrative drama. Benjamin Bennett makes this point with specific reference to Nietzsche's texts. He argues that being a masculine reader of Nietzsche's later texts, "a qualified reader, a reader addressed by the text and in a position to understand it, denies one the possibility of making any reasonable historical use of one's understanding." Being a "disqualified" reader, on the other hand—a woman, a reader "excluded from the text's projected community of understanding"— gives one an opportunity to "use" the texts for one's own revolutionary purposes (296). Nietzsche's phrases about woman suddenly sound very different when they are repeated by a woman. The change of the speaker's gender automatically brings a new, ironic perspective to bear on the gender-exclusive text.

Keeping in mind the privileges of the excluded reader—an ability to bring a different perspective to a text from which she is excluded, a perspective that may act as interpretive leverage—and recalling the text's generic possibilities as "Menippean satire" or as parody, let us take a closer look at some antithetical gestures that *Zarathustra* makes simply in terms of its address to readers, beginning with the subtitle: "A Book for Everyone and No One." On the one hand, the excluded reader here is every reader, including men. On the other, no one is excluded, including women. In setting this paradox on the very doorstep of the book, Nietzsche focuses attention on his readership, and on reading. Once inside, having taken up the invitation to be one with everyone, readers of both sexes find that Zarathustra addresses his discourses to men alone. By now it is too late. Women have entered, but as aliens, in a potentially subversive position. To be sure, some women readers may not notice that Zarathustra addresses only men; they may well be seduced by the narration to read from the male vantage point, and join the brothers. But those women who do notice their exclusion on the grounds of gender may well become voyeurs. They may form a skeptical claque. They may laugh. And outside the narrative frame, they can settle down irresponsibly to enjoy, and criticize, the show. Nothing is asked of them. They shouldn't even be there. They aren't there. If the ironies of this parodic text create a sense of freedom for a "qualified" reader, a masculine reader, then the effect may be intensified for women.

According to Ross Chambers, reading itself can produce opposition to structures of power that repress desire and oppress people. It can do so by virtue of the "room for maneuver" that is built into oppositional texts, wherein the text belongs to the power structures of its historical period and also transcends them through its use of irony and its "adroitness of address" (*Room for Maneuver* 2). In the case of *Zarathustra*, the text distances itself from the power structures of the historical periods of its parodic models, and through its narrative address to a strictly male audience it identifies women readers as interpretive subjects—that is, as readers defined oppositionally in relation to the text. As interpetive subjects, they are enabled to make conjectures about the text's intentions as "other" than these seem, producing oppositional readings.

Women's position as ironically privileged by their exclusion as narratees and actors in the text is subtly underlined by *Zarathustra*'s address to its model (or "implied") readers. These are readers outside the narrative toward whom the text is directed as the ones most likely to solve its riddles. Nietzsche places a major riddle at the center of the work, and before it is uttered, Zarathustra defines "the right" listeners, the ones capable of understanding it and who therefore have the best chance of solving it: "To you, the bold venturers and adventurers and whoever has embarked with cunning sails upon dreadful seas, to you who are intoxicated by riddles, who take pleasure in twilight, whose soul is lured with flutes to every treacherous abyss—for you do not desire to feel for a rope with cowardly hands; and where you can guess you hate to calculate—to you alone do I tell this riddle that I saw—" (Z 3 "The Vision and the Riddle" 1).

On a literal level, Zarathustra's narratees are at this point sailors on shipboard, but it is clear that Nietzsche is defining his model readers, for he repeats this description in general terms in *Ecce Homo* ("Why I Write Such Good Books" 3). Using a "rope" as guide is equivalent to "calculating"— that is, using science or logic—to solve a problem. By contrast, Zarathustra would rather have his readers "guess" or intuit their solutions to his textual enigmas. Indeed, they have little choice, for riddles cannot be "calculated." With this designation of his perfect reader, Nietzsche returns to the preference for the intuitive "feminine" Dionysian way to truth over Socratic "masculine" reasoning, a choice which informs *The Birth of Tragedy*. *Zarathustra*'s readers will be "intoxicated" by riddles, and "lured by flutes" to "treacherous abysses"—all Dionysian qualities; they will "take pleasure in twilight," that half-and-half state of nature, the gray area between logical oppositions, the area of ambiguity. In short, Nietzsche's perfect readers are happy with ambiguity and seek solutions to riddles in these terms. There is an obvious gender dimension to Zarathustra's description of his riddle-solvers: they exhibit, or have respect for, Dionysian qualities that culture has defined as feminine.

Zarathustra also addresses his listeners as "searchers and researchers" (*Sucher* and *Versucher*). *Versucher* means "attempter" as well as "researcher"— the former as in an experimenter who is ready to test his/her conjectures and to rethink his/her assumptions. However, Karsten Harries tells us that it also means "first of all" a tempter, or indeed *the* tempter: "The devil, who tempted Adam and Eve with the promise that their eyes would be opened and they would be like God, knowing Good and Evil, is the Versucher" (30). The tempter in the book of Genesis takes the shape of a serpent, a figure who beguiles the woman, who in turn beguiles the man. Stopping here, we can infer that Nietzsche's job description for the perfect reader and riddle-solver includes the characteristic of the "tempter," *Versucher*. In this capacity, the serpent and the woman both qualify as Nietzsche's readers, but the man does not.

Thus Spoke Zarathustra addresses men and boys inside the narrative and privileges women as oppositional readers. This address to model readers thus opens a line to women while not excluding men—unless, of course, the parodic Menippean turns of sexual/textual ambiguity have loosened and jumbled a reader's sense of sexual identity, and by doing so made it possible for a man to read as a woman, a woman as a man, or both to read as both, and neither.

"On Little Old and Young Women" and Zarathustra's Whip

Thus Spoke Zarathustra devotes only one chapter out of eighty to the subject of "woman," and its passing references to actual women are slighting. References to females are divided between "woman" (*das Weib,* the far larger group) and "women" (*die Frauen,* a courteous form of address); the latter refers to a class of females whom the reader might actually know, and occurs very seldom in this or any other Nietzschean text. When it does appear, the reader does well to heed the distinction its presence draws with the more common *Weib,* as, for example, in the line about the whip. Recall that this reads as follows—*Du gehst zu Frauen? Vergiss die Peitsche nicht!* ["Are you going to *women*? Don't forget the whip!"]—suggesting that one would need particularly to remember the whip with those women in one's acquaintance.

I'll begin this discussion with a survey of references to *das Weib,* "woman." To set the narrative scene: Zarathustra, type of the prophet and holy man, has come down from his mountain, encountered an old hermit in the forest, and preached the Übermensch to "many people assembled in the market square." Presumably the crowd is made up of villagers of both sexes. When they jeer and laugh at the message of the Übermensch, Zarathustra warns the crowd about the "Last Man," but still they laugh. And so Zarathustra leaves them, and decides henceforth to speak, not to the "herd," which despises him as a lawbreaker and a smasher of their tables of values, but to fellow creators, "those who inscribe new values on new tables." His decision, "I will not speak again to the people," henceforth excludes women as interlocutors; his own companions, "the lone hermit and the hermits in pairs" (a reference to brothers, or to gay couples, perhaps) from here on out will be males, to and with whom he speaks *about* woman (Z Prologue 3, 5, 9). When he speaks about woman, what does he say? Quantitatively, not very much— and qualitatively even less. In sequential order, and in a tone of voice and spirit reminiscent of Nietzsche's nasty letters to Salomé, "woman" appears thus:

1. *As pretty sweet little girls.* Halfway into part 1, in a chapter entitled "Of War and Warriors," we read: "'What is good?' you ask. To be brave is good. Let the little girls say: 'To be good is to be what is pretty and at the same time touching.'"

2. *As a lustful sexual being, a bitch.* In "Of Chastity" (Z 1), Zarathustra argues against chastity for most men, but nonetheless labels woman as temptress:

"Is it not better to fall into the hands of a murderer than into the dreams of a lustful woman? . . . And how nicely the bitch Sensuality knows how to beg for a piece of spirit, when a piece of flesh is denied her."

3. *As slaves, tyrants, cats, birds, and cows.* Of the twenty-seven aphorisms in the chapter on friendship ("Of the Friend," *Z* 1), four are devoted to woman, all of which develop the proposition that a woman cannot have, or be, a friend: "In woman, a slave and a tyrant have all too long been concealed. For that reason, woman is not yet capable of friendship: she knows only love. . . . Women still are cats and birds. Or, at best, cows." Then comes the reversal which, like the argument on chastity, is explicitly directed to men only: "Woman is not yet capable of friendship. But tell me, you men, which of you is yet capable of friendship?"

4. *As a little old woman, and as endless mothers.* These references occur in the chapter entitled "Of Old and Young Women" (*Z* 1)—also known as "On Little Old and Young Women" (*TSZ*)—which I will go on to discuss in further detail.

5. *As a piece of merchandise on the marriage market.* In the chapter called "Of Marriage and Children" (*Z* 1), which explicitly excludes women ("I have a question for you alone, my brother"), Zarathustra advises against buying damaged goods on the marriage market: "I have found all buyers cautious, and all of them have astute eyes. But even the most astute man buys his wife while she is still wrapped." Once married, the man may find that his package deal includes a goose, or a virago.

6. *As manly women.* These women need redemption (in other words, to be made pregnant) by real men. "There is little manliness here: therefore their women make themselves manly. For only he who is sufficiently a man will—*redeem the woman* in woman" (*Z* 2 "Of the Virtue that Makes Small"). This is recapitulated in *Ecce Homo*: "Has my answer been heard to the question how one *cures* a woman—'redeems' her? One gives her a child" ("Why I Write Such Good Books" 5).

7. *As breasts.* "And there are many things so well devised that they are like a woman's breasts: at the same time useful and pleasant" (*Z* 3 "Of Old and New Law-Tables" 17).

8. *As dancing mothers.* "This is how I would have man and woman: the one fit for war, the other fit for bearing children, but both fit for dancing with head and heels" (*Z* 3 "Of Old and New Law-Tables" 23).

9. *As wicked girls dancing naked*—referring to the Higher Men's lustful thoughts listening to the Sorcerer's song (*Z* 4 "Of Science")—and *as oriental dancing girls* in the Wanderer's song (*Z* 4 "Among the Daughters of the Desert").

There are a number of points to be made about these explicit references to woman as a generic class. The first is that there are so few; they occupy a small proportion of the text. The second is that they are caricatures, or masculine stereotypes; they do not refer to actual women, but rather parody cultural assumptions about the women of Nietzsche's time. The third is that we can discern something of the moralities of gender in Nietzsche's day between the lines of the caricature. Such a glimpse reveals a world where little girls are expected to be sweet and pretty and good; where women accord love the central part of their lives and are blind to all else; where women (like the little old woman) can be more misogynist than men; where women are kept under wraps until they are sold and bought on the marriage market, or otherwise displayed, bought, and sold as objects for men's sexual pleasure. It is a "man's world" where women are not much in evidence publicly, and where men speak to each other *about* women in conventional, stereotyped, and belittling or sexual terms, and congregate in separate schools, clubs, bars, jobs. Nietzsche's picture is beyond caricature; it is satire. The fourth is that, in degrading women, these references challenge the myth of the *Ewigweibliche,* the eternal feminine as moral guardian and redeemer of men, a dominant middle-class ideal across much of the Western world in the mid-nineteenth century. Far from redeeming others, these women are in need of redemption themselves, and not by being given a child (a point I think the text itself makes through its satire of "men on woman"). The fifth and final point is that the situation of the speaker in the text must be considered. He occupies a negative and reactive position in relation to real women: dogmatic and essentialist, Zarathustra believes that he knows what is good for "the true man" and how to solve the "riddle" of woman. When it comes to men and women, he holds to binary oppositions in their classical hierarchical form.

Like *The Birth of Tragedy, Thus Spoke Zarathustra* creates its myths, and undoes them, through patterns of repetition, association, similarities, and differences. One of its central myths is that of metamorphosis; as a process of internal transformation, this works textually, through metaphor, to highlight relations of similarity and difference. Zarathustra stresses the importance of transformation in the first of his discourses to his disciples, "Of the Three Metamorphoses." As we have noted in the previous chapter, he describes a spiritual movement from resentment (a resigned bearing of a load, metaphorized as a camel) to resistance (a refusal to continue bearing that load, represented as a lion) to a state of creative joy (which appears in the guise of a child). These constitute the ongoing cycle of "self-overcoming" that is Zarathustra's project. He speaks from all three places—often burdened with resentment, or with former values and old law-tables—frequently resistant of them all—and at times liberated, in a place of pure delight and affirmation.

The initial position—resentment—is that of the whip (whether used on oneself or another). I hold that the whip itself returns symbolically in a pattern of repetitions and differences and goes through two of the metamorphoses of the spirit—from being a tool of resentment, specifically of women and the feminine, to being a tool of resistance to that very resentment. The roar of the negative against the negative (saying No to no) successfully opens up a distance, creating a space for new creation, or new valuation. The negative flips over and becomes the positive, transforming itself as attitude or relation toward an "other."

The chapter entitled "On Little Old and Young Women"[15] occurs near the end of part 1, as Zarathustra is nearing the end of his first descent from his mountain retreat into the valleys of human habitation and culture.[16] In the chapter immediately preceding it, Zarathustra preaches "Of the Way of the Creator" which, he tells his "brother," is marked by solitude. He describes the burdens of solitude, warning that this state can produce its own special types of resentment. The solitary creator is assaulted by love, Zarathustra says, and "extends his hand too quickly to anyone he meets"— but apart from those whom he loves and then despises ("What does he know of love who has not had to despise precisely what he loved?"), he will always be his own worst enemy. As he observes: "You yourself will lie in wait for yourself in caves and forests. Solitary one, you are going the way to yourself! And your way leads past yourself and your seven devils" (Z 1 "Of the Way of the Creator"). By the beginning of the chapter on little young and old women, Zarathustra is observed uncharacteristically "slinking" or "stealing" shyly or cautiously through the twilight with something hidden "carefully" under his cloak.

His observer is also a "brother," one of his disciples, who asks him whether what he is hiding under his cloak is "a treasure someone has given you? Or a child that has been born to you?" Or, if neither, is Zarathustra now a thief? Zarathustra replies that the disciple's first two guesses are more or less correct; it is a treasure that has been given to him, as well as a "little truth" that is like a little child. We are in the generic realm of poetry, where truth is personified as a child small enough to be hidden beneath a cloak: that is, a baby truth. Zarathustra's attitude toward this baby is one of furtiveness, leading the disciple to suspect that he is carrying an illegitimate child. Zarathustra confirms that the little truth is, if not illegitimate, most certainly unruly, and given to crying "too loudly." The baby truth disturbs the peace; Zarathustra's response to the crying is to "stop its mouth."

This opening constitutes the first frame of the subsequent discourse on woman, and is accompanied by a second. Zarathustra tells his "brother" the story of how he came by the little truth: "Today as I was going my way alone, at the hour when the sun sets, a little old woman encountered me and spoke thus to my soul: 'Zarathustra has spoken much to us women, too, but he has never spoken to us about woman.' And I answered her: 'One should speak about women only to men.' 'Speak to me too of woman,' she said; 'I am old enough soon to forget it.'" ("Woman" and "women" here are *Weib* or *Weibern*.)

The actual discourse on woman and the occasion of the little old woman's parting gift are told in flashback. Chronologically, (1) Zarathustra encounters the little old woman, who asks him to speak to her about woman; (2) he does so; (3) she thanks him and gives him the "little truth"; (4) he steals through the twilight with the little truth under his cloak; and (5) he meets a disciple who asks him what he is doing. The story doubles back on itself in the telling. There is much to suggest that Zarathustra's encounter with the "little old woman" is illusory, and that among the doubles of this chapter, the little old woman is Zarathustra's. The dual frame around the actual "sayings" on woman has the effect, as frames do, of intensifying and distancing that which is framed, and of accenting its nature as artifice. Both narrative frames specify the time of day as twilight, a period of visual deception with connotations of ambiguity; neither day nor night, twilight is the in-between or liminal state, and as such is a witching hour, a time of magic. It is the time of day Zarathustra designates explicitly as pleasing to his perfect readers, those "who are intoxicated by riddles, who take pleasure in twilight" (Z 3 "Of the Vision and the Riddle"). Then the little old woman, accosting Zarathustra like a goblin in a fairy tale, speaks to his soul. She is the only character to do so (apart from Zarathustra himself, who does once address his sayings to his soul [Z 3 "Of the Great Longing"]).

The meeting with the little old woman is precisely the sort of "encounter" Zarathustra warned his brother about in "Of the Way of the Creator"—a meeting in the wilderness with one of his own seven devils, the worst enemies he can "encounter," who lie in wait for him. He names each of these—a heretic, a witch, a prophet, a fool, a doubter, an unholy one, and a villain—and tells his disciple that "you would create a god for yourself out of your seven devils." This sort of creation involves metamorphosis—transforming disparate parts of oneself into a whole "god," a liberated creator. On an allegorical level, the little old woman cast as one of his seven devils (the witch, most likely) joins the other fragments of Zarathustra that float through the text. Rather than treat her as an enemy, as by rights he ought to given his previous advice, he "obliges" her by speaking to her, as she requests, about woman.

The Whip as a Joke

In his conversation with Haussmann in Sils-Maria, Nietzsche characterized the line about the whip as a joke, and an "exaggerated, symbolic mode of expression," and said that it had arisen from a "personal memory." Taking the whip as a joke, the setting of "On Little Old and Young Women" is farcical, parodic. Zarathustra steals along like a villain in melodrama, concealing something under his cloak; the little old woman pops up out of nowhere and promises she is "old enough" to hear Zarathustra speak about woman— so old in fact that she'll forget whatever he says anyway! At this witching hour in this secluded place, he then begins to talk in a formal and rhetorical manner, in measured antitheses as from a rostrum. The formality of the speech is out of place, jarring, and calls attention to itself as parody.

Much of what is relayed is consistent with Judeo-Christian teachings on woman. In part 3, Zarathustra tells us that he sits and waits, "old shattered law-tables around me and also new, half-written law-tables" ("Of Old and New Law-Tables" 1). One of these is the curse that God utters as he expels Adam and Eve from paradise: "I will greatly multiply your pain in childbearing, in pain you shall bring forth children, yet your desire shall be for your husband, and he shall rule over you" (Gen. 3:14-16). Obedience was a long-established cardinal virtue of a Christian woman, included in her marriage vows, with procreation her justification. Zarathustra inflects the injunction to obedience thus: "'Behold, now the world has become perfect!'— thus thinks every woman when she obeys with all her love." In Christian doctrine, "perfect love" means perfect obedience and reflects the Holy Church's love for her bridegroom Christ. Zarathustra's redrafting of the old rule retains the principle that love and obedience are commensurable, but secularizes it—demonstrating that our "deepest feelings" have a history, and are rooted in our cultural past. That a woman should have the "flash of a star" glittering in her love, and that the star should be her hope that she may bear the Übermensch, the new redeemer, emphasizes that we are tied to the old stories, as the star is patterned on the star of Bethlehem, and the hope on the redeemer Jesus. This association casts doubt on the Übermensch as a "new" savior. As readers of this treatise on "woman," we are positioned among old law-tables—the very ones Zarathustra wants us to break. He doesn't smash them for us; rather, he hands them to us, as the old woman subsequently hands Zarathustra the whip.

Zarathustra's speech—laying down the law on the nature of woman as antithetical to that of man—similarly parodies Schopenhauer's diatribe "On Woman." The two texts share a number of common assertions: the wife should be submissive to the husband; she should "amuse man in his hours of recreation" (Schopenhauer 105, 108) and be a "dangerous plaything" (Nietzsche). The shade of difference here is worth noting; as in the *Weiblein* of the title, Nietzsche's expression is jocular in contrast to Schopenhauer's solemnity, and whereas their playthings are both dolls, Nietzsche's is likely to explode. Nietzsche's parody also streamlines Schopenhauer's verbosity. Where Schopenhauer observes, "Women exist in the main solely for the propagation of the species, and are not destined for anything else" (112), Nietzsche succinctly notes, "Everything about woman has one solution: it is called pregnancy." In Schopenhauer's estimation, "A man tries to acquire *direct* mastery over things, either by understanding them or by forcing them to do his will. But a woman is always and everywhere reduced to obtaining this mastery *indirectly*, namely through a man" (113); for Nietzsche, "The man's happiness is: I will. The woman's happiness is: he wills." For Schopenhauer, woman is childish and remains in a "stage between the child and the full-grown man" all her life (108); in Nietzschean terms, "man is more childlike than woman."

Ultimately, by having the line about the whip spoken by the woman, Nietzsche parodies Schopenhauer's thought that the "natural feeling" between women is enmity, caused by "trade-jealousy," one that "embraces the entire sex" (112). With this trade-jealousy in mind, having a woman suggest taking a whip to women is a kind of joke, and a long-standing one at that. This Nietzsche demonstrates in *Beyond Good and Evil,* where he quotes an old Italian proverb, *"Buona femmina e mala femmina vuol bastone"* ["Good women and bad women need beating"], which he prefaces by the tag, "From old Florentine novels, moreover—from life" (147).[17] This is the self-same life about which the old woman knows something. Never mind Zarathustra's fine words, which are "nice," she says, "especially for those who are young enough for them." Aphorism 64 from *The Gay Science,* briefly mentioned in the last chapter, provides the best gloss on her attitude toward his speech: "I am afraid that old women are more skeptical in their most secret heart of hearts than any man: they consider the superficiality of existence its essence, and all virtue and profundity is to them merely a veil over this 'truth,' a very welcome veil over a pudendum—in other words, a matter of decency and shame, and no more than that."

The old woman is the skeptical audience (unlike the disciples; she may model the "model readers" as women) who knows that the words about woman are a "veil" over a "pudendum." She proceeds to pass this "little truth" along in the form of a little child who cries too loudly: "You are going to women? Do not forget the whip!" It is this little truth, a "treasure," a gift, which Zarathustra conceals under his cloak at the start of the chapter. The little old woman indicates her attitude toward Zarathustra's speech on woman by calling the women he might visit Frauen. "Woman" is an abstract concept, through which one can make up any number of pleasant or unpleasant fictions. Real women, Frauen, are flesh and blood and *pudenda* (both the female genitals and an attitude toward them—shame, modesty). In contrast to the discourse, the whip suggests actuality, physicality, pain—bodies; the old woman may be winking to Zarathustra, hinting that the present is secretive and hypocritical about sex, especially about its nastier sexual habits. Perhaps Zarathustra himself would enjoy being whipped? Or doing the whipping? There is a public/private dichotomy at work in this chapter, in the public aphorisms, the traits of the eternal feminine, proclaimed formally by Zarathustra, opposed by the notion of private vices, a nitty-gritty, not-very-"nice" reality that one accepts but then discretely and very carefully conceals.

A final point here about skepticism. It is a quality Nietzsche praises consistently throughout his works. In *The Anti-Christ* he writes, "One should not let oneself be misled: great intellects are skeptics. Zarathustra is a skeptic" (54). As one of his seven devils, the little old woman presents the skeptical side of Zarathustra. She is allied to truth, not only in aphorism 67 of *The Gay Science,* but also in the poem "In the South," which closes the second edition of the work: "Up north—embarrassing to tell— / I loved a creepy ancient belle: / The name of this old hag was Truth."

The Whip as an "Exaggerated, Symbolical Mode of Expression"

If the little old woman is a figment of Zarathustra, then their conversation has curious psychological dimensions. She is a devil, thus a tempter; he is seduced by her request and "falls" for it. Like Adam, he is overcome by the serpent/woman. Ricoeur's analysis of the serpent as an externalization of desire, temptation by a part of ourselves we do not recognize (*Symbolism of*

Evil 255), is helpful here. Zarathustra is intellectually aware that solitude encourages self-temptations, but when confronted by just this occurrence, and right after mentioning it, he does not recognize it. After all, why should the request to speak "about woman" be regarded as a temptation?

According to Jung, whose two-volume study of *Thus Spoke Zarathustra* is the most exhaustive analysis of the text in print, the book's parts are connected as in a dream by a "logical series of images" (748); this is accomplished by the dreamer, Nietzsche, who identifies with Zarathustra. For Jung, the little old woman is a manifestation of Nietzsche's "anima," the feminine side of his personality connected to a universal archetype. As an archetype, "the anima is the deposit of the age-old experience of man with woman" (735)—a storehouse of clichés, of worn-out metaphors, upon which a man always draws in his relations with women. (A woman similarly draws upon her storehouse of clichés about man, known as the "animus," in her relations with men.) Jung claims that "a man always projects his anima when talking to a woman because that is the only way he can reach her. . . . If there is no anima, there is absolutely no contact, no bridge, and inasmuch as his anima is maya, illusion, the relation between the sexes is illusion" (734). However, the archetype is the necessary illusion, the function that connects the unconscious with the conscious.

Nietzsche foreshadows Jung when he writes in *The Birth of Tragedy* that a poet's images are "projections" of himself, that the Apollonian world of illusion is necessary for human understanding, and in *The Gay Science* that man's construction of woman is his own masculine ideal. Nietzsche's *Ewigweibliche*, the eternal feminine, as repository of cultural myths of woman, is a precursor of Jung's unconscious anima. Nietzsche jokes about woman's belief in an "eternal masculine" (*BGE* 235); Jung tells his *Zarathustra* seminar, "A woman simply cannot understand a man without the help of the animus, because the man in her helps her to understand the man outside; the less that system plays a role, the less she meets the real man." To this he adds, "This only proves how difficult it is to establish a real relation between the sexes" (734). Jung's interpretation of the anima/animus offers us one way of understanding the little old woman as a part of Zarathustra's unconscious that is not particular or individual—a way that I think the text itself indicates through its very hackneyed assertions about woman.

Jung suggests that the anima directs Zarathustra's discourse on woman, and that his first statement ("Everything about woman is a riddle, and every-thing about woman has one solution: it is called pregnancy") contains a "shocking paradox": though the first part is true ("men understand nothing about a woman"), the second contradicts it as "a man's prejudice." Just because he understands nothing, he has an answer prepared: "Oh, she just wants a child" (734). "This is just anima talk," Jung says; "The anima always tries to convince a man of his extraordinary depths and what a hell of a fellow he is, in order to envelope or entangle him. . . . He is simply a fool caught in his own cage and driven around by his anima that has become like those women in the circuses who go around with a whip" (741).

Nietzsche's practice here prefigures Jung's theory. He sets up the chapter on woman as a potential encounter between Zarathustra and one of his own devils, and frames it twice to foreground its irony. When cornered on the subject of woman, Zarathustra spouts truisms, including the line about the whip. Jung says of this line, "Do not forget thy whip! This is what a man never knows and it is the first thing he has to learn in analysis: Remember thy whip. But the whip is for his anima and not for women" (743). Here it seems to me that Jung is inconsistent, for he reads the little old woman's advice as anti-anima talk—a moment of truth in which Zarathustra escapes the anima's snares. To pursue this line of thought— if the whip is to be used on the anima, then Jung's interpretation agrees with that of R. Hinton Thomas (120); the whip is for Zarathustra to use on himself, to whip himself into shape, as it were, to say No to the camel-load of cultural baggage he carries on the subject "woman." This load is heavy, for it consists of petrified concepts—including the concept "woman" itself.

The whip is an image. Taking the text as a dream, the whip is a dream symbol of a serpent. For Freud, the serpent is always phallic, but for Jung, its symbolic meaning is more ambiguous, often suggesting biblical and other ancient mythic links to femininity and the earth. Nietzsche joins serpent and woman in his explanation of Genesis 1–3 (A 48), and substitutes serpent-woman-God (HAH 2:274; EH "Beyond Good and Evil"). If the whip can indeed be glossed symbolically as a serpent, then clearly we are dealing with "exaggerated symbolic" matters here.

Taking the line about the whip as "an exaggerated, symbolical mode of expression," I find Jung's analysis of the "little truth" as a "little child" suggestive, given the ways in which the text already parodies Christian doctrine. Literally, the whip is an object not to be forgotten in the presence of women. Figuratively, it is a gift that the old woman gives to Zarathustra through his ear. Jung suggests that because Zarathustra is hiding the child, it is illegitimate; its mother is the anima (the old woman as part of Zarathustra) and its father "the unconscious animus" (the archetype of the wise old man, also a part of Zarathustra). This story, Jung says, suggests the myth of Mary, "the illegitimate mother made pregnant by the animus," or spirit, and who also conceived through the ear: "Now here, the anima has heard something, she had an audition, she conceived the Word. . . . She has been impregnated, and we don't know what that child might be, but apparently it is a lively child and it wants to make itself heard. And a child that has been conceived by the Word will be a *logos, a word of authority*" (733).

The text itself hints that we should consider the "little truth" both as an illegitimate child and as a gift, a treasure *(ein Schatz)*. As a parody of the Annunciation, this announcement is very strange and even very funny. The old woman, like a mother, gives Zarathustra a piece of advice on the order of reminding him not to forget his umbrella in case of rain, only here the umbrella is a whip should he "go to women." As is characteristic of Menippean satire, the line is both humorous and serious. Shapiro makes a number of points with regard to this text: the old woman's gift is one of very few that Zarathustra accepts, and it is "double-edged," ambivalent; the very next chapter, "On the Adder's Bite," is about a serpent's gift of poison; and the subsequent gift is the staff his disciples give Zarathustra, which has a serpent coiled around the sun emblazoned on its golden handle (*Alcyone* 31–32).

Conventions of allegory and dream symbolism make it possible for the whip as a baby truth to transmute into another symbolic form, a serpent, and to grow up into the nauseating thought of the eternal return (at least for Zarathustra)—a serpent with its tail in its mouth, an age-old symbol of eternity. The old woman—as part of Zarathustra, one of his "devils," perhaps the key devil, the serpent—tempts him to talk about woman in order to give him the gift of herself as serpent and as the symbol of eternal return. In the coils of the whip, she symbolizes resentment of women, something that Zarathustra must overcome, because resentment of women equals resentment of life, and of himself. As the serpent of wisdom, which is Zarathustra's own talismanic animal, the old woman is transformed into Wisdom/Life—the gift, the treasure, the sweetheart—and in choosing this Zarathustra also chooses death.[18] The most obvious symbolic form of the whip, however, is phallic. If the little old woman reminds Zarathustra that the phallus might be useful when he visits women, we find ourselves again, as indeed we always have been, in the realm of Menippus.

The Whip as a "Personal Memory"

The line about the whip has a biographical provenance. In my estimation, recognizing its origin in real life complicates and broadens but does not override interpretations of the statement as joke and symbol. Biographical particulars open a layer, archeologically, to my thoughts about the text, and answer some questions that other interpretations strain to consider. It is curious, for instance, that in "On Little Old and Young Women," only the old woman appears, and she merely mentions women who may be "young enough" to appreciate Zarathustra's thoughts on woman. Scanning the biographical horizon, we find more particular figures—Lou Salomé, who actually had some thoughts like these and jotted them down in her notebook, and Elisabeth Nietzsche, who despised her. As an exercise in autobiography, the chapter tells the sorry story of Fritz, Lou, and Lisbeth the Lama (Nietzsche's pet name for his sister), from start to finish.

Recall that Zarathustra furtively hides something under his cloak; he tells his "brother" that it is an "unruly little truth," and that it will "cry too loudly" if he does not stop its mouth. Remember too, that Nietzsche tried to keep Lou Salomé a secret after they met. Binyon, quoting from Salomé's letters, notes that she wanted to "cry aloud" for joy that her Roman dream of studying in a threesome with Nietzsche and Rée was "coming true," but Nietzsche objected; "I like concealment in life," he wrote to her in June, 1882, thus effectively "stopping her mouth." At the same time, Nietzsche says that he hopes she will be his philosophical "heir": "I am now seeking people who could be my heirs; I carry something around with me absolutely not to be read in my books—and I am seeking the finest, most fertile soil for it" (Binyon 67). In the text, Zarathustra, "carrying something around" with him, is pregnant (presumably with the idea of eternal return). The baby truth that Zarathustra is hiding is thus a complex collation of Nietzsche's hidden love and his unwritten thought, disguised as an idea about whips and women—whips, because, through Lou's persuasion, Nietzsche agreed to having that telltale piece of evidence, a photograph, taken in Lucerne. Nietzsche himself arranged the image; according to Salomé, he rushed about finding some lilac with which to adorn her whip as she sat in the cart (*Looking Back* 48). He was clearly, already, ironically distancing himself, or protecting himself, from a problem, and laughing both at himself and at Rée.

In June of 1882, after the group photograph was taken in Lucerne, Nietzsche visited his family in Naumburg, and during his stay Elisabeth read Turgenev's novella *First Love* aloud to him (since his eyesight was by this time perennially bad). Elisabeth offers an account of this in the second volume of her biography of Nietzsche, in order to explain the line about the whip in *Thus Spoke Zarathustra*. In the Turgenev story, the lover of a beautiful young coquette takes the riding whip to her. "My brother," Elisabeth reports, "accompanied the reading with all kinds of humorous remarks, but at this scene he expressed his disapproval of the lover's behavior. So I could not avoid reminding him by a few examples we know that there simply happen to be female natures who are held in check only by a brutal stressing of power on the man's part." She eventually goes on to note, "At this mention, however, he leaned back on the sofa, and cried out with well-feigned astonishment: 'Thus the Lama advises the man to use the whip!'" When part I of *Thus Spoke Zarathustra* appeared in print, Elisabeth tells us, she recognized the reference: "'Oh Fritz,' I exclaimed in alarm, 'I am the old woman!' My brother laughed and said he would not betray that to anyone. Meanwhile, Fritz might have changed his view of women somewhat or learned something new since reading that novella, so that now in the whip story he felt the need to stress it especially strongly" (in Gilman *Conversations* 123–25).

This comment demonstrates Elisabeth's egotism and revengefulness, for she hints that after the reading the novella, her brother discovered that his paragon Salomé was the sort of woman who needed the whip after all. The little old woman's attentiveness as Zarathustra has his say about woman accords with the episode at Tautenberg, when Nietzsche and Salomé discussed and scribbled their thoughts about woman, and other things, in their notebooks, with Elisabeth attentively listening at a distance (sometimes no farther than a keyhole). The old woman's advice not to forget the whip accords with Elisabeth's advice regarding Lou. Elisabeth had herself, in fact, taken a verbal whip to Salomé, and persuaded Nietzsche to do the same—handing him the coils by pouring poison into his ear.

The line about the whip, like the text in which it is embedded, is vastly overdetermined: it derives from a multitude of sources and explodes with many possible interpretations. As part of the parody of "old law-tables" on "Woman," and Zarathustra's apparent subscription to them, it is a joke. As an embryonic hint of Zarathustra's future transformation, it is an exaggerated, symbolic mode of expression. And as a personal memory, it is raw emotion—anger, lust, resentment. This personal memory, Dionysian in character, fuels the production of the text, which is exceptional in several respects. Unique among chapters of *Thus Spoke Zarathustra*, it has a double frame, a flashback, and the sole instance of a woman character and narratee. Furthermore, and not coincidentally, it is the only chapter in the book that directly addresses women readers, where Nietzsche/Zarathustra speaks to an extra-diegetic audience—listeners outside the narrative frame, beyond the text. Here Zarathustra discusses woman's understanding of children, saying, "A child is concealed in the true man: it wants to play. Come, women [*ihr Frauen* (*KSA* 4:85)], discover the child in man!" (*Z* 1 "Of Old and Young Women). It is clear that Nietzsche knows actual women are listening, and reading.

An oppositional, ironic reading of the chapter calls on us to examine each of its propositions and to ask a number of questions. From whose vantage point is this text positioned? Whose truth is this? Who is wielding the whip? The frames around the discourse on woman, the twilight setting, the fairy tale crone as character—all of these serve to hedge this chapter with qualifications and with hints that we must seek for ironies. The content of the discourse, it subtly suggests, must be qualified by its outcome: the gift of the whip. The discourse is "nice," while the whip is vulgar and ugly, a symbol of brute force and domination. Like other oppositions in Nietzsche's texts, this one dissipates on close inspection. The discourse itself is symbolic of man's domination of woman and has served, like a whip, to keep her in her place: loving, obeying, sacrificing, and pregnant.

6

"All Things Are Enchained, Entwined, In Love"

Zarathustra's Eternal Return

IN *Thus Spoke Zarathustra* (as in *The Birth of Tragedy*), women are hardly represented at all, but those characteristics conventionally associated with the feminine—nature, the earth, the body, emotions, dreams and the unconscious—are established as sources of self-trust, self-confidence, and self-worth. The very absence of women as characters and models, in fact, makes possible the transfer of feminine characteristics to male characters; in the simplest way, the absence challenges the heterosexual dichotomy by eliminating it as a narrative possibility.

This radical solution to the "cardinal problem" of "man and woman" (*BGE* 239) enacts the masculine fantasy that wishes to expunge women from existence, and *Zarathustra* can be interpreted as Nietzsche's indulgence of this misogynistic fantasy. It can also be interpreted as going beyond this fantasy to another radical solution: the elimination of both genders as they are presently constituted. The second is my choice. For me, Nietzsche's narrative challenge to the heterosexual dichotomy clears a space for new ways to think about what it is to be human, which is the main goal or purpose of *Thus Spoke Zarathustra*.

Like its embedded reflection in the narrative of the old woman and the whip, the book is both humorous and serious at the same time. It unfolds its meaning and achieves its end progressively and, like the Pythia of Heraclitus, it speaks its message through hints and riddles rather than through straightforward exposition. As a type of Menippean satire, *Zarathustra* works to achieve its coherence in the manner of a "specular text," through "repetition, reflection, and mirroring of all kinds" (Chambers *Story and Situation* 28). Like the models it parodies, it purports to convey wisdom, but what exactly that wisdom *is* remains enigmatic, not directly spelled out but rather hinted at and gestured toward through the symbolic devices of the text's central prophecies—the Übermensch and the eternal return—and through its narrative events.

Like many other readers of Nietzsche, I have been enlightened by Martin Heidegger's interpretation of these prophecies in the short essay, "Who is Nietzsche's Zarathustra?" Heidegger reads the narrative as a process whereby Zarathustra has to overcome the horror of his task in order to become who he is, where the task and who he is are the one in the same. Late in the story, Zarathustra announces that he is "the advocate of life, the advocate of suffering, the advocate of the circle" (Z 3 "The Convalescent"), and then he summons his "abysmal thought," which has been "burrowing" inside him but which he hasn't had the courage, until that moment, to evoke. This is the thought of eternal recurrence. "Zarathustra is the teacher whose doctrine would liberate previous reflection from the spirit of revenge unto a *yes* to the Eternal Recurrence of the Same," Heidegger writes (74); the spirit of revenge is the will's aversion to transience (73). Because of this aversion, the will has created eternal ideals as absolutes, "compared with which the temporal must degrade itself to actual non-being" (73). For Zarathustra, thinking must be so free of revenge that it welcomes transience-as-being. Welcoming transience is the work of the Übermensch, the one who "*surpasses* man as he is up to now, for the sole purpose of bringing man-till-now into his still unattained nature, and there to secure him" (67). For Heidegger, "Zarathustra does not teach two different things as the teacher of the Eternal Recurrence and the Superman. What he teaches belongs internally together, because each demands the other in response" (74).

Heidegger claims that "the Superman surpasses previous and contemporary man, and is therefore a passage, a bridge." In order to become who he is, Zarathustra—and, by extension, all of us—must get onto this bridge of the Übermensch. We are once again in the realm of metaphor, but Heidegger does not look at the metaphor as metaphor. Rather, he notes that in order to comprehend Superman-as-bridge, we must understand three things: "(1) That from which the person passing over [the bridge] departs; (2) The bridge itself; (3) The destination of the person crossing over." "Who is Nietzsche's Zarathustra?" submits the case that the person passing over is departing from revenge, or the will's aversion to transience, and is "on the way to his authentic nature" (68), a state of affirmation of transience—of life, suffering, the circle. In Heidegger's view, Zarathustra does not make it across the bridge, and "his doctrine does not bring deliverance from revenge" (76), because the doctrine is still metaphysical. "Metaphysical thinking," Heidegger writes, "rests on the distinction between that which truly is and that which by comparison does not constitute true being" (77). Because Heidegger thinks Nietzsche casts Zarathustra from a "Dionysian" perspective, and contrasts that perspective with the Christian, he holds that Nietzsche is still operating within a metaphysical system, retaining a distinction between a true (Dionysian) and a false (Christian) world, and thus, remains revengeful.

Heidegger maps out the two sides or ends of the bridge of becoming—one end revenge against and the other acceptance and affirmation of what is—but he does not take up the question he poses regarding the character or status of the bridge itself. Whatever it may signify, the bridge, textually, is a metaphor, interactively carrying associations both ways, from revenge at one end to acceptance at the other, and from acceptance to revenge, partaking of and motivated by both. Zarathustra likens "man" (not the Übermensch, as per Heidegger) to a bridge; as man proceeds by willing, the bridge could serve to symbolize will to power in human nature. Because will to power has both reactive and affirmative valences, it is difficult for Zarathustra to free himself completely from the side of the bridge that constitutes revenge, even though he sees that he should, and wishes that he could. He knows that he should proclaim the prophecy of the eternal return, but his very "bridgeness"—his connection at the near end to revenge, the "reactive" force in the will to power—prevents him from doing so until late in the narrative. Then, at last, when he sings that "all things are enchained, entwined, in love" (Z 4 "The Drunken Song"), the metaphorical bridge along with the metaphysical dualism give way to a precious, completely affirmative moment. For the sake of this moment, Zarathustra wills to live his selfsame life all over again.

It is important that the teacher, Zarathustra, teaches "something twofold that belongs together," the eternal return and the Übermensch, according to Heidegger, who notes that "in a sense, Zarathustra himself is this belonging-together" (77). This assertion might well suggest the basic twofold belonging-together of the human race, man and woman, were it not for the fact—as Derrida points out in Spurs (84–85)—that Heidegger's analysis of Nietzsche leaves out the feminine, even when it is there in the text. Appreciating the role of the feminine deepens our understanding of Zarathustra's journey, and of his central prophecies. In shedding the metaphysical and recovering the feminine—paired tasks in the project of accepting the temporal world—Zarathustra is a model for modernity.

The Feminine in *Thus Spoke Zarathustra*

Ostensibly, *Thus Spoke Zarathustra* is a pep talk for men. This becomes wholly evident in part 4, the "satyr play" that parodies parts 1–3, which are already satiric and parodic. In the first three parts of the book, Zarathustra encourages his disciples to "become hard": "Why so soft, so unresisting and yielding? . . . For creators are hard" (Z 3 "Of Old and New Law-Tables" 29). Having done so, he then goes on to stress their failings in his long speech to the Higher Men gathered for "the Last Supper" in his cave, and tells them frankly that they are not the men for whom he waits; "you," he asserts, "are not high and strong enough." As he goes on to note, "For he who himself stands on sick and tender legs, as you do, wants above all . . . to be *spared* . . . I do not spare *my warriors:* how, then could you be fit for *my* warfare? . . . He who belongs to me must be strong-limbed and nibble-footed, merry in war and feasting, no mournful man, no dreamy fellow, ready for what is hardest as for a feast, healthy and whole" (Z 4 "The Greeting"). "Healthy and whole": this quest for wholeness is also Zarathustra's, as he tells his disciples that his aim is "to compose into one and bring together what is fragment and riddle and dreadful chance." He finds, he says, nothing but "the fragments and limbs of men" in both the past and the present; "the terrible thing to my eye is to find men shattered in pieces and scattered as if over a battle-field of slaughter." Everywhere, he observes, he finds "fragments and limbs and dreadful chances, but no men!" (Z 2 "Of Redemption").

Zarathustra's cure, the recipe for making men "better and more evil" (Z 4 "Of the Higher Man" 5), whole and not fragmented, includes the following ingredients: laughter, dance, pain and suffering, pregnancy, childbirth, intoxication, solitude (private space), desire, love, attention and loyalty to the body and the earth. Over time, cultural repetition has marked many of these elements as "feminine." Zarathustra claims them for men. At one point, he suggests that "man" has been depleted of the "woman" in him by God's creation of Eve from one of Adam's ribs: "'Ah, how you stand there, you unfruitful men, how lean-ribbed!'. . . . And they have said: 'Perhaps a god has secretly taken something from me there as I slept? Truly, sufficient to form a little woman for himself!'" (Z 2 "Of the Land of Culture"). The passage hints that present-day men are unfruitful, perhaps because they have been robbed of their "fruitful" part, their femininity, and suggests that Zarathustra finds modern men inadequate, weak, pusillanimous.

In his very first public appearance, Zarathustra promotes the earth and the body (as opposed, metaphysically, to heaven and the soul): "I entreat you, my brothers, *remain true to the earth,* and do not believe those who speak to you of superterrestrial hopes!" He tells the people in the market-place to overcome man and to reach and create beyond themselves—specifically, the Übermensch: "The Superman is the meaning of the earth.

Let your will say: The Superman *shall be* the meaning of the earth!" (Z "Pro-logue" 3). As long as readers assume (and why shouldn't they?) that "the Superman" is a man, then not only are Zarathustra's parodic models and his narratees masculine, but so too is his prophesied future for humanity. But Zarathustra hardly ever attributes masculine characteristics to this prophecy; rather, he fills out the definition of the Übermensch as the mean-ing of the earth by likening it to a sea, to lightning, to madness—all of which are Dionysian properties. What is the meaning of the earth?: this is a good riddle. It is a goal, the opposite of heaven; it is where humanity needs to direct its thoughts.

Dying, in the new dispensation of the Übermensch, means "going under" *(Untergehen)*, gladly, into the earth: "Thus I want to die myself, that you friends may love the earth more for my sake; and I want to become earth again, that I may have peace in her who bore me" (Z 1 "Of Voluntary Death"). The earth is given its pre-Christian designation here, as mother—womb and tomb alike.[1] Bachofen's work makes the point that the Greeks reversed the order of priority from women/earth to men/sky; Nietzsche reverses the reversal, returning values from father heaven to mother earth.

Zarathustra's commendation of the body accomplishes a similar rever-sal, valuing the flesh above the soul: "'I am body and soul'—so speaks the child. And why should one not speak like children? But the awakened, the enlightened man says: 'I am body entirely, and nothing beside'. . . . The body is a great intelligence, a multiplicity with one sense, a war and a peace, a herd and a herdsman. . . . There is more reason in your body than in your best wisdom" (Z 1 "Of the Despisers of the Body"). The narrative of *Zarathustra* here demonstrates that the body, or more particularly Zarathustra's body, is a multiplicity, and the herdsman is, radically, not consciousness or the "ego" but "the Self. He lives in your body, he is your body." Zarathustra's Self is an important character in the psychodrama; it leads and organizes, but in a completely non-authoritarian way, the herd that he is, including his ego: "You say 'I' and you are proud of this word. But greater than this—although you will not believe in it—is your body and its great intelligence, which does not say 'I' but performs 'I.'" Here again, the text emphasizes the distinction between saying (Zarathustra's discourses) and doing (the actions Zarathustra performs). The ego, our consciousness, maintains boundaries and constructs identity; our Self includes this ego and comprises our body, which has its own great intelligence.

As for living, a man must become a creator; he must know how to go across the metaphoric bridge from animal to Übermensch, and he must face "the abyss" without fear. The abyss is the "empty space" created by the death of God the Father and Creator, and in psychoanalytic terms it symbolizes the male fear of castration. If God is imagined as male, then his departure from the scene of creativity leaves a gaping hole in sexual as well as ontological terms. For Zarathustra, though the abyss has its horrors, its very perils offer opportunities for heroism. Extolling courage, Zarathustra observes: "Courage also destroys giddiness at abysses: and where does man not stand at an abyss? Is seeing itself not—seeing abysses?" (Z 3 "Of the Vision and the Riddle" 1). Finally, he addresses the sky (former home of God the father) as an abyss: "Yes, if only you are around me, you pure, luminous sky! You abyss of light!—then into all abysses do I carry my consecrating declaration Yes" (Z 3 "Before Sunrise"). Joan Stambaugh takes note of the contradictions of this text—"abysses are traditionally beneath one, and they are dark"—and concludes, "When the heaven, the abyss of light is about him, [Zarathustra] is transformed into a figure of affirmation; in a sense difficult to articulate he himself becomes a kind of heaven" (137–38). Having faced the terror of the abyss, that special empty space which causes vertigo, Zarathustra and his male followers can lose their fear (of nihilism, of castration, of women), affirm that which formally terrified them, and become genuine creators, valuing and validating the earth, the material world, transient reality.

Zarathustra's birth metaphors are abundant, but as good an example as any occurs right at the beginning of the text: "I tell you, one must have chaos in one, to give birth to a dancing star" (Z "Prologue" 5). Chaos is not confusion; chaos is—and the text makes this clear in many ways—deferral of meaning, the state of possibility. A dancing star may be an Übermensch. The text reveals several times that, however the Übermensch is metaphorized, it is always Zarathustra's creation, his baby. Jung comments on one of its obvious aspects: "The essence, the very principle, of creation would be man-beyond-himself" (49); with God dead, "man . . . becomes the creator of himself" (52) and also creates "beyond" or "over" (über) himself. Zarathustra says of the creator: "For the creator himself to be the child new born he must also be willing to be the mother and endure the mother's pain" (Z 2 "On the Blissful Islands"). Thus he gives birth to himself; such self-creation is painful, but the pain is both necessary to self-overcoming and entwined with joy.[2]

Pregnancy is especially significant: "For one loves from the very heart only one's child and one's work; and where there is great love of oneself, then it is a sign of pregnancy" (Z 3 "Of Involuntary Bliss"). One's child, here, is one's work; Nietzsche draws his metaphor from Plato's *Symposium*, where Socrates proposes, through his feminine mouthpiece Diotima, that spiritual creativity or pregnancy of soul is the height of erotic self-expression, "according to a model of erotic responsiveness whose central terms are fecundity, conception, gestation, and giving birth" (Halperin 277). As a student, Nietzsche loved the *Symposium*, and the maternal metaphor remained powerful, and fecund, for him. "What keeps me living?," he writes in his notebook. "Pregnancy: and every time the work is born, my life hangs by a flimsy little thread" (*KSA* 10:119). More generally, he asks: "Is there a more holy condition than that of pregnancy? To do all we do in the unspoken belief that it has somehow to benefit that which is coming to be within us! . . . Everything is veiled, ominous, we know nothing of what is taking place, we wait and try to be *ready*. . . . 'What is growing here is something greater than we are' is our most secret hope. . . . It is in this *state of consecration* that one should live!" (*Daybreak* 552).

This last aphorism is called "Ideal selfishness", a paradoxical title for a paradoxical state of being—two in one, responsible yet not responsible for what goes on. Sheridan Hough argues that pregnancy is "Nietzsche's metaphor for the ideal individual and the ideal life," through which he challenges "our sense of autonomy, and calls into question the absolute authority of reason"; by embodying at least two in one, a pregnant person is simultaneously looking to the future to effect change, raise questions, and propose new answers, and "celebrating his or her strengths and powers in a way that is wholly noninstrumental" (xxv).[3] As he drafts *Zarathustra*, Nietzsche records his own "conceiving" of the eternal return (which, like the Übermensch, is also his baby): "Immortal is the moment when I engendered the Return. For this moment's sake I can bear to will the Return" (*KSA* 10:210).

Throughout much of his book, Zarathustra is pregnant, heavy with the future, and he urges metaphoric pregnancies on his male followers. The final chapter of part 3 (which Nietzsche had originally planned as the book's ending) is a free-verse poem and an extended apostrophe to Eternity—the only woman by whom Zarathustra wants children. In this poem, he again affirms pregnancy—but it is his and not hers: "If I be a prophet and full of that prophetic spirit . . . pregnant with lightnings which affirm Yes! laugh Yes! ready for prophetic lightning flashes: but blessed is he who is thus pregnant!" (*Z* 3 "The Seven Seals" 1).

Eternity joins other allegorical women who share Zarathustra's company; he has two mistresses, Wisdom and Life, and he confesses that he has also been caught by Happiness because he does not run after women;

"happiness, however, is a woman" (*Z* 3 "Of Involuntary Bliss"). Life—the seductive, modest, mocking veiled woman of the *vita femina* aphorism (*GS* 339)—speaks the message of perspectivity and gender difference in *Thus Spoke Zarathustra.* When Zarathustra accuses her of being unfathomable, she replies, "All fish talk like that," and says "I am merely changeable and untamed and in everything a woman, and no virtuous one. Although you men call me 'profound' or 'faithful', 'eternal', 'mysterious'. But you men always endow us with your own virtues—ah, you virtuous men!" (*Z* 2 "The Dance Song"). Life herself is "merely" changeable, but she speaks for women. "You men always endow *us,*" she says—the reference here is not to "me," Life, but to "us," women. In this speech, Life answers the sage of aphorism 68 in *The Gay Science;* she understands that man "creates for himself the image of woman" (*GS* 68) and has no intention, herself, of living up to the virtues with which man has endowed her.

The statement "wisdom is a woman" is of course a metaphor. The attributes of Zarathustra's Wisdom are not reason, knowledge, the branches of the seven liberal arts, or omniscience or serenity; they are wildness, passion, anger, jealously, changeableness, and defiance. Furthermore, there arises the possibility that Wisdom is false. Life is, of course, his other mistress; Zarathustra explains the triangle in the following terms: "This then is the state of affairs between us three. From the heart of me I love only Life,—and in truth, I love her most of all when I hate her! But that I am fond of Wisdom, and often too fond, is because she very much reminds me of Life!" (*Z* 2 "The Dance Song").

The description of Zarathustra's mistresses appears midway through part 2. At this point the metaphors that compare wisdom and life to women are only partly activated—that is, our sense of the meaning of the abstract concepts of life and wisdom is probably somewhat transformed, but that of woman rests securely and tediously on received knowledge about her nature (she is temperamental, changeable, emotional). Only gradually does it become apparent that we must read these figures as extensions of Zarathustra himself. There are a number of passages that make this clear; consider for instance that in which Zarathustra speaks of his loneliness, his work, and his future. He is completely alone, and observes: "Yes, you too, my friends, will be terrified by my wild wisdom; and perhaps you will flee from it altogether with my enemies. . . . My wild Wisdom became pregnant upon lonely mountains; upon rough rocks she bore her young, her youngest" (*Z* 2 "The Child with the Mirror"). It is only when we understand that Wisdom and Life are Zarathustra—they are *his* wisdom and *his* life—that the metaphors are fully activated; the "woman" half of the comparison then obviously undergoes a complete inversion, which participates in the metamorphosis of Zarathustra himself. "To metaphorize well," said Aristotle, "implies an intuitive perception of the similarity in dissimilarity" (in Ricoeur *Rule of Metaphor* 9). The tension between identity and difference, and the way in which Nietzsche, intuitively or consciously, manipulates it, is revealed most clearly through Zarathustra's relationships with the women in his life. Gradually we come to understand them as fully allegorical—that is, as functioning in a unified network of metaphors that tells a story, in this case, that of Zarathustra's own self-overcoming as he moves through the landscape of modernity.

At the outset of the narrative, Zarathustra leaves his mountain retreat because he is overfull, overladen with wisdom—very pregnant—and ready to give birth, that is, to communicate it to his fellow humans. He begins by telling people in the marketplace about the Übermensch—to follow the metaphor, his first "brain child"—but this is unacceptable to the general populace (the "rabble") and so Zarathustra moves away from the crowd and communicates his wisdom only to a select group of followers. Eventually he leaves even this small group, returns to the mountains, and communes with himself; at this point the discussions become lively, as he is not merely lecturing (as to his disciples), but engaging in give-and-take with the women in his life who are implicit in his Self.

What Is the Eternal Return?

Like the biblical prophets who are his prototypes, Zarathustra must speak a message that he is reluctant, indeed terrified, to impart. What this is and why he is so terrified of it remains vague until near the end of part 3, when it emerges, like a baby from its mother's entrails, as the eternal return, twin and double of the Übermensch. My answer to the riddle, "What is the eternal return?," is suggested by Bachofen's descriptions of the tellurian world of nature. *Mother Right* sets up a distinction between the imperishable and the perishable that figures too in *Zarathustra*. Bachofen tells the story of Bellerophon, who in bemoaning his fate "is blind to the innermost laws of all tellurian life, the law to which he himself belongs, the law that governs the womb. Only in the halls of the sun, which he vainly seeks to reach, do immortality and imperishable existence reign; under the moon the law of matter prevails, with death assigned as twin brother to all life. . . . The transience of material life goes hand in hand with mother right. Father right is bound up with the immortality of a supramaterial life belonging to the regions of light" (127, 129).

Zarathustra explicitly denounces visions and parables of the transcendental in "On the Blissful Islands," where he contrasts gods and the Übermensch, offering in the process another hint or two about the significance of the Übermensch as the meaning of the earth. Whereas you, he says to the disciples, could not create a god, "you could surely create the Superman"—or at least, "you could transform yourselves into forefathers and ancestors of the Superman." Having spoken these words, in apposition with this transformation, Zarathustra goes on to direct the disciples to will that "everything shall be transformed into the humanly-conceivable . . . the World should be formed in your image by your reason, your will, and your love!" The Übermensch is human potential, "beyond" present-day humans, who could thus be its ancestors. God, by contrast, is an anguished supposition: "God is a thought that makes all that is straight crooked and all that stands giddy. What? Would time be gone and all that is transitory only a lie?" (Z 2 "On the Blissful Islands"). The transitory and the perishable, rather than the imperishable "halls of light" that have symbolized eternity in the past—this is where Zarathustra's Übermensch will be at home.

The text plays with the ending of Goethe's poem *Faust,* where Faust's soul is saved from the devil and "drawn upward" to heaven by the love of a pure woman, as the mystical chorus eulogizes the "intransitory" and the "eternal feminine" that draw us ever upward. The "eternal feminine" in *Zarathustra* is the "eternal return," which draws us ever downward, to the earth, to time, to the transitory. "I call it evil and misanthropic," Zarathustra tells his disciples, "all this teaching about the one and the perfect and the unmoved and the sufficient and the intransitory. All that is intransitory—that is but an image! And the poets lie too much. But the best images and parables should speak of time and becoming: they should be a eulogy and a justification of all transitoriness" (Z 2 "On the Blissful Islands").

In "Of the Bestowing Virtue," the last chapter in part 1, Zarathustra takes leave of his disciples to return to his mountain; they in turn present him with the staff topped by the golden image of a serpent coiled about the sun. Zarathustra then discusses images, and says, "Whenever your spirit wants to speak in images, pay heed; for that is when your virtue has its origin and beginning" (Z 1 "Of the Bestowing Virtue"). He interprets the images of sun and serpent on the staff: "It is power, this new virtue; it is a ruling idea, and around it a subtle soul: a golden sun, and around it the serpent of knowledge." Perhaps Zarathustra is hinting here that his spirit, by employing images that, like Heraclitus's Pythia, hint but do not speak out directly, is doing the only thing it can to express "the new virtue." It is easier to tear down than to build; here Zarathustra, who is in the process of demolishing old ideals, is simultaneously trying to create—to give birth to—a new one.

What is this serpent of knowledge? In *The Birth of Tragedy*, Nietzsche refers to knowledge of the abyss as "Dionysian." It is knowledge so horrible that words cannot describe it: it is imageless. It is the nauseating feeling that existence is meaningless suffering, which the Greeks experienced as "the terror and horror of existence," "the keenest susceptibility to suffering," "a hidden substratum of suffering and of knowledge." It is the wisdom of Silenus that it is best not to be, *to be nothing;* or second best, soon to die (*BT* 3). It is the glance into "gruesome night" that calls for the remedy of Apollonian illusion, saving art. When Apollonian illusion mates with Dionysian truth, the paradoxical tragic synthesis is "born." This synthesis revalues, or reinterprets, Dionysian truth, converting No to Yes. A tragic interpretation of life says Yes to transience, because it believes in life's indestructibility. "'We believe in eternal life,' exclaims tragedy" (*BT* 16)—not the eternity of the individual, but of the whole. "In spite of fear and pity, we are the happy living beings, not as individuals, but as the *one* living being, with whose creative joy we are united" (*BT* 17). In this work, Nietzsche associates the "eternal same" of life with "the eternally creative primordial mother, eternally impelling to existence, eternally finding satisfaction in this change of phenomena!" (*BT* 16). When the serpent of knowledge—knowledge of impermanence, transience, of the eternal return—is paired with the golden sun of power, then knowledge becomes courageous, and powers its own revaluation from resentment and fear of life (and death) to its affirmation.

Such, at least, is the theory; *Thus Spoke Zarathustra* shows us that the practice is something else again. For Zarathustra, knowledge of the eternal return is initially as nauseating as the wisdom of Silenus. If we believe what Zarathustra's spirit of gravity and his animals (the eagle and the serpent, which will be discussed in the next part of this chapter) tell him, the eternal return means that he will die, but he will return to live "this identical and self-same life" (*Z* 3 "The Convalescent" 2) again and again. All his good and all his evil, and the knowledge that chokes—all will return with him. The thought that his life will recur in identical terms in all details, with no finality, no closure, is so disturbing to Zarathustra that he simply cannot "get it out." Rather, he hears it boring within, his unconscious reveals it to him through his vision in the moonlight, and his animals tell him about it.

As many commentators have remarked, Zarathustra himself never speaks the "thought" of the return, in a conceptual manner. Instead, he expresses his interpretation of it in figures of speech and in narrative actions. This dramatized answer to the riddle of the eternal return differs from the answer proposed by Zarathustra's animals. The animals, of course, are also parts of Zarathustra's Self; it is interesting that their interpretation is incorrect, as though Zarathustra, still resentful, needs to defend himself against the knowledge of the "return." As the text makes clear, the "return" is ironic; Zarathustra's is a journey of no return. While Life in general returns, the narrative suggests that Zarathustra's life will end. Perhaps that thought is what Zarathustra (like the rest of us) finds almost impossible to accept.

From Whip to Eternal Return: "Of the Vision and the Riddle"

In "Of the Vision and the Riddle" (Z 3), Zarathustra relates the most excessive riddle in the work and in the entire Nietzschean oeuvre. Zarathustra's first "saying" on woman, "everything about woman is a riddle," appears again in this chapter, reversed, as in a mirror: everything about this riddle is a woman. Other Zarathustrian riddles reappear and merge in this one— the Übermensch is the meaning of the earth; woman is a riddle whose solution is pregnancy; when you go to women, don't forget the whip. The riddle's content links the eternal return and the Übermensch—this much seems clear. The rest anybody's guess—a fact Zarathustra himself brings to the fore and in which he takes decided pleasure.

The riddle's immediate setting places Zarathustra on board a ship, bound away from the Blissful Islands where he has preached to his disciples, en route back to his mountain cave; as we have seen, he starts by addressing the narratees as interpreters, and defines as his ideal among these someone who is "intoxicated by riddles," who prefers twilight, abysses, and the intuitive guess to the rational calculation—someone, in short, whose qualities are mythically Dionysian and conventionally feminine. Through his opening address to his audience, both of narratees and of implied readers, Zarathustra constructs a frame around the already embedded riddle. This framing of the riddle mirrors the framing of the chapter on "little old and young women," and in each case Zarathustra's address to his audience intensifies the textual or specular nature of what is to follow. Repetition of the framing device brings the two chapters into relation.

In "On Little Old and Young Women," Zarathustra reveals that he has a "gift" hidden beneath his cloak, which he discloses as the secret of the whip that he should not forget when he goes to women. We are really not much wiser for this revelation, for it answers an enigma with another enigma. Furthermore, the thing that he hides under his cloak is by turns compared to a small child, a little truth, and a treasure, yet it looks ugly, snarling, violent, negative. As something hidden, it carries connotations of shame. The other thing that is hidden, secret, ugly, and negative in *Thus Spoke Zarathustra* is the thought of the eternal return. The whip (in connection with women), and Zarathustra's hidden, secret nausea (a result of his gestation of the eternal return), are woven together poetically through the repetition of images that take on symbolic value. These images issue forth in Zarathustra's visionary riddle, where not only are they disclosed as one, but are transformed, and revalued from negative to positive.

Zarathustra leads up to this climax gradually, producing one riddle that is symbolically related to another. The first of these is a vision of a gateway inscribed "Moment," where a road traveling infinitely into the past meets a road traveling infinitely into the future. Zarathustra interprets the vision of the gateway intellectually as symbolic of the eternal return: "Must we not return and run down that other lane out before us, down that long, terrible lane—must we not return eternally?" (*Z* 3 "Of the Vision and the Riddle" 2). He also describes his affective responses to the experience: fear, doubt, and pity for a howling dog. The gateway disappears, and Zarathustra turns to the second vision and riddle: "Had I been dreaming? Had I awoken? All at once I was standing between wild cliffs, alone, desolate in the most desolate moonlight." The ambiguity of the scene is underscored by the blurring of dreaming and waking states, and by the iconography of the landscape, which is that of the romantic gothic. This genre, particularly favored in Germany, gives form to repressed sexuality through its use of conventions of the grotesque and of melodrama. In Zarathustra's vision, the imagery suggests a repressed feminine.

The disappearing gateway that might or might not have been dreamed has feminine connotations, which under the influence of Christianity become negative. We don't need Freud to tell us that the gateway (any door or archway) symbolizes in dreams the female genital opening, egress from the womb into the world, and ingress from the world back into the womb. Peter Brown notes that during the early Christian centuries, "Christian men used women 'to think with' in order to verbalize their own nagging concern with the stance that the Church should take to the world. For ancient men tended to regard women as creatures less clearly defined and less securely bounded by the structures that held men in place in society. The woman was a 'gateway.' She was both a weak point and a bridgehead.

Women allowed in what men did not permit to enter. For the morose Tertul-lian, women needed to be reminded that they might be Eve, 'the devil's gateway.'" (153). Much before this, the tribal shaman used the gateway and its analogue, the mouth, to move (as through a portal) between worlds or levels of reality; "the vagina is seen in many cultures as the ultimate portal between worlds." In shamanistic cultures, "portals demarcate the qualities of transition" (MacDonald et al. 40-47). In the Eleusinian mysteries, where the Baubo figure represented the vagina, the qualities of this particular gateway and the gateway itself were still venerated. And in ancient China, Lao Tsu describes the "valley spirit" that "never dies. It is the woman, primal mother. Her gateway is the root of heaven and earth" (*Tao Te Ching* number 6).

Zarathustra's gateway is in good company, and since it stands for the conjunction of past, present, and future in "the moment," it carries the same sort of cosmic profundity as in other cultures. That Christianity debased the female gateway is part of Zarathustra's message; this is clearly articu-lated in "Of Immaculate Perception," to which we will shortly turn. For Freud as for Lao Tsu, valleys signify the woman ("'Valley' is a frequent female symbol in dreams" [*Interpretation of Dreams* 374]); recall that in the vision, we find Zarathustra located between wild cliffs, in a valley, at a time of day and by the light of the celestial body traditionally associated with woman. The howling dog is Hecate's sign.[4] The scene is permeated with Yin, the female principle, and Zarathustra is "most desolate" there.

He describes what he sees in this place: a "young shepherd" was lying prone on the ground, "writhing, choking, convulsed, his face distorted; and a heavy, black snake was hanging out of his mouth." Zarathustra the visionary/dreamer comments on his own dream-response—"Had I ever seen so much disgust and pallid horror on a face?"—and on his action:

> My hands tugged and tugged at the snake—in vain! they could not tug the snake out of the shepherd's throat. Then a voice cried from me: "Bite! Bite!
> "Its head off! Bite!"—thus a voice cried from me, my horror, my hate, my disgust, my pity, all my good and evil cried out of me with a single cry.

The shepherd then bites with a good bite, spits out the snake's head, and springs up:

> No longer a shepherd, no longer a man—a transformed being, surrounded with light, *laughing*! Never yet on earth had any man laughed as he laughed!
> O my brothers, I heard a laughter that was no human laughter—and now a thirst consumes me, a longing that is never stilled.

> My longing for this laughter consumes me: oh how do I endure still to live!
> And how could I endure to die now!
>   Thus spoke Zarathustra. (Z 3 "Of the Vision and the Riddle" 2)

The vision seems to present a recapitulation of the progress of humanity, from the earthbound tellurian stage of feminine materiality to the "imperishable" halls of light, as described by Bachofen. Other interpretive possibilities of this riddle, which are drawn from traditions that *Zarathustra* parodies, align with this view. The serpent, the shepherd, and the apotheosized shepherd belong to both scriptural Christian and ancient Greek traditions. A straightforward allegorical reading in the Christian tradition offers the following associations: the shepherd is the old Adam, unregenerate man; the serpent is guilt, sin and death that have eaten their way into his flesh; the shepherd's bite is the surmounting of those things by faith; and the apotheosized shepherd is the redeemer, Christ. The classical tradition produces a different interpretation: the shepherd is Apollo Nomios, he of the pastures, physician of his flock; the serpent is Python, who barred Apollo's way to Delphi; the shepherd's bite is Apollo's defeat of Python; and the transfiguration is the sign of the god's prophetic relationship to the truth. In Zarathustra's riddle, the laughing figure, "no longer human," suggests that we, as readers and interpreters, may be taking this vision far too seriously, and that we should perhaps lighten up.

The central horrifying image in the riddle is the long black snake, about which there is nothing very funny, unless the snake is not a snake. There is every indication, however, at least in one manifestation, that the snake *is* a snake—and hence a quick review of the lore of the serpent may prove useful. Serpents are very ancient, bivalent symbols, and in *Zarathustra* they exhibit three values: there are good snakes, bad snakes, and snakes that are not clearly good or bad. The first serpent we encounter is introduced as one of Zarathustra's two faithful animals (the other animal is the eagle; for Zarathustra they are the wisest and the proudest animals under the sun ["Prologue" 10]). This is clearly a "good" snake, aligned with Dionysian wisdom. It is joined by its artistic double when Zarathustra's disciples give him the staff, which has on its haft the emblems of a "serpent of knowledge" coiled around a sun. Serpents have been associated with cosmic creation and with knowledge or wisdom in the ancient myths of many cultures. This is dual knowledge, like that of Zarathustra, associated with birth and death. The cosmic serpent of ancient Egypt, for example, the "provider of attributes," is two headed, fork tongued, and has a double penis; this last characteristic does not represent a double dose of virility, but rather bisexuality, or the duality of life itself, depending on the manifestation (Narby 102).[5] Zarathustra's talismanic serpent descends from what was clearly an ancient tradition for even the Hebrews and ancient Greeks.

The other serpents in *Thus Spoke Zarathustra* carry either negative or ambiguous connotations. As Jung points out, once the whip appears as an image in part I, it is immediately followed by—or, more accurately, is transformed into—an adder in the next chapter, and proceeds to bite Zarathustra in the neck; he then persuades it to take back its poison. Zarathustra uses the story as a parable about revenge—"A little revenge is more human than no revenge at all"—and notes that it is better to return a curse with a curse (Z I "Of the Adder's Bite"), thus reversing Christ's injunction to turn the other cheek. The book of Genesis establishes a connection between the snake and revenge as a law of nature. "The Lord God said to the serpent, 'Because you have done this [tempted Eve to disobey God and eat of the forbidden fruit], cursed are you among all animals and among all wild creatures; upon your belly you shall go, and dust you shall eat all the days of your life. I will put enmity between you and the woman, and between your offspring and hers'" (Gen. 2:3, 14-16). This enmity is the very spirit of revenge—woman and her offspring, the human race, against the serpent and its connotations: the earth, sex, the lower parts of the body.[6] Nietzsche's text reproduces this negative spirit and its hostile attitude to woman, encapsulated in the line about the whip. Whip and serpent are connected not only iconographically, but through their conventional, cultural relationship to revenge and to woman.

Several more serpents populate part 2 of *Zarathustra*. The chapter entitled "Of Immaculate Perception" discusses the hypocrisy of Christian contemplatives: "Your spirit has been persuaded to contempt of the earthly, but your entrails have not: these, however, are the strongest part of you!" (Entrails are symbolically serpents.) As he tells these "pure ones":

> Only dare to believe in yourselves—in yourselves and in your entrails! He who does not believe in himself always lies.
> You have put on the mask of a god, you "pure": your dreadful coiling snake has crawled into the mask of a god." (Z 2 "Of Immaculate Perception")

The shepherd with the snake hanging from his mouth in the vision mirrors this earlier prophecy of Zarathustra, or fulfills it. In "Of Immaculate Perception," the allegorical "dreadful coiling snake" is a bad snake, symbolizing the hypocritical lies told by the "contemplatives" of "pure knowledge" who are ashamed of their entrails—their "lust"—and who disguise their desire by the "noble words" in their mouths. Zarathustra also tells the "pure" ones that innocence must now be defined as "begetting" for life's sake, creating "beyond" oneself, loving and perishing: "Loving and perishing: these have gone together from eternity. Will to love: that means to be willing to die, too." This is the message of Dionysus, "cut to pieces [as] a promise of life: it [life] will be eternally reborn and return again from destruction" (*WP* 1052).

Other passages in part 2 adumbrate the serpent of the vision and riddle. In "The Child with the Mirror," Zarathustra is impatient to rejoin his disciples and wants to reach them quickly. "I leap into your chariot, storm! And even you I will whip on with my venom!" This mixed metaphor connects the whip and the snake, the snake and Zarathustra himself, and recalls the extratextual photograph of Lou Salomé in the "chariot" with her whip. The venom in this case is efficacious, capable of energizing even the horsepower of a storm.

In "Of the Rabble," Zarathustra describes the sensation of being choked or gagged by his feelings of loathing for "the rabble"—people who are most concerned with themselves and their own comfort and do not think beyond themselves:

> That was not the mouthful that choked me the most.
> But once I asked, and my question almost stifled me: What, does life have *need* of the rabble, too?"

Being choked or stifled by one's distaste for those persons or attitudes of which one disapproves is also a common metaphor that plays into the vision and riddle, where the serpent becomes the representative of all that is hateful. Because of the connections the text has drawn, lightly, between the whip and the serpent, the serpent in the mouth of the shepherd also suggests that woman or women are part of what is most hateful to Zarathustra—least able to be "swallowed," most stifling.[7] (Recall here that the biographical particulars of this period of Nietzsche's life, which we surveyed in the previous chapter, compare his struggles with the women around him to Laocöon wrestling with his serpents.)

These associations exist in the text, but what stands out about the serpent figures or their substitutes is that they clearly symbolize Zarathustra's *other* prophecy, the eternal return. Whereas Zarathustra has no trouble articulating the prophecy of Übermensch, eternal return prompts in him a reaction of fear and loathing characteristic of the agony of the Hebrew prophets. In "The Wanderer" (the chapter that precedes "Of the Vision and the Riddle"), he says that he knows he must descend "deeper into pain than I have ever descended, down to its blackest stream"; then the eternal return "appears" to Zarathustra in the vision of the gateway that precedes and evokes the riddle of shepherd and snake. In "Of Involuntary Bliss" (the chapter that follows "Of the Vision and the Riddle"), Zarathustra explains the riddle: "In symbols everything called to me . . . But I—did not hear: until at last my abyss stirred and my thought bit me. . . . Even your silence threatens to choke me, you abysmal, silent thought. . . . Your heaviness has always been fearful for me" (Z 3 "Of Involuntary Bliss"). Later in part 3 (in "The Convalescent"), he refers to "my abysmal thought, a worm" and "that monster crept into my throat," where the monster personifies his "grand disgust" and weariness with man but substitutes for the black snake (Z 3 "The Convalescent").

One more contribution to serpent lore seems to epitomize the archetypal significance humans have always ascribed to these most inscrutable, most numinous of animals, and to connect with Zarathustra's strange vision. This is Francis Huxley's summary of ancient meanings of "primal serpents": "The main characteristic of primal serpents is their habit of swallowing everything, so that they have to be killed to make themselves disgorge. This is traditionally interpreted in one of two ways: either the killing of the serpent and the resultant flood of waters signifies the birth of a child from its mother, or it refers to the symbolic ejaculation of the Sky Father, which produces rain and children impartially." To this Huxley adds one further detail: the soul of a "dead man is regularly figured as a snake or dragon. The dragon brings children, as it does to the Aborigines, which tells us that the dead are also the unborn" (89). The connection between the dead and the unborn, mediated by the serpent, seems a good description of Zarathustra's eternal return.

As in a dream, the images of the vision externalize and symbolize the psychological state of the dreamer. In this case, the dreamer is Zarathustra, who is also the shepherd; Zarathustra "sees" and "speaks" and *is* the message. He is split, fragmented, doubled, and redoubled; within the riddle, he is a reporter/observer, but with agency, the ability to change his own dream, to act on his own fate, which the dream is prophesying. He is like the poet in *The Birth of Tragedy* who, completely absorbed in his vision, "is at once subject and object, at once poet, actor, and spectator" (*BT* 5). The imagery of the vision's setting suggests a repressed feminine at the outset, and the serpent, symbol of the earth and of sexuality, stands for the thought of eternal return, which has fastened itself onto the prophet's vocal chords and prevented him from speaking the message. The vision tells Zarathustra, who is his own best reader, that transformation will occur when he frees himself from his abysmal thought, and that in order to free himself from it he must bite into it. We might say go right into it, right through it with no evasion, where "it" stands for pain, depression, disgust, or nausea—the heavy—the difficult—meaningless death—but ultimately, for Zarathustra, his own particular demise. Actually accepting one's own mortality, rather than merely talking about doing so and theorizing its consequences, is as hard, and as repulsive, as biting the head off a snake, the riddle seems to say.

It is also as physical as the pain of childbirth. Clearly, childbirth is one of the referents for this riddle, where the prone shepherd is the woman, the mouth is the vagina (a common dream transposition from the lower to the upper part of the body[8]), the serpent is the umbilicus, the bite cuts the umbilicus, and the laughing figure is the child. A point of reference or a model for such a birth might be that of the *Theogony,* where Kronos gives birth to his children through his mouth. Using Huxley's account of the myth of freeing the waters, the serpent has to be cut into (or in two) in order to release the new life.

Zarathustra tells his animals that he finds the thought symbolized by the snake "abysmal." Nausea at the futility of life's suffering and the great disgust at man recalls Heidegger's theory that the revenge against the transience of time is what must be overcome. In "Of Redemption," Zarathustra explains that the will, which could be a liberator, is also a "malefactor" because "it is sullenly wrathful that time does not run back." It cannot change the past, and therefore it becomes revengeful; in fact, "this alone is *revenge* itself: the will's antipathy towards time and time's 'it was.'" The will takes out its revenge on time by willing punishment: "Where there was suffering, there was always supposed to be punishment." Because life involves "eternal suffering," we humans, who suffer, must deserve this lot—therefore we must deserve punishment. "Because there is suffering in the willer himself, since he cannot will backwards—therefore willing itself and all life was supposed to be—punishment!" And so, Zarathustra says, we arrive at the belief that "everything passes away, therefore everything deserves to pass away" (Z 2 "Of Redemption"). For the will to be a liberator, it must "unlearn the spirit of revenge" by saying to time, "But thus I willed it!" Indeed, "But I will it thus!"

How does the shepherd summon the will to bite into the serpent? A passage from *On the Genealogy of Morals* reads: "The active force . . . precisely that instinct for freedom (in my language, the will to power) . . . takes delight . . . in imposing a form upon itself as heavy, recalcitrant, passive matter, in branding into itself a will, a critique, a contradiction, a contempt, a *No*" (2:18). If we take it that the will to power wills the negative, and let the serpent for the moment represent that negative (the whip as resentment of women, for example), then the bite is the "*no!*" to the negative constructed by the will itself, taking sides against itself. It is the will of the lion, the second metamorphosis of the spirit, willing to be free from its load of resentment, summoning up the energy to confront its most difficult task. The shepherd is the will to power which, as a force, is manifested in the vision first as reactive—passive, lying down, and beset by the negative which, the vision shows, attacks internally. Zarathustra, as onlooker, cannot dislodge the power of the negative; the shepherd has to do it himself. However, Zarathustra is also the shepherd, and he tells us that at this critical moment, he summons up "my horror, my hate, my disgust, my pity, all my good and evil" to cry out with a single word: "Bite!" The negative and the moral in Zarathustra provide the energy to command the bite, and they turn back upon themselves at the moment it occurs. In that instant, reaction becomes action and affirmation.

In the passage about the active force from *On the Genealogy of Morals,* the "No" to the self which divides the self becomes the "bad conscience"; the bad conscience becomes "the womb of all ideal and imaginative phenomena" and brings forth "an abundance of strange new beauty and affirmation" (2:18). Once again, if the serpent/whip is the thought of eternal return as the "baby truth" that Zarathustra guards under his cloak—that attaches itself inside Zarathustra's throat as in a womb and is in this manifestation valued negatively by the shepherd—then the act of biting off its head is the cutting of the umbilical cord, the "freeing of the waters" as in ancient birth myths, the "disgorging" of the primal serpent, which transforms the shepherd into the Übermensch. Following Zarathustra's formula for self-overcoming by willing the past, and therefore all of time, we could say that the occasion of the shepherd's bite is the moment of acceptance of transience and the earth, which is the time when resentment falls away and the negative is revalued as affirmative. Then it is possible to say "Yes" to all of life, including death; the unborn and the dead are part of the same ongoing, eternally transforming Dionysian existence.

The "vision" shows that, having bitten into the thought of eternal return and by so doing overcoming resentment of time, the shepherd is transformed into something over, or beyond, himself—that surpasses human "gravity," that rejoices in laughter. In an earlier analogy, Zarathustra compared this

"something" to a child, who is "innocence and forgetfulness, a new beginning, a sport, a self-propelling wheel, a first motion, a sacred Yes" (Z 1 "Of
the Three Metamorphoses"). This "third metamorphosis of the spirit,"
beyond contradiction and the negative, beyond irony and metaphor, creates from affirmation alone.

Time and the feminine are bound together, for Nietzsche, due to woman's ancient links to birth and death, the primary events that mark human
life. In *Zarathustra,* as in *The Gay Science,* Life is a woman. When the will
becomes "reconciled" to time, it is thus "reconciled . . . and higher things
than reconciliation" (Z 2 "Of Redemption") to woman as well. Zarathustra's
strange dream vision is saturated by woman and the feminine—from the
valley setting by moonlight to the shepherd struggling to give birth to the
triumphant birth of the Übermensch, celebrating the supreme human
achievement of acceptance of the transience of material life. In this way,
the vision signifies Nietzsche's choice of the tellurian world of the mothers,
rather than the imperishable halls of light of the fathers.

How, then, does the light surrounding the laughing figure, and the
figure itself, tally with this interpretation? I suggest that these images
similarly evoke a feminine context for Nietzsche. In the summer of 1883,
he recorded in his notebook what seems a revelation: "I have discovered
Hellenism: they believe in the eternal return! It is the faith of the mysteries"
(*KSA* 10:340). At the time he was busy drafting the second part of *Zarathustra.*
He had himself "discovered" the eternal return two years earlier, and had
whispered it to Lou Salomé on Monte Sacro the following May; here in the
notebooks he connects it with the Eleusinian mysteries. Eureka. What he
had described in *The Birth of Tragedy* as tragic joy, the faith in the permanence
of time itself, strong enough to accept death; the sameness of the ever-
changing material world; all that he had imagined as the "eternal return"—
these he now "saw" as the faith of the mysteries, the ritual, feminine celebrations of fertility.

Zarathustra's riddle parodies what Nietzsche knew of the Eleusinian
mysteries; he mentions the "grotesque hieroglyphics of their rites" (*PTAG*
33) and then produces a "vision" to which these terms clearly apply. Certainly the shepherd choking on a long black snake is grotesque. Laughter
has ancient associations with fertility; gazing on Baubo's belly or pubis,
Demeter, so the story goes, burst out laughing and thus broke the drought,
restoring fertility to the land. The vision at the mysteries was accompanied, according to sources, by a dazzling light. If the laughing figure sur-
rounded by light symbolizes the Übermensch, then the Übermensch is joy

that comes with woe (the serpent), transforms the woe, and joyfully, laughingly, affirms life as its own justification. It is hard to imagine this kind of laughter, unless one thinks of the wholly joyful laugh of a baby. After all, Zarathustra's vision is a prophecy and the beginning of a new ideal—or the reintroduction of a very old one—that is desperately difficult for Zarathustra to articulate. However, this prophetic ideal tells Zarathustra, and us, that he will overcome the horror of his task and become who he is: the advocate of life, the advocate of suffering, the advocate of the circle.

The Eternal Return as Life

Like an unrepressed Dionysian, the "thought" of the eternal return makes its way into Zarathustra's consciousness, until as a "convalescent" he listens to his animals sing about it. In the third-last chapter of part 3, he has a dialogue with his soul, acknowledging that she is now perfectly ripe, like golden grapes, and that she is longing to board the golden boat of free will that will, freely, be commanded by the master who has the vine knife. In essence, Zarathustra tells his soul that she—and by extension that he—is ready to die. In this regard, Gary Shapiro comments that Zarathustra's soul has been transformed, and that Zarathustra's praise of his soul here is a kind of love song to himself. It is not "the triumphant cry of the hegemonic, imperial self but the joy felt upon the release from the constrictions of a narrowly defined identity" (*Nietzschean Narratives* 93). It is self-acceptance, self-forgiveness—a condition, indeed the only condition, that makes acceptance of a return to this "self-same life" possible. Zarathustra asks his soul to sing for him, and she offers "The Second Dance Song," which constitutes the second-last chapter of part 3.

This song is full of images of the Dionysian and the Apollonian as they interact, at first "openly at variance," inciting each other to new creation as in *The Birth of Tragedy*, until the characters of the song finally come together in loving reconciliation. The song begins with Zarathustra gazing into Life's eyes: "I saw gold glittering in your eyes of night. . . . I saw a golden bark glittering upon dark waters, a submerging, surging, re-emerging golden tossing bark." Dark waters, golden boat: the images conjure Dionysian/Apollonian, at variance yet equally present in Life's eyes, which themselves mirror Zarathustra's own state of becoming. In the previous chapter he refers to the golden boat of free will, ready to put out on the "sea of longing and desire" *to die* (Z 3 "Of the Great Longing"); here that boat is tossing on the sea of longing and desire *for Life*. Since it's the same sea, we sense that death and life are being drawn closer together. The tossing bark metamorphoses into Zarathustra's feet, "tossing in a mad dance" with Life. In the dance, the partners do not move in harmony; the dance is "mad," and thus Dionysian, and Life becomes Dionysus/Medusa, whose serpent locks force Zarathustra to "retire." With this, she then advances—and so it goes, this dance of contradictions: "Your fleeing allures me, your seeking secures me," you, "whose coldness enflames, whose hatred seduces, whose flight constrains, whose mockery—induces." Zarathustra fancies himself the hunter, but Life becomes a "supple snake and slippery witch" that eludes and bites him. Exasperated, he tells her, "I am truly weary of being your shepherd," and he threatens her with the whip: "To the rhythm of my whip you shall shriek and trot! Did I forget my whip?—I did not!" (Z 3 "The Second Dance Song" 1).

The allusion to the advice offered in "On Little Old and Young Women" draws a parallel between the old woman and Life, and the references to Life as a "supple snake" associate the whip and the serpent. Furthermore, the fact that Zarathustra calls himself Life's shepherd, and that she, in serpent form, bites him, forces a reinterpretation of the "vision and the riddle." The song suggests that the serpent in the vision is Life herself. (Should we require further evidence of this association, we need only consider this entry in Nietzsche's spring/fall 1887 notebooks: "Against the value of that which remains eternally the same . . . , the values of the briefest and most transient, the seductive flash of gold on the belly of the serpent *vita*—" [WP 577].) The associations between shepherd and serpent life in "The Second Dance Song" identify Life with the eternal return.

The allusion to the whip in this text brings the mad dance to a conclusion. Whereas the first part of the poem has been more Dionysian than Apollonian, now Life says, "O Zarathustra! Do not crack your whip so terribly! You surely know: noise kills thought." Life has reverted to the form of a woman who desires thought, the Apollonian; she tells Zarathustra that the two of them have much in common, that she is jealous of his Wisdom, and that her jealousy actually fixes her love for him. She also accuses Zarathustra of "thinking of leaving me soon," to which he responds by whispering something in her ear. What he whispers remains a secret, but the very act is reminiscent of the gift—the "little truth"—that the old woman softly speaks in Zarathustra's ear, and of its real-life original, Nietzsche's whispered communication to Salomé of his idea of eternal return. Life responds thus to Zarathustra's whispered message: "'You *know* that, O Zarathustra? No one knows that.' And we gazed at one another and looked out at the green meadow, over which the cool evening was spreading, and wept together. But then Life was dearer to me than all my Wisdom had ever been. Thus spoke Zarathustra" (Z 3 "The Second Dance Song" 2).

Critics have generally assumed (and I agree) that Zarathustra tells Life about the eternal return, about which of course, she already knows (though no one else does). Maudemarie Clark suggests that the text then offers us a clue about how we might respond to the thought of the return—we might weep—and that this gives us a clue as to its nature (*Nietzsche on Truth and Philosophy* 263-64). Why would we weep if we knew we would meet again, the next time round? It seems evident that the content of the eternal return is neither cosmological, nor scientific, nor "true." The eternal return is "a parable," and like all good Zarathustrian parables, it speaks of time and becoming. Clark holds that the eternal return is a hypothesis, a test of one's ability to affirm life (262). Zarathustra finds that he cannot affirm "the small man's" return, that this thought nauseates him. He is able only gradually to overcome his nausea and affirm emotionally that which he knows is the truth—nothing returns, except life itself. "The return to the same," Paul Valadier observes, "is a return to the same affirmation. . . . Yea-saying entails its return, the 'one-time' wills the 'second time'" (254-55). David Wood suggests that it is not the actual details of experience that repeat, in eternal return, but rather its "dynamic structure"—"the rhythm, the pulse of excitement and fatigue, of arousal and consummation, of exhilaration and passivity, of the rising and setting of the passions. It is thus *movement*, the movement of becoming, that is repeated eternally" (52).

The partners in "The Second Dance Song"—Zarathustra and Life—act out those rhythms, whose structure is based on a set of binary oppositions, the principal one being man/woman. The constituent elements change their substance but remain opposed throughout the first part of the song; then, at the sound of the whip, they are brought into contiguous rather than antagonistic relation. In this, the oppositions are finally dissolved and the principals end up united in tears and love. In keeping with Nietzsche's typical pattern, the structural opposition breaks down and gives way to interrelationship between the former antagonists. In this case the interrelationship is identity: Zarathustra becomes his Life.

By using these figures, Nietzsche asks us to read the text as allegory. Zarathustra's relationship with his own Life is one of romantic love; he clearly feels passionately about Life, most especially when he hates her. In "The Second Dance Song," Life initially dominates the relationship, leading Zarathustra in a dance up hill and down dale until he has had enough and pulls out his whip. We use the allegory ourselves in everyday speech, when we say that life is getting out of hand or assert that we need to take control of our lives. Nietzsche simply dramatizes our common figures of speech. The assertion that life is a woman complicates this, however, because it tempts us to see her as a figure to whom Zarathustra takes the whip; from this vantage point, he is violent and misogynistic. Even the act of seeing her as the feminine in Zarathustra serves to confine her to a role—a problematic association, as I rather think she represents an externalization of Zarathustra's life. Bearing this in mind, I think that we might take the text to read that Zarathustra is not in charge or control of his Life until he takes his whip to her/himself/it. The crack of the whip symbolizes the will to power's sharp call to order, whereby it exercises its force to gain self-mastery.

And then—presto—there is a change. The sequence of events in the song replicates those in the "vision," where Zarathustra (the shepherd) is passive and life (the serpent) has the advantage—that is, until he bites off her head (a metaphoric expression for delivering a sharp rebuke) with a symbolic crack of the whip, which is the moment of transformation in both instances. It is not that life or the serpent symbolizes the negative; the negative exists solely in the shepherd's/Zarathustra's attitude toward life's recurrence. The bite, or the crack of the whip, symbolizes the will to power's response—the "No"—to this negative attitude. The effect of the whip/bite in both the vision and the song is Apollonian and creative. In the vision, it produces the laughing affirmation of the Übermensch. In the song, order is restored to the relationship between Zarathustra and Life, with the result that the two rationally discuss their situation and share their knowledge, which is that of eternal return—the serpent's knowledge. After the momentary No to the no, Zarathustra is able to think things out clearly and calmly, and finds that his resentment—of life, of woman, of time—has been transformed into love. At the end of the song, it is Zarathustra who gives voice to his love of Life, and the tag "Thus spoke Zarathustra" underlines the fact that Zarathustra—or rather, his soul—is the sole actor, the only spokesperson, in the chapter.

The text does not "speak out," but merely hints to us, its readers, that Zarathustra's transformation from a resentful, aging prophet to an even older, loving one has taken place. Recall that in "On Little Old and Young Women" (in part 1), Zarathustra is seen hiding the little truth under his cloak and "slinking" through the twilight—a gesture that we can easily read as one of shame. In Zarathustra's love song to his soul, "Of the Great Longing" (in part 3), he says, "O my soul, I washed the petty shame and corner-virtue away from you and persuaded you to stand naked before the eyes of the sun." Here the shame is gone, and the soul, like truth, stands naked, with nothing to hide. As he accepts the gift of the staff from his disciples, Zarathustra comments on the images, comparing the serpent of knowledge to "a subtle soul." If we take this to be self-referential, then we once more see the union of knowledge and power in Zarathustra, his soul standing forth naked and unashamed.

Similarly, at the start of part 3, we discern that allegorical figures we have met as separate entities in the text are in the process of merging. Zarathustra informs us that this is happening: "It is returning, at last it is coming home to me—my own Self and those parts of it that have long been abroad and scattered among all things and accidents" (Z 3 "The Wanderer"). This self-fulfillment occurs without Zarathustra's intervention. Whereas he has willed the roadblock of the eternal return and used his will, as well, to overcome it, his Self draws together of its own accord. The act of willing is necessary, but it is insufficient to create a whole Self. Once Zarathustra "bites into" the serpent in his vision, and later consciously summons his thought, his Self does the rest without his conscious control. But what parts are coming home to him? If Life and Wisdom are bound together by their love for Zarathustra and jealousy of each other, and if they closely resemble each other; if Life is the "supple snake" of "The Second Dance Song," and Zarathustra's soul is also the serpent of knowledge—if all these hold true, then his Life, his Wisdom, and his soul are the same, and they all represent the eternal return. Thus it should come as no surprise or shock when, in the song that ends part 3, after declaring his love to Life, Zarathustra tells us: "Never yet did I find the woman by whom I wanted children, unless it be this woman, whom I love: for I love you, O Eternity!" (Z 3 "The Seven Seals"). Eternity—by his special definition, now fairly clear to us as time—includes everything else: his Life, Wisdom, soul, conscience, happiness, sensuality, all his good and all his evil. All are one as Zarathustra. They have returned to him as he in turn returned to himself, by welcoming eternity—that is, by welcoming life exactly as it is. This is the way, Zarathustra suggests, to bring about constructive change.

For Alexander Nehemas and for Maudemarie Clark, eternal recurrence "is not a theory of the world but a view of the ideal life" (Nehemas 7); it is "an ideal that takes us beyond the ascetic ideal," as Nietzsche's "proposed solution to the problem of nihilism" (Clark *Nietzsche on Truth and Philosophy* 166n, 253). For Clark, it is a "test for the affirmation of life": "Affirming eternal recurrence depends in no way on believing recurrence to be true, probable, or even logically possible. It requires the willingness to live one's life again, not the belief that one will" (251–52). It also calls upon the willingness to affirm death. In "The Second Dance Song," Clark holds that Zarathustra tells Life "that to affirm life, one must affirm the recurrence of everything, including death" (263). Like *The Birth of Tragedy, Thus Spoke Zarathustra* also poses the question of how to accept death out of love of life.

Life tells Zarathustra that she knows he is thinking of leaving her when the old midnight bell strikes twelve. Each line of Zarathustra's poem, which comprises the third part of "The Second Dance Song," is set to the stroke of the bell, tolling between one and eleven. There is no text at the stroke of twelve, implying the possibility of Zarathustra's death. There follows the "eulogy" of the last song, praising eternity with "The Seven Seals" (a reference to the seven seals of the Apocalypse). By the title of this last song, Nietzsche overturns Christian teleology in favor of eternal return. When he finished part 3 of *Zarathustra,* Nietzsche wrote to Franz Overbeck, his friend in Basel, that he had brought to completion something he had started in his earliest years in that city. I suggest that the thing he felt he had finally accepted was the Dionysian feminine, the perishable world of time and change, as the tragic condition of human endeavor. And it is here, with the eulogy to time and change, that Nietzsche might have left Zarathustra. But he did not. Rather, he went on to add part 4, a satyr play, a strange coda, to the tragicomic, Menippean trilogy.

Zarathustra's Irony and Its Mastered Moment

Although I find it a delight, indeed a wonder, and the best part of *Thus Spoke Zarathustra,* I shall restrict my discussion of part 4 of the work to questions of sex-gender and genre.[9] By the end of part 3, the feminine, implicit in Zarathustra's major prophecy of eternal return and in his self-overcoming, has become assimilated as an important, major part of his Self. If Life is a woman, and if she is Zarathustra's very own life, then the logic of Zarathustra's self-identity as a male has opened out into a pluralism that is neither man nor woman, but human and inclusive. The oppositional categories simply don't apply anymore. In part 4 Nietzsche gives us a reworking of that thought, emphasizing the ironic, parodic gap between the reader and the text that liberates the reader from the authority of Zarathustra and his prophecies.

This final part of the work is obviously parodic, and though some of the events therein caricature well-known storied traditions of Western culture (one chapter is called "The Last Supper," for example), its main focus is—as befits such a thoroughly self-reflexive text—parts 1-3. Because it introduces a number of different voices, it is dialogic in the Bakhtinian sense; its varying perspectives "[liberate] the object from the power of language in which it had become entangled as if in a net; they [destroy] the homogenizing power of myth over language; they [free] consciousness from the power of the direct word" (60). Nietzsche's irony "cuts remorselessly" into his own text—as Socrates' irony did into his own flesh and that of the Athenian nobles, according to Nietzsche (*BGE* 212), or as the shepherd bit into the serpent with his teeth. This is creative cutting, pain akin to childbirth, once again—healing and liberating, if it doesn't kill you ("What does not kill me makes me stronger" [*TI*, "Maxims and Arrows" 8]).

When we encounter him in part 4, Zarathustra is an old man with white hair, sitting on his mountain, waiting for his "children" to appear. The text offers various hints to indicate (to me at any rate) that his children are actually philosophers of the future, philosophers of the "dangerous perhaps" (*BGE* 2) who will have read his "prophecies" (Nietzsche's books, that is) and carried his ideas further across the metaphorical bridge to the Übermensch. As he waits, he receives a motley collection of masculine characters (a pessimistic prophet, two former kings, a former pope, a sorcerer-musician, a philosopher-scientist, a deformed person, and his own shadow) who have sought him out for help and comfort. Zarathustra invites them up to his cave for a meal, for which his poor distracted animals-cum-servants have to go out and hunt. Because they echo Zarathustra's sayings, these Higher Men can be understood as Nietzsche's first readers, and Zarathustra's mixture of dismay and sympathy for them as "firstlings" of a new order reflects Nietzsche's anxieties about his reception and influence. Each one of them echoes a piece of Zarathustra's philosophy, and either distorts it by inflecting it his own way, or is himself misshapen, or both.

Zarathustra here succumbs to his great temptation, which is "pity for the higher men." Gary Shapiro has suggested that Zarathustra responds to the "cries of distress" of the Higher Men in exactly the way a mother responds to crying infants—running hither and thither, gathering them together and "reassuring the criers with a promise of food, rest, and play" (*Alcyone* 73). For Shapiro, these Higher Men are Zarathustra's parasites. For Caroline Picart, they are his abortive children. Their appearance in the text supports Picart's argument that Zarathustra's illness, his resentment of women in particular (his "lust for and envy of the maternal womb") is based on his inability to give birth to the Übermensch, and his capacity to produce only the distorted "monstrous higher men" (110). On one level, I see these as the first, clumsy attempts at giving expression to a new myth, rather like the monsters of Hesiod's *Theogony,* which Homer's retellings later perfected. In *Beyond Good and Evil,* Nietzsche stresses the strangeness of things at their beginning: "It seems that, in order to inscribe themselves in the hearts of humanity with eternal demands, all great things have first to wander the earth as monstrous and fear-inspiring grotesques" ("Preface"). The Higher Men would serve as yet another of Nietzsche's masks, another way to call attention to and at the same time parody his own work as a great new thing. On another level, however, I see the title "Higher Men" as ironic, and parodic of the nineteenth-century concern with evolutionarily "higher" (and lower) living things. The "Higher Men" are simply human males looking for help and comfort, trying to grasp Zarathustra's teachings. Zarathustra's concern for them is something that demonstrates for us (rather than merely telling us) that he has overcome resentment, and has become a good teacher.

As caricatures of Zarathustra's teachings, the Higher Men are the clearest instance of doubling in the text. They embody a Nietzschean quality that Zarathustra himself recommends to them: "Learn to laugh at yourselves as a man ought to laugh!" (*Z* 4 "Of the Higher Man" 15). References to manliness occur several times in part 4, for Zarathustra wants his followers to be strong men, and clearly detects in them some effeminacy, or perhaps a measure of sexual ambiguity. It is hard to decide where self-mockery begins and ends in the early sections here, so apt is the text to turn and bite its own tail. If the Higher Men are caricatures of Zarathustra, then what is said of them may be understood to apply to him, their distortions only emphasizing, perhaps, his distinguishing features.

The text establishes its mirror-play in the scene where the first of the Higher Men—the world-weary prophet—appears before Zarathustra. At first their shadows appear side by side; then Zarathustra (who is a prophet himself) springs up and observes the other prophet's battered face with alarm. "The prophet, who had perceived what was going on in Zarathustra's soul, wiped his hand across his face, as if he wanted to wipe it away; Zarathustra did the same" (*Z* 4 "The Cry of Distress"). This mimetic gesture demonstrates that each is the other's mirror image.

We become reacquainted with old friends in this final part of *Zarathustra.* The content of the vision and the riddle appears once more, for example, this time in a bad verse "wailed" by the sorcerer, who mimes the agony of the shepherd in the riddle: "Spread-eagled, shuddering, / Like a half-dead man. . . . / Pursued by you, my thought! / Unutterable, veiled, terrible one!"

(*Z* 4 "The Sorcerer" 1).[10] The sorcerer lampoons Zarathustra, who in turn beats him with a stick for his efforts. The sorcerer then plays liar's paradox with Zarathustra, as Zarathustra has played it with his disciples. "Such things are part of my art," he tells Zarathustra, explaining that he was only feigning torment; "I wanted to put you yourself to the proof when I gave you this exhibition!" Yes, I was lying, he admits. He knows Zarathustra, as Zarathustra knows him, by this accusing the sorcerer of deception: "You . . . *must* deceive: I know you so far. You must always be ambiguous, with two, three, four, five meanings!" (*Z* 4 "The Sorcerer" 2). Thus does Zarathustra accuse the sorcerer, but because of the mirror-effect established between the two, and because we know Zarathustra's own words are ambiguous and carry several meanings, the accusation boomerangs.

In a later chapter, the sorcerer gives an overtly sexual expression to Zarathustra's word "ambiguous," such that textual and sexual ambiguity become explicitly analogous. Introducing his "melancholy song" to the company assembled in Zarathustra's cave, the sorcerer warns them thus: "But already *he* is attacking me and compelling me, this spirit of melancholy, this evening-twilight devil: and truly, you Higher Men, he has a desire—just open your eyes!—he has a desire to come *naked*, whether as man or woman I do not yet know" (*Z* 4 "The Song of Melancholy" 2). The sorcerer twice mentions that he does not know which sex his melancholy spirit will adopt for his/her appearance, drawing attention to the sexual ambiguity of creative—especially poetic—activity. (The other "twilight devil" in the text is the little old woman Zarathustra meets in part 1, who, as an extension of Zarathustra, had already multiplied his sexual identity.) Here the sorcerer introduces his twilight devil as man or woman (he doesn't know which, and could appear as either), and his desire to appear naked parodies Zarathustra's song to his soul.

Ambiguity is the subject of a conversation between Zarathustra and a former pope about the nature and purpose of the old God, now dead. Zarathustra observes that God had something of the priestly nature about him: "He was ambiguous. He was also indistinct. How angry he was with us, this snorter of wrath, because we mistook his meaning! But why did he not speak more clearly? And if our ears were to blame, why did he give us ears that were unable to hear him properly?" (*Z* 4 "Retired from Service"). This is a lovely, multileveled comment on the "undecidable" nature of God's word, the *logos*—why on earth didn't God just say what he meant?—a criticism leveled at Nietzsche during his own time, and ever since. The comment compares Zarathustra and God (Zarathustra invoked the Gospel's "He who has ears to hear, let him hear" to underline his own ambiguity [Z 3 "Of the Apostates" 2]), and picks up on Zarathustra's constant complaint about ears ("They do not understand me: I am not the mouth for these ears" [Z 1 "Prologue" 5]). Whose fault is this, the speaker's, or the listener's? In the topsy-turvy world that marks this final part of the work, Zarathustra blames the speaker (and the creator of ears); hitherto his usual practice has been to blame the listeners for being so very obtuse, so unprepared, so badly educated, so habit-ridden, so media-plagued, so long (ass)-eared, and so on.

Much of the irony characteristic of part 4 is situational and depends on repetition. The two unemployed kings who figure in the third chapter use Zarathustra's words to complain of the rabble, and one of them says, "It is this disgust that chokes me . . . faugh, to live among the mob! . . . Ah, disgust! disgust! disgust!" (Z 4 "Conversation with the Kings" 1). Here, as elsewhere in this last part of the work, readers experience the shock of recognition with each of the Higher Men, who throw Zarathustra's words back to him as in an echo chamber. In the epilogue to *The Gay Science* (written after the fourth part of *Zarathustra* appeared), Nietzsche hears laughter all around him, and remarks that "the spirits of my own books are attacking me, pull my ears, and call me back to order" (GS 383). In the chapters that constitute part 4 of *Zarathustra,* the Higher Men, like the spirits of his book, lampoon Zarathustra's sayings and pull his ears. At the same time, structural irony erects a framework around the text. The events are treated as significant religious occasions; third-person narration is used, and characters other than Zarathustra sometimes act as narrative focalizers. It is carnival, it is fun, and it is effective. As so often with Nietzsche's texts, it performs or enacts, textually, its meanings. I would argue that, rather than providing a generic contrast to parts 1–3, part 4 actually intensifies and foregrounds the parody that has been implicit throughout the work. The space that the use of irony opens up—producing a text that can mean two or more different things at the same time through its clash of perspectives—informs readers that reality is multiple and complex. That the Higher Men mime Zarathustra's words, and that we discern that they—like the allegorical figures—"belong to" Zarathustra, shows us that internal reality is similarly complex. But as with parts 1–3, so too in part 4 the complexity is slowly organized, and in the end, the ironies of an ironic text are mastered.

In his treatise on the subject, Kierkegaard concludes that the negativity of irony, which serves to defend the subject from reality through alienation, by creating distance between the subject and the world, can be overcome. Irony remains, as the necessary space of conscious thought, but its negativity is mastered: "Irony as a mastered moment exhibits itself in its truth precisely by the fact that it places due emphasis upon actuality." As Kierkegaard notes, in this way actuality acquires its validity "as a history wherein consciousness successively outlives itself, though in such a way that happiness consists not in forgetting all this but becoming present in it" (341). Consciousness becoming present in the moment, dwelling in actuality, bringing memory (of the past) and hope (for the future) to the constitution of the present—this characterization is akin to Zarathustra's eternal return.

The narrative in part 4 of *Thus Spoke Zarathustra* is marked by a number of surprising and atypical developments:

First, we see Zarathustra from the outside for the only time in the text. The first sentence of the part's first chapter reads: "And again months and years passed over Zarathustra's soul, and he did not heed it; his hair, however, grew white" (Z 4 "The Honey Offering"). This physical detail serves at the start to distance us from the character and enables us to see him not as a Dionysian Übermensch, but as an aging human being.

Second, though the visitors to his mountainside are called "The Higher Men," they too are elderly and in various states of infirmity. Though some of them have held society's highest rank, they are all called upon to help prepare the supper and pitch in with the communal work, as at a summer camp. Against the explicit exhortations of his discourses, here in part 4 Zarathustra sets on democratic par the noble and the plebian.

Third, and once again contrary to the spirit of his discourses, Zarathustra is overcome with kindred feeling, which he calls "pity," for these elderly men. But his pity, if pity it be, soon turns to affection. They cheer him up; several times in the course of their shared adventure he utters words to this effect: "What good things this day has given me . . . as recompense for starting out so badly! What strange discoursers I have found!" he notes in "The Ugliest Man." This is echoed in the one of the final chapters: "O my new friends . . . , you strange men, you Higher Men, how well you please me now, since you have become joyful again!" (Z 4 "The Ass Festival" 3).

Fourth (and finally), toward the end of the book, the text's doubleness, its obvious irony, disappears. After the Last Supper, Zarathustra's guests wander out of the cave; it is close to midnight: "Meanwhile, however, one after another had gone out into the open air and the cool, thoughtful night; but Zarathustra himself led the ugliest man by the hand, to show him his nocturnal world and the big, round moon and the silver waterfalls beside the cave. There at last they stood silently together, just a group of old folk, but with comforted, brave hearts and amazed in themselves that it was so well with them on earth" (Z 4 "The Intoxicated Song" 1).

This passage is narrated with an almost childlike simplicity (indicating perhaps that the third metamorphosis of the spirit is at hand) and it purports to tell the truth about real people, who experience the immanent, finite world and find it to be good. These are not "prophets" and "higher men"; they are "just a group of old folk." There is only one story in this passage and no ambiguity at all; "the creator" is speaking his message clearly. Here is the mastered moment, in my view the one toward which the entire narrative of *Thus Spoke Zarathustra* has labored, capped by "The Intoxicated Song" that closes the chapter, where Zarathustra sings that "all things are chained, entwined, in love" (Z 4 "The Intoxicated Song" 10). It has taken Zarathustra a lifetime to reach this point of acceptance and affirmation.

In this celebratory "Intoxicated Song" that is the penultimate chapter of the book, difference collapses—not into identity, but into simultaneity: "My world has just become perfect, midnight is also noonday, pain is also joy" (Z 4 "The Intoxicated Song" 10). Focusing on this passage, Stambaugh comments that Nietzsche's use of the word "perfect" echoes that of Spinoza, for whom reality and perfection are the same thing. When Zarathustra says that the world has become perfect, "he means it has become totally real" (25). At this point—rhetorically—metaphor, which needs the space of difference separating its terms in order to function, collapses; "the bridge" ceases to act as a space between two ends; the space disappears, and the two ends meet (in Zarathustra, Nietzsche comments, "all opposites are blended into a new unity" [EH "Thus Spoke Zarathustra" 6]). Here at last, in "The Intoxicated Song," Zarathustra sings as the advocate of life, of suffering, and of the circle, where life circles back and affirms itself in death.

Because it is the story of an individual, *Thus Spoke Zarathustra* makes clearer and more forceful the point it shares with *The Birth of Tragedy*—that is, the suggestion that individuals are multiple Selves and bring together in one person qualities that society has labeled "masculine" and "feminine." In the sets of opposition that are united in "The Intoxicated Song," Zarathustra does not say "a man is also a woman." Nonetheless, in the course of the book, which describes a process of internal change, the development and growth of the subject which is open and endless, we begin to see Zarathustra figuratively, as both/and—or rather, and more accurately, as fully human, beyond man and woman.

Nietzsche's "Dangerous Perhapses"

"Supposing truth to be a woman—what? Is the suspicion not well founded that all philosophers, when they have been dogmatists, have had little understanding of women?" (*BGE* Preface). Truth is the last great allegorical woman in Nietzsche's armory, and the biggest troublemaker. This isn't her fault; when he writes the following line in *Beyond Good and Evil*—"From the very first, nothing has been more alien, repugnant, inimical to woman than truth—her great art is the lie, her supreme concern is appearance and beauty" (232)—Nietzsche inscribes woman in both columns of this binary opposition, just as he does by dividing attributes of his "Greek woman" between the Dionysian and the Apollonian in *The Birth of Tragedy*. Little wonder that the poor dogmatist is confounded in his wooing, if woman is both the truth and the lie.

Woman as truth is the Sphinx, whom Nietzsche describes in *The Birth of Tragedy* as being "of two species" (9); her "nature" as nature is already divided and "unnatural," since she combines human and animal. She is the Sphinx of Nietzsche's early notebooks whose beauty seduces and "masks" the realities of suffering, the ugly, and the questionable. She confounds easy classification; human or animal, beauty or ugliness, life or death—she is both, and all. She appears before the philosopher at the start of *Beyond Good and Evil*, as the polyvalent truth that woman might be, if truth were a woman. The story of Oedipus and the Sphinx is "already a long story," Nietzsche writes, as he glimpses a few more questions posed by his enigmatic interlocutor. "That this sphinx should teach us too to ask questions? *Who* is it really who here questions us? . . . Which of us is Oedipus here? Which of us sphinx?" (*BGE* 1). In Nietzsche's early scenario, the Sphinx is the riddler, nature, overthrown by Oedipus the scientist, but she reemerges in *Beyond Good and Evil* to teach Oedipus to ask the riddles, so that he too can play the Sphinx. And as the Sphinx, who is also truth as woman, Oedipus asks his first riddle: What is the value of truth? Why do we prefer it to untruth?

Nietzsche/Sphinx/Oedipus suggests that the dogmatist's problem lies in his dependence on "antitheses," the either/or premise of logic that creates exclusive categories based on self-identical concepts. The dogmatist asks, "How *could* something originate in its antithesis? Truth in error, for example?" Answering his own rhetorical question, he goes on to assert, "Things of the highest value must have another origin *of their own*—they cannot be derivable from this transitory, seductive, deceptive, mean little world! This confusion of desire and illusion!" (*BGE* 2). We know that Nietzsche's truth, if she is a woman, lives and breathes only in this transitory, mean little world, and that deception is part of her nature. The fact that truth deceives is the paradox of a truth that goes beyond, or undoes, conceptual antitheses, and subsumes deception as part of a larger whole. "For it may be doubted whether there exist any antitheses at all," Nietzsche grandly writes, from there proceeding to argue that moral values like "good" may have their origin in "evil": "It might be possible that *what* constitutes the value of those good and honoured things resides precisely in their being artfully related, knotted and crocheted to these wicked, apparently antithetical things, perhaps even in their being essentially identical with them. Perhaps!—But who is willing to concern himself with such dangerous perhapses!" (*BGE* 2). Nietzsche clearly answers his own rhetorical question; the ones who will concern themselves with such dangerous perhapses are a new breed of philosopher, "philosophers of the dangerous 'perhaps' in every sense."

I have argued that the construct of truth as a woman has a scholarly genealogy in Nietzsche's work. She begins as the maternal principle of Bachofen's tellurian phase, whose "realm is not being but becoming and passing away," where death is "not the opposite but the helper of life" (33–34). This truth of life takes on ritual attributes in the Eleusinian mysteries, whose symbol is Baubo: "Perhaps truth is a woman. . .? Perhaps her name is—to speak Greek—*Baubo*?" (*GS* "Preface for the Second Edition" 4). Here truth is the ongoing celebration of life and death embodied by a woman in childbirth. Truth then enters Nietzsche's work as Life, whose seductive veil—the veil of maya, of sensation and form, of metaphor, of art—keeps us in love as we work through our difficulties in accepting Life as serpent—changeable only, and connected to time and the earth.

This truth, as Zarathustra shows us, involves affirmation of eternal return. As Debra Bergoffen notes, "Nietzsche's Zarathustra would undo the Oedipus complex. His memory of the will remembers the woman at the beginning. As the one who teaches the eternal recurrence of the *same,* he remembers that his desire returns upon itself. . . . When he supposes that truth is a woman, he names her Baubo, the hole, the void, the nothingness" (230). For Bergoffen, naming truth as a woman also commits Zarathustra to the roll of the dice, "where chance, not his will, prevails. In calling the origin chance or woman, Zarathustra . . . names an other out of his control. As out of his control, this other cannot be appropriated" (231). As truth, woman "names the abyss. She figures it as the unanchored field of possibilities of the sensual" (233). Bergoffen suggests that, simply by supposing truth to be a woman, Nietzsche returns us to questions of origin and makes philosophy "a matter between man and woman" (227). As sympathetic as I am to Bergoffen's arguments about woman as metaphor for truth (with the emphasis on woman), I hold that philosophy, as a matter between man and woman, is exactly what Nietzsche's project makes impossible.

I believe that Luce Irigaray is perfectly right when, in her book on Nietzsche, she condemns him for omitting her-as-woman, for not "sharing" but taking the "whole" of the world for himself (*Marine Lover* 19ff.). I am aware of no part of Nietzsche's work that even hints that "man" and "woman" might share anything, save the "will of the two to create the one that is more than those who created it" (*Z* 1 "Of Marriage and Children"), possibly in some utopian future. "Man" and "woman" are joined in "the most abysmal antagonism" (*BGE* 238) throughout, and the image of them peacefully reading philosophy together seems quite absurd. That is the point. As long as we think in terms of dichotomous gender, of "man" and "woman," and of the relationship between man and woman, we can easily slide toward defining and enacting the relationship as an "abysmal antagonism."

In her critique of Nietzsche's treatment of woman, Lynne Tirrell asserts that, because he combats dualism in general, so Nietzsche could and "should have" argued against sexual dualism (167). What prevents her from thinking that he did combat the sexual dualism is his "overtly misogynistic remarks" (159). It seems to me that his hyperbolic and illogical remarks about women accomplish precisely the job of disrupting the sexual dualism that Tirrell requires.

Nietzsche's passages on "man and woman" (a pairing he tends to set together in quotation marks, to emphasize its constructed nature) exhibit a pattern similar to those in which he surveys historical "woman" alone. I have hitherto considered most of these passages individually; here I will draw them together and examine them as a class or paradigm in which explicitly sexual binary logic is upset and overthrown. To establish this approach I draw on Bianca Thiesen's discussion of binary logic in "Rhythms of Oblivion" (1994). According to Thiesen, binary logic posits that something either is or is not: "This logic is based on two values that are mutually determined through negation; A (truth) is designated through not-A (non-truth) and not-A through A" (84). In *Beyond Good and Evil*, woman is inscribed metaphorically as both truth and non-truth—a logical impossibility. If A is Woman/truth, then Woman cannot be Woman/non-truth: "A cannot simultaneously occupy the position of not-A—as Nietzsche suggests, when 'woman' stands in for both truth and non-truth" (Thiesen 84). By placing "woman" on two sides of the binary divide, Nietzsche splits the concept as self-identical, thereby destroying the concept "woman-as-such." I suggest that Nietzsche also undercuts sexual binary logic in his "overtly misogynistic" passages, by demonstrating that the basis upon which the opposition rests is tenuous and wholly dependent on human evaluation.

In *The Gay Science,* Nietzsche has to invent a third sex for "small women," as they don't fit the category "woman" (*GS* 75). In aphorism 363, "How each sex has its own prejudice about love," the man who loves like a woman is not considered a man, whereas the woman who loves like a woman is a more perfect woman. Nietzsche demonstrates that the categories are inadequate to describe the realities of love, which are in any case "prejudiced" by the demands of conventional roles. And in the aphorism about the sage and the youth ("Will and willingness," *GS* 68), he once again divides women, this time four ways, leaving her with no essence.

Section 238 in part 7 of *Beyond Good and Evil,* one of the most "overtly misogynistic" among the passages Nietzsche labels "my truths" about woman, similarly fits my paradigm. The passage begins by asserting the "necessity" of "an eternally hostile tension" between "man and woman," and goes on to call a thinker "shallow" who "dreams" things might be otherwise. A few lines on, however, the "abysmal antagonism" between man and woman has disappeared, and the tension (which R. J. Hollingdale reminds us might have been considered creative in other Nietzschean contexts [*BGE* "Commentary" p. 232]) has given way to total appropriation of the woman by the man. This shift repeats that found in aphorism 363 of *The Gay Science,* where, in order to accommodate Man's prejudice, Woman conveniently—willingly, unselfishly—disappears altogether.

Last but not least, in section 5 of *Ecce Homo*'s "Why I Write Such Good Books," Nietzsche divides "woman" into two groups, those who are "perfect" and exemplify the ideals of the "eternal feminine," and those who are "abortive" females, the "'emancipated' who lack the stuff for children." One group is labeled "woman," and the other "not-woman." Barring acceptance of this absurd distinction, or the formulation of a "third sex," we must clearly question the characterizations of this notoriously misogynistic passage. Here we find that the "perfect" woman "tears to pieces when she loves.—I know these charming maenads." The "perfect" woman is also "indescribably more evil than man" and "good nature" is with her a form of degeneration. Then comes the slippage, and the introduction of a *tertium datur* ("a third value of a different logical type" [Thiesen 84]): "In all so-called 'beautiful souls' something is physiologically askew at bottom." The beautiful-souled woman (the woman of the Goethean eternal feminine who acts as an inspiration to man) is not really a woman either, or not so much a woman as the "dangerous, creeping, subterranean little beast of prey" who is the "woman who is turned out well." There are degrees of being a woman, it seems: "Woman, the more she is a woman, resists rights in general hand and foot." At the same time, the "emancipated," the "abortive woman," "instinctively" hates and resents "the woman who is turned out well," who is the beast of prey, who can be "redeemed" only by being "given" a child. (And it follows that if redeemed, then she is no longer a beast of prey, no longer "turned out well," no longer a woman [*EH* "Why I Write Such Good Books" 5]).

As Nietzsche observes: "The emancipated are anarchists in the world of the 'eternally feminine,' the underprivileged whose most fundamental instinct is revenge." We know that the world of the eternally feminine is one where "idealism" is the rule, and that—even if he hadn't shown us this world in this passage—Nietzsche believes it should be exposed as "lie." He here exposes it as contradictory at the very least, and not "one" and self-identical, and we see that he has been the chief anarchist in the world of the eternal feminine, which puts him and the "emancipated" on the same side.

If we read section 5 of "Why I Write Such Good Books" from start to finish, we find that the passages on "woman" appear in the middle of the text, bookended by paragraphs dealing with (1) wholeness of being (that is, the importance of being an independent self-confident individual first, and only after that of being a lover—"one must stand bravely on one's own two legs, otherwise one is simply *incapable* of loving"), and (2) the praise of "what is natural in love." Taken as a whole, the section moves from advocacy of self-love, to advocacy of "giving a woman a child," to advocacy of sex. In making his positive claims, Nietzsche opposes the false morality that presumes love is something unegoistic. He opposes any sort of idealization of "woman," including that of the emancipated as "female idealists." And he opposes "every kind of antinature" in sexual love: "Every kind of contempt for sex, every impurification of it by means of the concept 'impure,' is the crime *par excellence* against life—is the real sin against the holy spirit of life" (*EH* "Why I Write Such Good Books" 5).

Whereas the middle paragraphs of section 5 contain logical riddles, and a suspicious plethora of punctuation—dashes, exclamation marks, and question marks—to alert us to double meanings and perspectival thinking (including that of the physicians, those scientists who describe to us the "nature" of women), the closing discussion of "what is natural in sexual love" and the opening consideration of self-reliance show no signs that they are intended ironically. The middle undermines the gender dichotomy by making a mockery of the category "woman." The text joins with other seemingly misogynistic passages that cancel "woman" out, or exceed her as a concept—an awkward absence if a man's job (as in Nietzsche's Germany) is to give a woman a child. Without a woman present, a man can't be present either. The bookends of section 5, however, indicate that individual people, standing on their own two feet and enjoying "what is natural in love" (a loaded phrase, since Nietzsche has shown that what is "natural" is impossible to separate from what is cultural) are the harbingers of the future.

This future is risky. The danger of such a Nietzschean assault on the sexual dichotomy is a strategic one for women especially. Rosi Braidotti has consistently expressed the concern that the "trend in modern thought" toward "becoming woman"—a trend whereby male writers, Nietzsche exemplary among them, incorporate aspects of femininity in their metaphors to break down sex-gender distinctions—ends up cancelling women out. "Isn't it strange," she asks ironically, "that it is precisely at the time in history when women have made their voices heard socially, politically and theoretically, that philosophical discourse—a male domain *par excellence*—takes over the 'feminine' for itself?" (37). It is not at all coincidental that men are moving to explore the "woman" in themselves, and in their "discourse," as women gain power in the world. It seems to me an inevitable response, but in this not a very dangerous one, as women can oppose it if they choose. In fact, I rather think it a desirable development from the "value perspective" that I have maintained Nietzsche's texts endorse—that of the creation, through training, of whole multivalent individuals, who have overcome resentment of themselves, others, and life, and have learned to love.

Let me take up two additional scholarly caveats to the argument that Nietzsche displaces the dichotomy man/woman. The first holds that this displacement doesn't exist in Nietzsche's work and that he opposes it in general. Adrian Del Caro argues that Nietzsche's texts engage in a critique of the roles occupied by man and woman throughout history (a particularly apt characterization, to my way of thinking) and that Nietzsche "feared that reversal of these roles contributes to the displacement of both man and woman" (140). In Del Caro's view, Nietzsche was "the sworn enemy of neutrality" (136)—an assessment that also seems accurate to me. Nietzsche never argues or even hints that role reversal would be a good thing; eliminating the dichotomy obviates reversing it, and does indeed "displace" both man and woman—though it does not result in one "neuter" being, or in neutrality toward sex.

"Displacement" seems to worry Alison Ainley as well, who thinks that by "taking up the metaphoric potentials of pregnancy and femininity," Nietzsche effects a "strategic parody" of sexual difference—the second caveat. As she concludes: "It is a dangerous move to see the strategic, textual freedom of masks and changeability as a freedom from sexual difference. . . . This move apparently frees men and women to appropriate or open up strategies of sexual difference in a space of interchange. But the space . . . is empty" (126). Here Ainley quotes from aphorism 363 of *The Gay Science,* where Nietzsche (as a prejudiced "man") asks what would happen if a man and a woman felt an equal impulse to renounce themselves, leaving an empty space. I will not reiterate the particulars of this passage, which we considered at length in chapter 4, except to say that rather than clinching Ainley's argument, the quotation destroys it. Nietzsche, the philosopher whose truth is a woman, the philosopher of the dangerous perhaps, is not afraid of the empty space. As Bergoffen notes, he names it Baubo—woman—in praise and celebration of the human "being," particularly in its feminine aspects; it is the space of possibility for those who love.

For Nietzsche, the power of love is transformative and is capable of filling the empty space with new forms, meanings, and values. He observes in *Beyond Good and Evil:* "That which is done out of love always takes place beyond good and evil" (153). And in *The Will to Power,* he makes this profession: "Do you desire the most astonishing proof of how far the transfiguring power of intoxication can go?—'Love' is this proof: that which is called love in all languages and silences of the world. In this case, intoxication has done with reality to such a degree that in the consciousness of the lover the cause of it is extinguished and something else seems to have taken its place" (808). Referring to this passage, Martha Nussbaum writes of Nietzsche's "remarkable account of the ways in which the intoxication of passion transfigures the self, producing a being who is fictional and yet also real, transformed and transforming, an object of art and an artist . . . —in short, a lover" (38).

A passage in *On the Uses and Disadvantages of History for Life* similarly insists on the social and historical necessity, and near impossibility, of overcoming nihilism by love. "History brings to light," Nietzsche writes, "so much that is false, crude, inhuman, absurd, violent that the mood of pious illusion in which alone anything that wants to live can live necessarily crumbles away: for it is only in love, only when shaded by the illusion produced by love . . . that man is creative. Anything that constrains a man to love less . . . has severed the roots of his strength" (7). In this early work, Nietzsche links love and illusion—both necessary, both good. But in the philosophical progression through to *Thus Spoke Zarathustra,* Nietzsche dispenses with illusion as part of a false dichotomy. At the moment in "The Intoxicated Song" when oppositions collapse, or at Life's unveiling in *The Gay Science,* truth stands naked, whole and unafraid. In that instant, she is joy. At the last, Zarathustra, as foreshadowed in "One must learn to love" (GS 334), becomes a person for whom love and truth are not opposed to hate and illusion, but have rather subsumed them.

The empty space, the open horizon, the clear skies and open seas which figure in Nietzsche's works—these are the spaces that the future will fill, those of human potential directed, via the symbol of the Übermensch as a self-conscious goal, to the meaning of the earth. Such spaces are constantly being filled with human interpretations. Nietzsche was aware that he wrote for posterity, and he knew his prescriptions could wait to be filled. A passage in *Daybreak* in fact cautions against filling them too quickly:

> If a change is to be as profound as it can be, the means to it must be given in the smallest doses but unremittingly over long periods of time! Can what is great be created at a *single stroke*? So let us take care not to exchange the state of morality to which we are accustomed for a new evaluation of things head over heels and amid acts of violence—no, let us continue to live in it for a long while yet—until, probably a long while hence, we become aware that *the new evaluation* has acquired predominance within us and that the little doses of it *to which we must from now on accustom ourselves* have laid down a new nature in us. (D 534)

Let us for the sake of argument interpret the empty space as the one created by the elimination of the sex-gender dichotomy that has legislated social behavior for millennia. The dissolution of this opposition, which occurs very slowly, is already under way. It is evident as we become accustomed to women's voices and visibility in the public and political arenas, as we increasingly speak and think in a nonsexist language, as we grow used to seeing more men in what were traditionally "woman's" professions (kindergarten teaching, nursing, home care), and as we consider gay marriage. These are first steps in the gradual process that constitutes a real social revolution. This is not unfolding peacefully as Nietzsche hoped, as sexual

violence of all kinds, including murder, continues unabated, but his revaluation of "the feminine," and his gestures toward the conflation in whole
individuals of traits the culture has labeled "masculine" and "feminine,"
are already yielding results.

To gauge the extent to which Nietzsche's works were prophetic of social
change, or of scholarly trends in the area of gender studies, let us briefly
survey academic work on gender toward the end of the second millennium
CE. Since the 1960s, feminist writers across a very wide spectrum of interests
and from a variety of perspectives have questioned the verities of conventional gender roles, and fought over the probities of sexual difference. More
recently, work on masculinity[1] and queer theory[2] has gone "beyond man
and woman," and by advocating an end to the categorical or conceptual
dichotomy of two opposite and discreet sex-genders has exemplified the
very argument I've made for Nietzsche's texts. Studies of bisexuality similarly vitiate the straight/gay dichotomy.[3] The provocative research of Anne
Fausto-Sterling (1985, 2000) and Edward Stein (1999) has examined the
biological basis of the division of humans into two sexes. Stein argues that
"our current views about what biological features distinguish males from
females might be mostly wrong" (1999 33), while Fausto-Sterling holds that
a body's sex is "simply too complex" to fall neatly into two chromosomal
categories, male and female: "There is no either/or. Rather, there are shades
of difference" (*Sexing the Body* 3). The existence of people with abnormal
chromosomal arrangements and people with ambiguous external genitalia
means that we cannot rely on such a strict dichotomy without excluding
or wrongly cataloguing people. Furthermore, "gender identity," or the sense
of belonging to a particular gender, is sometimes independent of a person's biological sex. Thus it is possible for a man who feels like a woman to
be attracted to women; "such a man would say that he feels like he is a
woman who is attracted to women and, hence, really a lesbian" (Stein 35).
It seems there may be nothing "given" about sex-gender.

Such a sign of the times appeared in the popular press at the turn of the
millenium. In May, 2000, the *New York Times Magazine* carried an account
about the lover of one Barry Winchell. Winchell, who was in the army, was
murdered because he was gay, but he "wasn't really gay—at least not in
the traditional Harvey Fierstein sense of the word. He was in love with a
pre-operative transsexual, part male and part female, falling into the gray
in-between" (France 27). As the account of the killing succinctly observed:
"In order to turn the murdered soldier Barry Winchell into a martyr for
gay rights, activists first had to turn his girlfriend, Calpernia Addams, back

into a man" (24). Addams preferred to be identified as "a transgendered woman": "As in the film *Boys Don't Cry*,[4] whose doomed transgendered character generated an Academy Award this year, almost every element of the Winchell case falls into the gray in-between. The biologist Anne Fausto-Sterling, in her new book, *Sexing the Body*, says that this state of being 'either/or, neither/both' is increasingly common" (26).

We clearly live in a world in which the dichotomous conventions of sex and gender no longer completely apply: "At the University of Minnesota's Program in Human Sexuality, one of the largest transsexual centers in the country, administrators now routinely admit patients who take only half the journey from one sex to the other, choosing hormones without surgery, or surgery without hormones, says Bean Robinson, Ph.D., the associate director. 'We see there's a lot more complexity to the world,' she says" (France 26). In the midst of such dizzying changes, there are equally those for whom "shattering the old law tables" that enforce the codes of two separate and incommensurable sexes is still an anathema. In the case of Barry Winchell, the reporter discovered that "all this postmodern gender parsing" did not go down well at the base. Winchell was bashed to death in July, 1999, for being a "faggot" (28–29).

These stories, as told by scientists, academics in the humanities, filmmakers, and reporters, and lived in vivid terms by real people, throw retrospective light on Nietzsche's textual experimentalism, which continues to encourage new ways of thinking about sex-gender that break the rigid boundary between masculine and feminine. Yet questions remain beyond the narratives. Why do this? Why break down the categorical boundaries that demarcate the space and habits of men and those of women, and by so doing confound the orbits of Mars and Venus? Won't this boundary destruction imperil human survival on earth, which depends on sexed and sexy difference? And why do it now, when women are finally gaining independent status? Nietzsche's writings suggest and support the following responses:

First, that open minds and bodies do not lead to extinction of the species, but quite the contrary. Maintaining the categorical boundaries does produce injustice for many, and ends in murder for some. As the example of Barry Winchell makes clear, the problem is not one of openness; it stems rather from rigid and dogmatic assertions of identity that are based on fear and resentment.

Second, that detaching femininity from the bodies of women and making its attributes available to men—the opportunity to cry, for example, or to be gentle and nurturing—does not negate sexuality unless we want it to. This holds for women as well—detaching attributes of masculinity from the bodies of men and making them available to women need not eliminate sexuality unless we wish it. The June 4, 2000, *New York Times Book Review* announced a forthcoming book by Karen Karbo, entitled *Motherhood Made a Man out of Me*. If Nietzsche encourages men to be more like women in certain respects, he leaves women on their own about taking up masculinity. Karbo's title plays on doing just that, emphasizing that the binary oppositions of gender are constructed, detachable from bodies, and useful for self-understanding, at least for the time being.

Third, that women have nothing to lose and much to gain by freeing up the categories. Indeed, their new status has derived from their assumption of roles and qualifications that, even fifty years ago, would have been considered "masculine." If we define "autonomy" as a state of being self-governing or morally independent, then clearly women of all social classes in many countries around the world enjoy greater autonomy as individuals than they did a century ago, when Nietzsche's works first appeared. On the one hand, these works may be read as a summary guide to moral conduct of the individual, with self-governance, self-acceptance, and self-love as the foundation of resentment-free behavior. On the other hand, the texts provide interpretive histories of conduct and critiques of morality. Women who read Nietzsche have valued and continue to draw inspiration from these aspects of his texts.

Fourth, and finally, that the doubleness of the texts, their presentation of various perspectives and alternatives, works not only to cancel out binary oppositions but also to promote a rational consideration of real alternatives, leaving readers to articulate the Nietzschean "quintessence of our wisdom" for themselves. In so doing, Nietzsche's work invites many interpretations—that is, presents multiple possibilities for interpreting texts, and bodies.

One final example illustrates these points, and others that I have introduced about language, sex-gender, and morality. It is found in *Daybreak*:

> *Everything has its day.*—When man gave all things a sex he thought, not that he was playing, but that he had gained a profound insight:—it was only very late that he confessed to himself what an enormous error this was, and perhaps even now he has not confessed it completely.—In the same way man has ascribed to all that exists a connection with morality and laid an *ethical significance* on the world's back. One day this will have as much value, and no more, as the belief in the masculinity or femininity of the sun has today. (*D* 3)

This passage embodies and enacts a mini-genealogy of language and morals. As with all of Nietzsche's aphorisms, it comprises at least a double meaning and three perspectives—past, present, and future. From the vantage point of the past, the attribution of sex to inanimate objects made sense. From that of the present, this no longer holds, replaced rather by the attribution of morality to things in the world. From that of the future, neither type of attribution seems sound (that is, describes the world accurately), in that both are anthropomorphic. So on the one hand, the aphorism directs us to the relativity and the historical contingencies of our beliefs ("everything has its day"). On the other, by placing an ancient belief in the sex of all things on an equal footing with belief in their moral natures, the text imposes a comparison and an evaluation in which the past does not fare worse than the present. If both beliefs are ridiculous, at least the past's is sexy and lively, while the present's is fear-producing and deadening.

Now to a concluding point (an arbitrary last, given that Nietzsche's aphorisms will go on revealing new facets and fostering new views). This assertion extends the aphorism's limits, perhaps, but I do not think it exceeds them; it is where I go with this aphorism. I suggest that we embrace the future's perspective, and in so doing imagine that assigning a sex to things (including humans) is in fact "an enormous error," something akin to attributing masculinity or femininity, or an ethical significance, to the sun. Let us consider for a moment the types of attribution that the aphorism suggests "man" has made to things—those of sex and morality. Perhaps Nietzsche wants us to comprehend that the two types of error are connected. Each one "lays" a significance "on the world's back"; the resulting image is that of a burden. By throwing off both of these weighty legacies—of "codes" of sexuality (which we would call "gender") and of "codes" of morality—we step beyond good and evil, and beyond man and woman, in one aphorism.

But do I wish to leave behind the sexiness that the aphorism teaches us to value in the past's attribution of sex to things? The text gives me a choice. By reading more closely the words comparing the character of the past's attribution with the present's, I find a "playfulness" in the former absent from the moral weight of the latter. Is it possible, I wonder, to keep, or reinstate, the sexual liveliness of all things in the world without assuming the burden of their fixed gender identities? Perhaps with these words Nietzsche is reminding us that sex is as basic as sunlight to the meaning of the earth, but that gender, its moral coding, is not. Like Galileo, we too may be discovering that the sun also rotates and is not a fixed star, and like Nietzsche, that the horizons are open.

Introduction

1. The terms *sex, gender,* and *sexuality* are all contested in feminist and gender studies; as Sedgwick notes, their "usage relations and analytical relations are almost irremediably slippery" (27). I slip and slide among them, using gender in my title, and *sex-gender* often but not always in my text. Nietzsche was most interested in gender, or the cultural construction of sexual difference as *man* and *woman*.

2. Women who were influenced positively by Nietzsche's books numbered among the leaders in socialist and feminist movements at the end of the nineteenth and beginning of the twentieth centuries (see Diethe, *Nietzsche's Women*). It could be argued that feminism's second wave was also strongly and positively influenced by Nietzsche's observations about such varied topics as men creating women in their own image, power, laughter that kills, resentment and slave morality, self-overcoming, and self-creating.

3. The argument that the feminine is central to Nietzschean philosophy, at least on the level of "style," is not original. Blondel's essay on the metaphor of the *vita femina* in Nietzsche ("Yes, Life is a woman!" *GS* 339) argues that "one could characterize Nietzsche's 'ontology' as feminine" ("Life as Metaphor" 156); Derrida draws connections between woman, truth/lie, and style in Nietzsche's texts *(Spurs),* and Pautrat draws them between Nietzsche's thought of eternal return and a maternal fetish ("Nietzsche Medused")—a thought (among others) Irigaray develops *(Marine Lover);* Kofman explores the complicated ambivalences toward women that Nietzsche's texts exhibit ("Baubô"). Krell's book on woman, sensuality, and death in Nietzsche observes that in the mid-1930s Karl Reinhardt had argued that following *Thus Spoke Zarathustra,* Nietzsche's philosophy underwent a metamorphosis which enabled him to "speak with the voice of woman," as Krell puts it *(Postponements* 20). Moving backward from the mid-1930s to the 1890s, and following the trace of the woman, one of the first books on Nietzsche, Lou Andreas-Salomé's 1894 [1988] *Friedrich Nietzsche in seinen Werken,* argues that Nietzsche's discursive divisions, including masculine/feminine, were self-divisions. In the last ten years, three collections of essays on Nietzsche's relationship with the feminine, and feminism's relationship with Nietzsche, have appeared: see Patton (1993), Burgard (1994), and Oliver and Pearsall (1998).

4. My thinking about step three, whereby the man/woman dichotomy collapses, is indebted to Maudemarie Clark's analysis of the "Real World" aphorism *(TI)* in *Nietzsche on Truth and Philosophy,* 109-14.

5. Nietzsche's friend Paul Deussen tells the story in its comic form: Members of Nietzsche's fraternity at Bonn visited a brothel in Cologne, taking Nietzsche with them. He was terrified by the ladies in their thin clothing and ran to the piano for relief, "the only living thing in the room," as he put it (in Pletsch 66-67). It has been widely believed that Nietzsche contracted syphilis at this time, which was the cause of his madness and death. See Gilman, *Inscribing the Other,* for an account of medical opinion on Nietzsche's illness.

6. Sedgwick also argues that Nietzsche was homosexual: "It seems patent that many of Nietzsche's most affective intensities of both life and writing were directed toward other men and toward the male body" (133).

1. Nietzsche's No to Woman

1. Laqueur cites the author of the leading nineteenth-century marriage manual in France; the 1850 edition "counsels women to fake orgasms if necessary and never to refuse their husbands" (195). Charcot's treatment of hysteria by hypnosis in France in the 1870s would have been reported, but according to Peter Gay, the medical community was not at all receptive to hypnosis: "Hypnotism was a fraud, a technique best left to charlatans at fairs" (xvi).

2. This sentence is misleadingly translated. The German reads: "Alle Menschen sind unschuldig für ihr Dasein, die Weiber aber sind unschuldig im zweiten Grade." A better translation might be: "Human beings are not guilty for their own existence [a swipe at the notion of Original Sin, guilt for having been born at all], but women are doubly innocent."

2. The "Secret Source"

1. The *Nachlass* have been published several times, most recently in what have become the standard editions, edited by Giorgio Colli and Mazzino Montinari. I use their paperback edition *Kritische Studienausgabe in 15 Einzelbänden* [*KSA*]; translations are mine.

2. See Janz, *Biographie* 1:313–16. Bachofen's work remains controversial. Lionel Gossman writes that histories of anthropology give Bachofen a brief mention for his "pioneering contribution to the popular nineteenth-century theory of matriarchy," for his correspondence with Lewis Henry Morgan, and for his influence on Engels's *The Origins of the Family* (*Orpheus Philologus* 1ff.). Classicists Sarah Pomeroy *(Goddesses, Whores, Wives, and Slaves)*, W. B. Tyrrell *(Amazons)*, and Froma Zeitlin *(Playing the Other)*, and anthropologist Joan Bamberger ("Myth of Matriarchy")—among others—take issue with Bachofen for using myth historically and for positing an actual historical matriarchal period where none can be proven to have existed.

3. In his discussion of the Oedipus myth in *The Birth of Tragedy*, Nietzsche follows Bachofen closely. The hero's actions confound natural and moral order, but they also "produce a higher magical circle of effects which found a new world on the ruins of the old one that has been overthrown" (*BT* 9).

4. Hartmann is named and quoted in notes for 1869 (*KSA* 7:65), 1873 (*PT* 115), and several times in 1883 (*KSA* 10:241, 312, 319, 324).

5. With one exception that I have noticed, reflecting admiration of Hartmann: in the notes for 1873, Nietzsche blames Hartmann's exclusion from a list of five great German thinkers on Hartmann's possession of spirit, and comments that "the Reich now belongs only to the poor in spirit" (*PT* 115).

6. In volume 3, Hartmann provides a chronological list of illusions that have comforted mankind over vast periods of time: the illusion that earthly happiness is attainable (represented by the Jewish-Greek-Roman worldviews); the illusion that happiness is attainable in a transcendent life after death (an anti-Christian diatribe accompanies the announcement of this phase); and the current illusion, that of progress

toward a better future (3:22–94). This list may well have provided Nietzsche with the idea for his own such chronology (*TI* "How the 'Real World' at last Became a Myth").

7. Bachofen anticipates Nietzsche, Freud, and Lévi-Strauss in attributing special significance to the myth. Lévi-Strauss proposed that "incest" is one of the terms mediating the nature/culture opposition, because the laws of exogamy are cultural but incest is natural. Note the similarity between Bachofen's and Nietzsche's interpretations and Lévi-Strauss's statement that "before [the prohibition of incest] culture is still non-existent; with it, nature's sovereignty over man is ended" (*Elementary Structures* 25 and passim). However, for Levi-Strauss "the field of sexual life" is already divided between nature and culture, since the sexual is "man's only instinct requiring the stimulation of another person" (12).

8. For example, in *Twilight of the Idols*: Schopenhauer values beauty "as redeemer from the 'focus of the will', from sexuality—in beauty he sees the procreative impulse denied. . . . Singular saint! Someone contradicts you, and I fear it is nature. . . . Art is the great stimulus to life" (*TI* "Expeditions" 22, 24, 80, 81).

9. "Wir dürfen keinen Abgrund der Betrachtung scheuen, um die Tragödie bei ihren Müttern aufzufinden: diese Mütter sind Wille, Wahn, Wehe" (*KSA* 7:93). The word *Wahn* is most difficult to translate. In *The Birth of Tragedy*, Kaufmann translates it "delusion," and speculates that the phrase about the mothers of tragedy sounds like an unintentional parody of Wagner (20). Krell translates it "will o' the wisp" and attributes the phrase to Schopenhauer (*Postponements* 34). In *Die Meistersinger*, a performance of which Nietzsche attended in Vienna in 1870 at the time of the drafting of this note, the central character Hans Sachs sings of the *Wahn* aroused by birdsong in spring—a semi-madness denoting love's necessity (Wagner here leaning on Schopenhauer). A note in the libretto of that opera at the word *Wahn* tells us that there are 43 columns in Grimm's dictionary devoted to defining the word, and that meanings range from "expectation" and "hope" to "illusion, delusion, madness, error" (Wagner *Meistersinger* 103).

10. The image of the abyss has been interpreted influentially, by Freud and his followers, as a symbol of the horror of the female genitals, which rather than presenting a "presence," a comforting penis, present a terrifying absence or gap where the penis should be. The "gap" is immediately papered over by cultural forms of all kinds, but it remains a repressed threat. Nietzsche explicitly repudiates in advance this interpretation on behalf of tragedy.

11. There are single-word references to the *Suidas* and to Hesykhius (*KSA* 7:56), ancient lexicographers and sources of the Baubo story: "The Alexandrian Hesykhios associated one of the meanings of this word with Empedocles: 'Baubo, nurse of Demeter; also means 'cavity' [*koilia*], as in Empedocles" (Olender 83–84). The *Souda* tells the story of the birth of a miraculous child who takes the "swollen breast" of Demeter as "Dionysos at the breast" (Olender 98–99).

12. See Lloyd, who quotes from this excerpt as an example not only of Nietzsche's misogynistic view of woman but of the long philosophical tradition in general (1). Keuls, for whom Nietzsche represents a class of "visceral misogynists" who have provided apologies for the Athenian phallocracy, writes that "in his essay 'The Greek Woman' he finds it inevitable that an advanced and creative culture should reduce its women to the status of vegetables" (9).

13. See also the praise of forgetfulness and other qualities of "The Greek Woman" in *On the Uses and Disadvantages of History*: "Forgetting is essential to action of any kind, just as not only light but darkness too is essential for the life of everything organic" (*UDH* 1).

3. *The Birth of Tragedy* and the Feminine

1. Kaufmann uses the German form in his translation "Apollinian"; I prefer to use the adjective "Apollonian" (from the English noun "Apollo").

2. There are exceptions, which have been helpful to me. Silk and Stern draw attention to the "omission" (173). Hatab (339) argues that Nietzsche's "respect for the tragic spirit is inspired by its recognition and acceptance of a primordial feminine principle" symbolized in qualities assigned to the Dionysian, an argument from which my own took off. Krell questions how Apollo and Dionysus are to mate, discusses the mothers of tragedy (*Postponements* 34–37), and returns to the question in "Orange Grove." Rathbone suggests that the "propriety of the oppositions around which [Apollo and Dionysus] are built are violated in the very moments of their self-articulation" (110). Staten calls the omission a "repression" (118). Picart advances an interesting argument, much like mine. For her, Apollo and Dionysus both possess masculine and feminine traits, and are each capable of autogenesis which "requires an internal duality." However, they require interaction with each other "in order to effect birthing" (42–43).

3. The "Orphic" mysteries are probably the same as the Eleusinian mysteries; a neoplatonic tradition "thought that Orphic literature contained the essential knowledge of Eleusinian and Dionysiac mysteries" (*Oxford Classical Dictionary* 1079).

4. Aristotle includes, in *Metaphysics* 1, a Pythagorean list of contraries that has become a prototype: "limit and unlimited, odd and even, one and plurality, right and left, male and female, resting and moving, straight and curved, light and darkness, good and bad, square and oblong" (1559).

5. "Mit unbewegtem Blicke" (*KSA* 1:118) might better be translated "with a steady gaze," since "unmoved" has connotations of a lack of sympathy, which the passage itself contradicts.

4. "Yes, Life Is a Woman"

1. My discussion of aphorism 60 of *The Gay Science* is indebted to that of Rosalyn Diprose, "Nietzsche and the Pathos of Distance."

2. In *Thus Spoke Zarathustra*'s "The Night Song," Zarathustra laments that he is always the giver; he'd like to be a lover, and to receive: "I do not know the joy of the receiver. . . . It is my poverty that my hand never rests from giving. . . . My joy in giving died in giving" (*Z* 2). The speaker of aphorism 363 in *The Gay Science* would identify Zarathustra's position here as that of a woman.

3. In *Death Is the Mother of Beauty*, Mark Turner identifies kinship as one of the most commonly used metaphors for describing relation and causation; mother and child, as metaphor, is the most frequently used kinship relation, and progeneration or the "marriage" metaphor is very common as well (55, 146). Nietzsche is extraordinarily fond of this "family" of metaphors.

4. Nietzsche did not originate the poetic anthropomorphism "God is dead"; Higgins refers to an essay on the origin of the phrase in Christianity (where God is Christ, and dies), in Luther, in Hegel, and in Heine (*Comic Relief* 96–98).

5. Before writing *The Gay Science,* Nietzsche summered as usual in the Alps, where he had his rarest insight, that of the eternal return, to which I think aphorism 339 refers. Describing this insight in *Ecce Homo,* Nietzsche writes: "The fundamental conception of this work [*Thus Spoke Zarathustra*], the idea of eternal recurrence, this highest formula of affirmation that is at all attainable, belongs in August 1881: it was penned on a sheet with the notation underneath: '6000 feet beyond man and time'" (*EH* "Thus Spoke Zarathustra" 1).

6. Here Nietzsche may be inverting Plato's suggestion in the *Symposium* that the ultimate beauty, "the Beautiful itself," seen "suddenly, in an instant . . . marvelous, beautiful in nature" is transcendental: "pure, unalloyed, unmixed, not full of human flesh and colors, and the many other kinds of nonsense that attach to mortality" (155–56). The point for Nietzsche is that ultimate beauty is, precisely, human and temporal.

7. This result bears out Turner's argument that "the meanings of kinship words are not free to commute away from their anchoring basic models and basic processes without some tension, friction, and resistence"—and that commutation helps us to see how our minds work (7–8).

5. Zarathustra's Whip

1. Well-known later members of this series are the two-volume study of *Thus Spoke Zarathustra,* edited from notes of the seminar given from 1934 to 1939 by Carl Gustav Jung, and the 1980 poststructuralist monograph *Amante Marine de Friedrich Nietzsche* [*Marine Lover of Friedrich Nietzsche*] by Luce Irigaray—both of which share characteristics of Salomé's study.

2. The best known of Salomé's other inspired admirers are Rainer Maria Rilke and Sigmund Freud, and there is a longer list of friends and lovers of both sexes who felt her personal charm, which must have been very great. All her biographers—Martin, Livingston, Binyon, and Peters—attest to it.

3. Details of the Nietzsche-Salomé relationship are offered by all of the biographers mentioned above. See also Siegfried Mandell's introduction to his translation of Andreas-Salomé's *Nietzsche.* Binyon gives the fullest account of Nietzsche's side of the affair, with quotations from unpublished material, and he is not altogether sympathetic to Salomé, his subject. See also *Looking Back,* Salomé's own memoirs.

4. For an account of the relationship that argues that both Nietzsche and Rée were gay and had a physical relationship together before Salomé came along, see Köhler, *Zarathustra's Secret.* That Nietzsche might have had strong homoerotic feelings and yet also have fallen for Lou Salomé is only problematic if strict definitions of sexual orientation are operating. Köhler asserts that during the period in question, Nietzsche "became hopelessly infatuated with Lou Salomé" (94).

5. "Der Stil soll dir angemessen sein . . . auf eine ganz bestimmte Person, der du dich mittheilen willst. (Gesetz der doppelten Relation)" (*KSA* 10:38).

6. Both Binyon (72) and Martin (84) tell us that Salomé wrote an essay on woman, of which the only surviving evidence is Nietzsche's rewrite in his notebook.

7. Note the implied gesture of continuing support, however, offered in "Of the Pale Criminal" (*TSZ* 1): "I am a railing beside the stream: he who can grasp me, let him grasp me! I am not, however, your crutch."

8. Binyon cites a letter from Gast, and comments by the Overbecks, crediting Salomé as "inspiration" for *Zarathustra* (102n). See also Klossowski: "The Lou experience" was the price Nietzsche paid for the "birth" of Zarathustra (190). Hayman notes: "The experience with Lou had jeopardized his ability to think well of himself, and *Also Sprach Zarathustra* is not merely the record of an attempt to build himself up again, but the tool for making the attempt" (258). Allison discusses the Salomé-Nietzsche relationship in detail as the background to the "deeply personal, largely hidden stratum to *Zarathustra*, where Nietzsche reflectively engages his own most personal, philosophical, and emotional concerns" (111–12ff.).

9. The book of adventure stories as "source" was discovered by Carl Jung, who describes his find, and his subsequent belief that Nietzsche had "cryptomnesia," the concealed recollection of a textual memory, to his seminar of fellow depth psychologists who gathered once a week between 1934 and 1939 to analyze *Thus Spoke Zarathustra*. The piece of text "secretly crept up and reproduced itself" in "Of Great Events" (*Z* 2). Jung recognized the story about seamen stopping on an island to hunt rabbits, having read it in his grandfather's library. He wrote Elisabeth Förster-Nietzsche, who confirmed that she and Nietzsche had read the same book in their grandfather's library, when Nietzsche was eleven. This, Jung informed his Zarathustra seminar, "shows how the unconscious layers of the mind work." He added, "the absolute parallel is of course formed by the rabbits" (1218).

10. I am indebted to Higgins, *Nietzsche's "Zarathustra"* and *"Zarathustra* Is a Comic Book,"* and Shapiro, *Nietzschean Narratives,* which have discussed *Thus Spoke Zarathustra* as at least partly parodic.

11. According to Gilman *(Nietzschean Parody),* Nietzsche was interested in parody from childhood, and composed musical versions of parody in which the melody is preserved and the words are altered. Gilman argues that young Nietzsche viewed parody as "a means of adaptation and alteration," not as negative criticism (15).

12. See Krell *Postponements,* 56 and passim, which discusses the scenarios and the fact that Nietzsche kept postponing Zarathustra's demise.

13. Julia Kristeva's uptake of Bakhtin, in her essay "Word, Dialogue, and Novel," refers to Nietzsche, loosely, in order to draw out Bakhtin's points, and is worth consulting for another interpretation of Menippean satire.

14. The one exception is "Of Great Events" at the beginning of part 2, where Zarathustra disappears and an omniscient narrator takes over for about a page. It is at this very spot, when Zarathustra mysteriously absents himself, that Jung detected Nietzsche's cryptomnesia (see note 9 above).

15. Hollingdale translates the chapter title as "Of Old and Young Women," but the German is *Von alten und jungen Weiblein—Weiblein* being a diminutive form of *Weib,* "woman." Kaufmann translates the title accurately as "On Little Old and Young Women," and comments that "the affectionate diminutive in the title suggests at once what is the main difference between this chapter and its vitriolic prototype, Schopenhauer's essay *Von den Weibern* [On Women]: a touch of humor" (*TSZ* 8).

16. I have profited in particular from discussions of this chapter by R. Hinton Thomas and by Jean Graybeal. Thomas casts doubt on a literal reading of the line about the whip, connects the little old woman with Life as one character, and argues that the whip is to be used by Zarathustra as a means of metaphorical self-flagellation when he finds himself sinking into a torrid emotional zone in relation to women (120–21). Graybeal examines nuances of language in the text, and positively relates Zarathustra's sayings on woman to concepts, like play, that Nietzsche treats affirmatively elsewhere. She emphasizes the overdetermination of the line about the whip, suggesting that, among other things, the whip could signify Zarathustra's "tongue," or ability to speak easily and fluently, in the presence of women (52–55).

17. Another object of parody or imitation, according to Köhler, is Sacher-Masoch's *Venus in Furs* (Leipzig, 1870), in which Sacher-Masoch considers Woman one of life's greatest riddles and has his Venus announce her arrival "with an instrument of torture, even if it be only a whip" (Köhler 72–73).

18. This is Dionysian wisdom, acceptance of the entailment of life and death. Freud interprets this entailment in his essay "The Theme of the Three Caskets," where the fairest woman is always death. Blondel makes the point that the *vita femina* metaphor (Life is a woman) is "the ultimate meta-phor of death," and refers to the Freudian explanation ("Life as Metaphor" 166).

6. "All Things Are Enchained, Entwined, In Love"

1. Nietzsche wrote in his notebook (November 1882–February 1883): "It should come to pass, that mankind's premier festivals are procreation and death" (*KSA* 10:202).

2. Critics have condemned Nietzsche/Zarathustra for the desire to give birth to himself. Among them, Luce Irigaray established the precedent in *Marine Lover* by accusing Zarathustra of being so self-absorbed that he forgets (represses) his own source in his mother, and of collapsing difference into the "sameness" of the eternal return out of resentment (41). See also Ansell-Pearson ("Nietzsche, Woman and Political Theory" 41), who accuses Nietzsche of womb envy, and Conway (43), for whom Nietzsche's "masculinist fantasies" derive from "primal fear of the maternal body."

3. There are many references to pregnancy throughout Nietzsche's works. Most compare pregnancy with an artist's love for his work (*GS* 72) or vice versa (*GM* 2:17, *GM* 3:4). Nietzsche writes of "contemplative types" as "male mothers" (*GS* 72), and considers a "continually creative person" as "a mother type in the grand sense" (*GS* 369). In *On the Genealogy of Morals,* pregnancy becomes a wider metaphor for the development of "bad conscience" in humans—thus, for creative self-division, consciousness itself (2:16, 19).

4. Hecate is a powerful and popular Greek goddess who became associated with witchcraft and magic, lunar lore, and creatures of the night, and—of significance for Zarathustra's vision—doorways and crossroads (*Oxford Classical Dictionary* 671). Hecate's attendant animal was the dog, which announced her coming by howling. The moon's supremacy as the primitive cosmic power is the counterpart of magical powers of primitive women (Briffault chap. 20).

5. Narby argues that the images of serpents that are a common feature both of ancient myth and of hallucinogenic visions are in fact early predictions of the aperiodic crystal of DNA.

6. "The serpent is the age-old representative of the lower worlds, of the belly with its contents and the intestines"; it is of the earth and sexuality" (Jung 18).

7. We now know that Nietzsche expunged from publication a section of *Ecce Homo* in which he declared that the thought of his mother and his sister seriously interfered with his own acceptance of the affirmation of eternal return: "I confess that the most profound objection to the 'eternal recurrence,' my truly *abysmal* thought, is always mother and sister" (in Graybeal 88). There has been critical discussion of this excised section of *Ecce Homo,* most of it psychoanalytic; see Graybeal chap. 4, Kofman "Fantastical Genealogy," and Oliver "Nietzsche's Abjection."

8. According to Freud (*Interpretation of Dreams* 387).

9. For a good summary of critical positions on part 4, and an interesting theory about its placement in the work, see Loeb.

10. In an essay pertinent to my argument, Bianca Thiesen shows how Nietzsche reinscribes the Sorcerer's song as "Ariadne's Lament," where the male figure becomes female ("Rhythms of Oblivion").

Conclusion

1. See, for example, Anthony Easthope's *What a Man's Gotta Do,* which argues that popular culture's holistic version of unproblematic masculinity is a role masking men's bisexuality.

2. For example, Michael Warner, *The Trouble with Normal.* Journals have appeared that are devoted to queer studies (e.g., *Journal of Gay, Lesbian and Bisexual Identity*).

3. For example, Clare Hemmings, *Bisexual Spaces.*

4. *Boys Don't Cry,* dir. Kimberly Pierce, Hart Sharp Productions, 1999.

BIBLIOGRAPHY

Works by Friedrich Nietzsche

The Anti-Christ, in *The Twilight of the Idols* and *The Anti-Christ*. Trans. R. J. Hollingdale. Harmondsworth: Penguin, 1968.

Beyond Good and Evil: Prelude to a Philosophy of the Future. Trans. R. J. Hollingdale. Harmondsworth: Penguin, 1973.

The Birth of Tragedy, in *The Birth of Tragedy and The Case of Wagner*. Trans. Walter Kaufmann. New York: Vintage Books, 1967.

The Case of Wagner, in *The Birth of Tragedy and The Case of Wagner*. Trans. Walter Kaufmann. New York: Vintage Books, 1967.

Daybreak: Thoughts on the Prejudices of Morality. Trans. R. J. Hollingdale. Cambridge: Cambridge University Press, 1982.

Early Greek Philosophy and Other Essays. Trans. Maximillian A. Mugge. In *The Complete Works of Friedrich Nietzsche*, ed. Oscar Levy. New York: Russell and Russell, 1964.

Ecce Homo: How One Becomes What One Is, in *On the Genealogy of Morals* and *Ecce Homo*. Trans. Walter Kaufmann. New York: Vintage Books, 1969.

Friedrich Nietzsche on Rhetoric and Language. Trans. Sander L. Gilman, Carole Blair, David J. Parent. New York: Oxford University Press, 1989.

The Gay Science. Trans. Walter Kaufmann. New York: Vintage Books, 1974.

Human, All Too Human: A Book for Free Spirits. Trans. Marion Faber and Stephen Lehmann. Lincoln: University of Nebraska Press, 1984.

On the Genealogy of Morals: A Polemic, in *On the Genealogy of Morals* and *Ecce Homo*. Trans. Walter Kaufmann. New York: Vintage Books, 1969.

On the Uses and Disadvantages of History for Life. In *Untimely Meditations*. Trans. R. J. Hollingdale. Cambridge: Cambridge University Press, 1983.

Philosophy and Truth: Selections from Nietzsche's Notebooks of the Early 1870's. Trans. Daniel Breazeale. London: Humanities Press International, 1979.

Philosophy in the Tragic Age of the Greeks. Trans. Marianne Cowan. Washington, D.C.: Regnery Publishing Inc., 1962.

Sämtliche Werke: Kritische Studienausgabe in 15 Einzelbänden. Eds. Giorgio Colli and Mazzino Montinari. Munich/Berlin: dtv/de Gruyter, 1988.

Selected Letters of Friedrich Nietzsche. Ed. and trans. Christopher Middleton. Chicago: University of Chicago Press, 1969.

Thus Spoke Zarathustra: A Book for Everyone and No One. Trans. R. J. Hollingdale. Harmondsworth: Penguin, 1969.

Thus Spoke Zarathustra: A Book for None and All. Trans. Walter Kaufmann. New York: Penguin, 1966.

Twilight of the Idols: or How to Philosophize with a Hammer, in *Twilight of the Idols* and *The Anti-Christ*. Trans. R. J. Hollingdale. Harmondsworth: Penguin, 1968.

The Will to Power. Ed. Walter Kaufmann. Trans. Walter Kaufmann and R. J. Hollingdale. New York: Vintage Books, 1968.

Other Works

Ackermann, Robert John. *Nietzsche: A Frenzied Look*. Amherst: University of Massachusetts Press, 1990.

Aeschylus. "The Eumenides." Trans. Richard Lattimore. In *The Complete Greek Tragedies*, ed. David Grene and Richard Lattimore. Vol. 1. Chicago: University of Chicago Press, 1959.

Ainley, Alison. "'Ideal Selfishness': Nietzsche's Metaphor of Maternity." In *Exceedingly Nietzsche: Aspects of Contemporary Nietzsche Interpretation*, ed. David Farrell Krell and David Wood. London: Routledge, 1988.

Allison, David B. *Reading the New Nietzsche*. New York: Rowman & Littlefield, 2001.

Andreas-Salomé, Lou. *Looking Back: Memoirs*. Ed. Ernst Peiffer, trans. Breon Mitchell. New York: Paragon House, 1991.

———. *Nietzsche* (orig. *Friedrich Nietzsche in seinen Werken*). Ed. and trans. Siegfried Mandell. Redding Ridge, Conn.: Black Swan Books, 1988.

Ansell-Pearson, Keith. "Nietzsche, Woman and Political Theory." In *Nietzsche, Feminism and Political Theory*, ed. Paul Patton. London: Routledge, 1993.

———. *Viroid Life: Perspectives on Nietzsche and the Transhuman Condition*. London: Routledge, 1997.

Aristotle. *The Complete Works*. Ed. Jonathan Barnes. Vol. 2. Princeton: Princeton University Press, 1984.

Bachofen, J. J. *Myth, Religion, and Mother Right: Selected Writings of J. J. Bachofen*. Trans. Ralph Manheim. Princeton: Princeton University Press, 1967.

Bakhtin, M. M. *The Dialogic Imagination: Four Essays*. Ed. Michael Holquist, trans. Caryl Emerson and Michael Holquist. Austin: University of Texas Press, 1981.

Bamberger, Joan. "The Myth of Matriarchy: Why Men Rule in Primitive Society." In *Women, Culture, and Society*, ed. Michelle Zimbalist Rosado and Louise Lamphere. Stanford: Stanford University Press, 1974.

Banham, Gary. "Creating the Future: Legislation and Aesthetics." In *Nietzsche's Futures*, ed. John Lippitt. London: Macmillan Press, 1999.

Barthes, Roland. *Mythologies*. Trans. Annette Lavers. London: Paladin, 1973.

Bennett, Benjamin. "Bridge: Against Nothing." In *Nietzsche and the Feminine*, ed. Peter J. Burgard. Charlottesville: University Press of Virginia, 1994.

Bergoffen, Debra B. "Nietzsche was no Feminist." In *Feminist Interpretations of Friedrich Nietzsche*, ed. Kelly Oliver and Marilyn Pearsall. University Park: Pennsylvania State University Press, 1998.

Binyon, Rudolph. *Frau Lou: Nietzsche's Wayward Disciple*. Princeton: Princeton University Press, 1968.

Black, Max. "More about Metaphor." In *Metaphor and Thought*, ed. Andrew Ortony. Cambridge: Cambridge University Press, 1993.

Blondel, Eric. *Nietzsche: The Body and Culture. Philosophy as a Philological Genealogy*. Trans. Sean Hand. London: Athlone Press, 1991.

———. "Nietzsche: Life as Metaphor." In *The New Nietzsche: Contemporary Styles of Interpretation*, ed. David B. Allison. Cambridge, Mass.: MIT Press, 1985.

Booth, Wayne. *A Rhetoric of Irony*. Chicago: University of Chicago Press, 1974.

Bordo, Susan. "The Cartesian Masculinization of Thought and the Seventeenth-Century Flight from the Feminine." In *Modern Engendering: Critical Feminist Readings in Modern Western Philosophy*, ed. Bat-Ami Bar On. Albany: State University of New York Press, 1994.

Braidotti, Rosi. "The Problematic of 'the Feminine' in Contemporary French Philosophy: Foucault and Irigaray." In *Feminine-Masculine and Representation*, ed. Terry Threadgold and Anne Cranny-Francis. Sydney: Allen and Unwin, 1990.

Branham, R. Bracht and Daniel Kinney. "Introduction." In *Satyrica* of Petronius, trans. R. Bracht Branham and Daniel Kinney. Berkeley: University of California Press, 1997.

Briffault, Robert. *The Mothers: The Matriarchal Theory of Social Origins.* Ed. G. R. Taylor. New York: Grosset and Dunlop, 1959.

Brown, Peter. *The Body and Society: Men, Women, and Sexual Renunciation in Early Christianity.* New York: Columbia University Press, 1988.

Burgard, Peter J., ed. *Nietzsche and the Feminine.* Charlottesville: University Press of Virginia, 1994.

Chambers, Ross. *Room for Maneuver: Reading (the) Oppositional (in) Narrative.* Chicago: University of Chicago Press, 1991.

———. *Story and Situation: Narrative Seduction and the Power of Fiction.* Minneapolis: University of Minnesota Press, 1984.

Clark, Maudemarie. *Nietzsche on Truth and Philosophy.* Cambridge: Cambridge University Press, 1990.

———. "Nietzsche's Misogyny." In *Feminist Interpretations of Friedrich Nietzsche*, ed. Kelly Oliver and Marilyn Pearsall. University Park: Pennsylvania State University Press, 1998.

Cocalis, Susan L. and Kay Goodman. "The Eternal Feminine Is Leading Us On." In *Beyond the Eternal Feminine: Critical Essays on Women and German Literature*, ed. Susan Cocalis and Kay Goodman. Stuttgart: Hans-Dieter Heinz, 1982.

Conway, Daniel W. "Annunciation and Rebirth: The Prefaces of 1886." In *Nietzsche's Futures*, ed. John Lippitt. London: Macmillan Press Ltd., 1999.

Del Caro, Adrian. "The Pseudoman in Nietzsche, or the Threat of the Neuter." *New German Critique* 50 (Spring/Summer 1990): 135–156.

de Man, Paul. *Allegories of Reading: Figural Language in Rousseau, Nietzsche, Rilke and Proust.* New Haven: Yale University Press, 1979.

Derrida, Jacques. *Spurs: Nietzsche's Styles.* Trans. Barbara Harlow. Chicago: University of Chicago Press, 1979.

Derrida, Jacques, and Christie V. McDonald. "Choreographies." *Diacritics* 12 (Summer 1982): 66–76.

Diethe, Carol. *Nietzsche's Women: Beyond the Whip.* Berlin: de Gruyter, 1996.

Dijkstra, Bram. *Idols of Perversity: Fantasies of Feminine Evil in Fin-de-Siècle Culture.* New York: Oxford University Press, 1986.

Diprose, Rosalyn. "Nietzsche and the Pathos of Distance." In *Nietzsche, Feminism and Political Theory*, ed. Paul Patton. London: Routledge, 1993.

Dodds, E. R. *The Greeks and the Irrational.* Berkeley: University of California Press, 1966.

Easthope, Anthony. *What a Man's Gotta Do: The Masculine Myth in Popular Culture.* London: Routledge, 1992.

Eco, Umberto. "The Frames of Comic 'Freedom.'" In *Carnival!*, ed. Thomas A. Sebeok. Berlin: Mouton Publishers, 1984.

Eliade, Mircea. *Myth and Reality*. Trans. Willard R. Trask. New York: Harper Colophon, 1975.

Evans, Richard. *The Feminist Movement in Germany 1894–1933*. London: Sage Publications, 1976.

Fausto-Sterling, Anne. *Myths of Gender: Biological Theories about Women and Men*. New York: Basic Books, 1985.

———. *Sexing the Body: Gender Politics and the Construction of Sexuality*. New York: Basic Books, 2000.

Felski, Rita. *The Gender of Modernity*. Cambridge, Mass.: Harvard University Press, 1995.

France, David. "An Inconvenient Woman." *New York Times Magazine*, May 28, 2000, 22–28.

Freud, Sigmund. *Civilization and its Discontents*. Trans. James Strachey. Standard Edition vol. 21. London: Hogarth Press, 1961.

———. *The Interpretation of Dreams*. Trans. James Strachey. Standard Edition vols. 4 and 5. London: Hogarth Press, 1953.

———. "The Theme of the Three Caskets." Trans. James Strachey. In *The Case of Schreber, Papers on Technique, and Other Works*. Standard Edition vol. 12. London: Hogarth Press, 1958.

Gadamer, Hans-Georg. "The Drama of Zarathustra." Trans. Thomas Heilke. In *Nietzsche's New Seas: Explorations in Philosophy, Aesthetics, and Politics*, ed. Michael Gillespie and Tracy Strong. Chicago: University of Chicago Press, 1988.

Gay, Peter, ed. *The Freud Reader*. New York: W. W. Norton & Company, 1989.

Gilman, Sander L. *Inscribing the Other*. Lincoln: University of Nebraska Press, 1991.

———. *Nietzschean Parody: An Introduction to Reading Nietzsche*. Bonn: Bouvier Verlag Herbert Grundmann, 1976.

———, ed. *Conversations with Nietzsche: A Life in the Words of his Contemporaries*. Trans. David J. Parent. New York: Oxford University Press, 1987.

Goethe, Johann Wolfgang. *Faust: Eine Tragödie*. Munich: dtv, 1977.

Gossman, Lionel. *Orpheus Philologus: Bachofen versus Mommsen on the Study of Antiquity*. Philadelphia: American Philosophical Society, 1983.

Granier, Jean. "Nietzsche's Conception of Chaos." In *The New Nietzsche: Contemporary Styles of Interpretation*, ed. David B. Allison. Cambridge, Mass.: MIT Press, 1985.

Graybeal, Jean. *Language and the Feminine in Nietzsche and Heidegger*. Bloomington: Indiana University Press, 1990.

Grundlehner, Philip. *The Poetry of Friedrich Nietzsche*. New York: Oxford University Press, 1986.

Guthrie, W. K. C. *Orpheus and Greek Religion*. London: Methuen & Co. Ltd., 1935.

Halperin, David M. "Why is Diotima a Woman? Platonic Eros and the Figuration of Gender." In *Before Sexuality: The Construction of Erotic Experience in the Ancient Greek World*, ed. David M. Halperin, John J. Winkler, and Froma I. Zeitlin. Princeton: Princeton University Press, 1990.

Harries, Karsten. "The Philosopher at Sea." In *Nietzsche's New Seas: Explorations in Philosophy, Aesthetics, and Politics*, ed. Michael Allen Gillespie and Tracy B. Strong. Chicago: University of Chicago Press, 1988.

Hartmann, Eduard von. *Philosophy of the Unconscious: Speculative Results According to the Inductive Method of Physical Science.* Preface by C. K. Ogden. London: Routledge and Kegan Paul Ltd., 1931.

Hatab, Lawrence J. "Nietzsche on Women." *Southern Journal of Philosophy* 19, no. 3 (Fall 1981): 333–345.

Hayman, Ronald. *Nietzsche: A Critical Life.* New York: Oxford University Press, 1980.

Heidegger, Martin. "Who is Nietzsche's Zarathustra?" In *The New Nietzsche: Contemporary Styles of Interpretation,* ed. David B. Allison. Cambridge, Mass.: MIT Press, 1985.

Hemmings, Clare. *Bisexual Spaces: A Geography of Sexuality and Gender.* New York: Routledge, 2002.

Henrichs, Albert. "'He has a God in him': Human and divine in the modern perception of Dionysus." In *Masks of Dionysus,* ed. Thomas H. Carpenter and Christopher A. Faraone. Ithaca: Cornell University Press, 1993.

Higgins, Kathleen Marie. *Comic Relief: Nietzsche's Gay Science.* New York: Oxford University Press, 2000.

——. *Nietzsche's "Zarathustra."* Philadelphia: Temple University Press, 1987.

——. "*Zarathustra* Is a Comic Book." *Philosophy and Literature* 16 (April 1992): 1–14.

Hough, Sheridan. *Nietzsche's Noontide Friend: The Self as Metaphoric Double.* University Park: Pennsylvania State University Press, 1997.

Huxley, Francis. *The Way of the Sacred.* Garden City: Doubleday and Co., 1974.

Irigaray, Luce. *Marine Lover of Friedrich Nietzsche.* Trans. Gillian C. Gill. New York: Columbia University Press, 1991.

——. *Speculum of the Other Woman.* Trans. Gillian C. Gill. Ithaca: Cornell University Press, 1985.

Jameson, Michael. "The Asexuality of Dionysus." In *The Masks of Dionysus,* ed. Thomas H. Carpenter and Christopher A. Faraone. Ithaca: Cornell University Press, 1993.

Janz, Curt Paul. *Friedrich Nietzsche: Biographie in Drei Banden.* Vol. 1. Munich: Carl Hanser Verlag, 1978.

Jenkins, Fiona. "Performative Identity: Nietzsche on the Force of Art and Language." In *Nietzsche, Philosophy and the Arts,* ed. Selim Kemal, Ivan Gaskell, and Daniel W. Conway. Cambridge: Cambridge University Press, 1998.

Jung, Carl G. *Nietzsche's Zarathustra: Notes of a Seminar Given in 1934–39.* 2 vols. Princeton: Princeton University Press, 1988.

Kerenyi, Karl. *Eleusis: Archetypal Image of Mother and Daughter.* Trans. Ralph Manheim. New York: Pantheon Books, 1967.

Keuls, Eva C. *The Reign of the Phallus: Sexual Politics in Ancient Athens.* New York: Harper & Row, 1985.

Kierkegaard, Søren. *The Concept of Irony, with Constant Reference to Socrates.* Trans. Lee M. Capel. Bloomington: Indiana University Press, 1968.

Klossowski, Pierre. *Nietzsche and the Vicious Circle.* Trans. Daniel W. Smith. London: Athlone Press, 1997.

Kofman, Sarah. "Baubô: Theological Perversion and Fetishism." Trans. Tracy B. Strong. In *Nietzsche's New Seas: Explorations in Philosophy, Aesthetics, and Politics,* ed. Michael Allen Gillespie and Tracy B. Strong. Chicago: University of Chicago Press, 1988.

——. "A Fantastical Genealogy: Nietzsche's Family Romance." In *Nietzsche and the Feminine,* ed. Peter J. Burgard. Charlottesville: University Press of Virginia, 1994.

——. *Nietzsche and Metaphor.* Trans. Duncan Large. London: Athlone Press, 1993.

Köhler, Joachim. *Zarathustra's Secret: The Interior Life of Friedrich Nietzsche.* Trans. Ronald Taylor. New Haven: Yale University Press, 2002.

Krell, David Farrell. *Postponements: Woman, Sensuality, and Death in Nietzsche.* Bloomington: Indiana University Press, 1986.

——. "To the Orange Grove at the Edge of the Sea." In *Nietzsche and the Feminine,* ed. Peter J. Burgard. Charlottesville: University Press of Virginia, 1994.

Kristeva, Julia. "Word, Dialogue, and Novel." In *The Kristeva Reader,* ed. Toril Moi. London: Basil Blackwood, 1986.

Lakoff, George, and Mark Johnson. *Metaphors We Live By.* Chicago: University of Chicago Press, 1980.

Lao Tsu. *Tao Te Ching.* Trans. Gia-Fu Feng and Jane English. New York: Vintage Books, 1972.

Laqueur, Thomas Walter. *Making Sex: Body and Gender from the Greeks to Freud.* Cambridge, Mass.: Harvard University Press, 1990.

Lévi-Strauss, Claude. *The Elementary Structures of Kinship.* Trans. J. H. Bell, J. R. von Sturmer, and R. Needham. Boston: Beacon Press, 1969.

——. *Structural Anthropology.* Vol. 1. Trans. Claire Jacobson and Brooke Grundfest Schoepf. Ringwood: Penguin, 1972.

Livingstone, Angela. *Salomé: Her Life and Work.* Mt. Kisco, N.Y.: Moyer Bell, 1984.

Lloyd, Genevieve. *The Man of Reason: "Male" and "Female" in Western Philosophy.* London: Methuen, 1984.

Loeb, Paul S. "The Conclusion of Nietzsche's *Zarathustra.*" *International Studies in Philosophy* 32, no. 3 (2000): 137–152.

Lungstrum, Janet. "Nietzsche Writing Woman/Woman Writing Nietzsche." In *Nietzsche and the Feminine,* ed. Peter J. Burgard. Charlottesville: University Press of Virginia, 1994.

MacDonald, George F., John L. Cove, Charles D. Laughlin, Jr., and John McManus. "Mirrors, Portals, and Multiple Realities." *Zygon* 24, no. 1 (March 1989): 39–64.

Maclean, Marie. *Narrative and Performance: The Baudelairean Experiment.* London: Routledge, 1988.

Mann, Thomas. "Nietzsches Philosophie im Lichte Unserer Erfahrung." In *Nietzsche, Also Sprach Zarathustra.* Baden-Baden: Insel Taschenbuch, 1976.

Martin, Biddy. *Woman and Modernity: The (Life)Styles of Lou Andreas-Salomé.* Ithaca: Cornell University Press, 1991.

Mosse, George. *Nationalism and Sexuality: Middle-Class Morality and Sexual Norms in Modern Europe.* Madison: University of Wisconsin Press, 1985.

Narby, Jeremy. *The Cosmic Serpent: DNA and the Origins of Knowledge.* New York: Tarcher/Putnam, 1999.

Nehemas, Alexander. *Nietzsche: Life as Literature.* Princeton: Princeton University Press, 1985.

Nussbaum, Martha C. "The Transfiguration of Intoxication: Nietzsche, Schopenhauer, and Dionysus." In *Nietzsche, Philosophy, and the Arts,* ed. Selim Kemal, Ivan Gaskell, and Daniel W. Conway. Cambridge: Cambridge University Press, 1998.

Olender, Maurice. "Aspects of Baubo: Ancient Texts and Contexts." In *Before Sexuality: The Construction of Erotic Experience in the Ancient Greek World,* ed. David M.

Halperin, John J. Winkler, and Froma I. Zeitlin. Princeton: Princeton University Press, 1990.

Oliver, Kelly. "Nietzsche's Abjection." In *Nietzsche and the Feminine,* ed. Peter J. Burgard. Charlottesville: University Press of Virginia, 1994.

———. "Who Is Nietzsche's Woman?" In *Modern Engendering: Critical Feminist Readings in Modern Western Philosophy,* ed. Bat-Ami Bar On. Albany: State University of New York Press, 1994.

Oliver, Kelly, and Marilyn Pearsall, eds. *Feminist Interpretations of Friedrich Nietzsche.* University Park: Pennsylvania State University Press, 1998.

Otto, Walter F. *Dionysus: Myth and Cult.* Trans. Robert B. Palmer. Dallas: Spring Publications, 1993.

Oxford Classical Dictionary. Ed. Simon Hornblower and Antony Spawforth. Oxford: Oxford University Press, 1996.

Patton, Paul, ed. *Nietzsche, Feminism and Political Theory.* New York: Routledge, 1993.

Pautrat, Bernard. "Nietzsche Medused." In *Looking After Nietzsche,* ed. Laurence A. Rickels. Albany: State University of New York Press, 1990.

Peters, H. F. *My Sister, My Spouse: A Biography of Lou Andreas-Salomé.* New York: Norton, 1974.

Picart, Caroline Joan S. *Resentment and the "Feminine" in Nietzsche's Politico-Aesthetics.* University Park: Pennsylvania State University Press, 1999.

Plato. "The Symposium." Trans. R. E. Allen. In *The Dialogues of Plato.* Vol. 2. New Haven: Yale University Press, 1991.

Pletsch, Carl. *Young Nietzsche: Becoming a Genius.* New York: Free Press, 1991.

Pomeroy, Sarah. *Goddesses, Whores, Wives, and Slaves: Women in Classical Antiquity.* London: Pimlico, 1975.

Rathbone, David. "Deconstructing Misogyny in Nietzsche." *Antithesis* 3, no. 2 (1990): 89–120.

Ricoeur, Paul. *The Rule of Metaphor: Multi-disciplinary Studies of the Creation of Meaning in Language.* London: Routledge and Kegan Paul, 1978.

———. *The Symbolism of Evil.* Trans. Emerson Buchanan. Boston: Beacon Press, 1967.

Schacht, Richard. *Making Sense of Nietzsche: Reflections Timely and Untimely.* Urbana: University of Illinois Press, 1995.

Schopenhauer, Arthur. "On Woman." In *Studies in Pessimism: A Series of Essays,* ed. and trans. T. Bailey Saunders. London: George Allen and Unwin, 1923.

Sedgwick, Eve Kosofsky. *Epistemology of the Closet.* Berkeley: University of California Press, 1990.

Shapiro, Gary. *Alcyone: Nietzsche on Gifts, Noise, and Women.* Albany: State University of New York Press, 1991.

———. *Nietzschean Narratives.* Bloomington: Indiana University Press, 1989.

Silk, M. S., and J. P. Stern. *Nietzsche on Tragedy.* Cambridge: Cambridge University Press, 1981.

Sissa, Giulia. *Greek Virginity.* Trans. Arthur Goldhammer. Cambridge, Mass.: Harvard University Press, 1990.

Spivak, Gayatri Chakravorty. "Displacement and the Discourse of Woman." In *Displacement: Derrida and After,* ed. Mark Krupnick. Bloomington: Indiana University Press, 1983.

Stambaugh, Joan. *The Other Nietzsche*. Binghamton: State University of New York Press, 1994.

Staten, Henry. *Nietzsche's Voice*. Ithaca: Cornell University Press, 1990.

Stein, Edward. *Mismeasure of Desire: The Science, Theory, and Ethics of Sexual Orientation*. New York: Oxford University Press, 1999.

Tacitus, Cornelius. *The Agricola and the Germania*. Trans. H. Mattingly. Harmondsworth: Penguin, 1970.

Thiesen, Bianca. "Rhythms of Oblivion." In *Nietzsche and the Feminine*, ed. Peter J. Burgard. Charlottesville: University Press of Virginia, 1994.

Thomas, R. Hinton. "Nietzsche, Women and the Whip." *German Life and Letters* n.s. 34, no. 1 (October 1980): 117–125.

Tirrell, Lynne. "Sexual Dualism and Women's Self-Creation: On the Advantages and Disadvantages of Reading Nietzsche for Feminists." In *Nietzsche and the Feminine*, ed. Peter J. Burgard. Charlottesville: University Press of Virginia, 1994.

Turner, Mark. *Death Is the Mother of Beauty: Mind, Metaphor, Criticism*. Chicago: University of Chicago Press, 1987.

Tyrrell, William Blake. *Amazons: A Study in Athenian Myth-Making*. Baltimore: Johns Hopkins University Press, 1984.

Valadier, Paul. "Dionysus versus the Crucified." In *The New Nietzsche: Contemporary Styles of Interpretation*, ed. David B. Allison. Cambridge, Mass.: MIT Press, 1985.

Wagner, Richard. *Die Meistersinger von Nurnberg*. Libretto. New York: Metropolitan Opera Libretto Series, 1992.

———. *Tristan und Isolde*. Libretto. Eng. trans. Lionel Salter. Hamburg: Deutsche Grammophon GmbH, 1997.

Warner, Marina. *Monuments and Maidens: The Allegory of the Female Form*. London: Picador, 1987.

Warner, Michael. *The Trouble with Normal: Sex, Politics, and the Ethics of Queer Life*. Cambridge, Mass.: Harvard University Press, 2000.

Williams, Bernard. *Shame and Necessity*. Berkeley: University of California Press, 1993.

Winninger, Kathleen J. "Nietzsche's Women and Women's Nietzsche." In *Feminist Interpretations of Friedrich Nietzsche*, ed. Kelly Oliver and Marilyn Pearsall. University Park: Pennsylvania State University Press, 1998.

Wood, David. "Nietzsche's Transvaluation of Time." In *Exceedingly Nietzsche: Aspects of Contemporary Nietzsche Interpretation*, ed. David Farrell Krell and David Wood. London: Routledge, 1988.

Zeitlin, Froma I. *Playing the Other: Gender and Society in Classical Greek Literature*. Chicago: University of Chicago Press, 1996.